THE MODERN LIBRARY
OF THE WORLD'S BEST BOOKS

THE GALLIC WAR
AND OTHER WRITINGS
BY JULIUS CAESAR

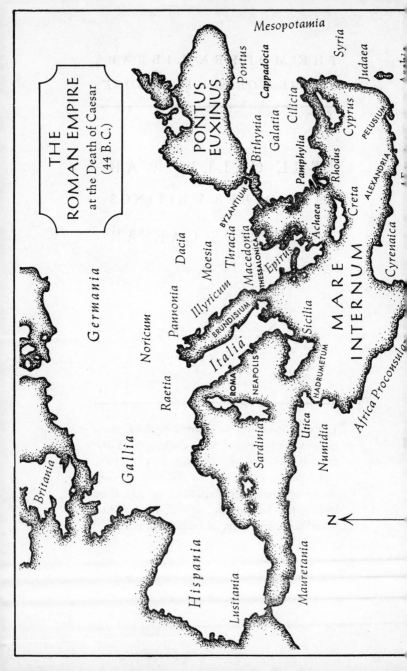

THE
ROMAN EMPIRE
at the Death of Caesar
(44 B.C.)

Britania

Germania

Gallia

Hispania

Lusitania

Mauretania

Raetia

Noricum

Pannonia

Dacia

Moesia

Illyricum

Italia

Sardinia

Sicilia

ROMA

NEAPOLIS

BRUNDISIUM

Thracia

Macedonia

THESSALONICA

Epirus

Achaea

BYZANTIUM

Bithynia

Galatia

Pamphylia

Rhodus

Creta

PONTUS EUXINUS

Pontus

Cappadocia

Cilicia

Mesopotamia

Syria

Judaea

Cyprus

ALEXANDRIA

PELUSIUM

Cyrenaica

MARE INTERNUM

Africa Proconsularis

Numidia

Utica

HADRUMETUM

N

THE GALLIC WAR
AND OTHER WRITINGS
BY JULIUS CAESAR

Translated, with an Introduction,

by MOSES HADAS,

Professor of Greek and Latin,

Columbia University

THE MODERN LIBRARY
NEW YORK

Random House IS THE PUBLISHER OF *The Modern Library*

BENNETT CERF · DONALD S. KLOPFER

Manufactured in the United States of America by H. Wolff

CONTENTS

Introduction   vii

GALLIC WAR   I (58 B.C.)   5
              II (57 B.C.)   39
              III (56 B.C.)   57
              IV (55 B.C.)   74
              V (54 B.C.)   94
              VI (53 B.C.)   127
              VII (52 B.C.)   152
              VIII (51-50 B.C.)   206

CIVIL WAR   I (50 B.C.)   207
              II (49 B.C.)   256
              III (49-48 B.C.)   284

ALEXANDRINE, AFRICAN,
AND SPANISH WARS   353

FRAGMENTS   355

              Gazetteer   357

              Maps: THE ROMAN EMPIRE AT
                      CAESAR'S DEATH   ii

                      GAUL   2-3

INTRODUCTION

If humanity truly abhorred Caesarism, if we were not
inured to chicanery and ruthlessness, we might deflate
Caesar as a cleverer Tamerlane or stronger Machiavelli.
But Caesar cannot be dismissed or evaded. Discredit the
traditional heroes of history as we will, there remains a
handful of demonic figures who have affected centuries
of history and millions of lives; and even the shortest
roster must include the name of Caesar. As a general or
as a statesman or as a writer or as a towering subject for
tragedy he may be matched; what makes him unique
is the conjunction of all these qualities with a pregnant
crisis in European history.

1

To appreciate the crisis we must take a rapid glance at
its historical background. The history of republican
Rome is an interweaving of two strands—the drive of
Rome to attain world dominion, and the drive of classes
and individuals within Rome to attain the direction of
that dominion. Republican officials were limited to one
year's tenure, and the militia they commanded in the
field were citizens who returned to their farms after each
campaign. But for operations in distant provinces this
system was impractical. The tenure of proconsuls and
propraetors was prorogued to enable them to finish
a given task, and armies became professional, with en-

listments running for sixteen or more years. It is inconceivable that an annual magistrate could lead a citizen army against Rome to enforce his own will; generals who had exercised autocratic authority in the provinces, leading armies who looked to them rather than to the state for bonuses and other rewards, eventually became stronger than the state itself and might use their individual power to enforce their will upon the state.

The magistracies were originally a prerogative of the patricians, which was broken only when marriage between patricians and plebeians was legitimized. But the internal struggle continued with a different alignment. On the one side was the virtual oligarchy of office-holding families, patrician or plebeian, called *nobiles,* and on the other the larger and less privileged group called *populares.* Beginning with the proposed agrarian reforms of the Gracchi, in 133 B.C. tension between the parties broke into violence, which continued intermittently for a century. The motives of the Gracchi, themselves aristocratic plebeians, are above question, but so much cannot be said for subsequent leaders of the *populares;* these were not revolutionaries in any real sense but merely used their leadership to supplant, not reform, the existing oligarchy.

In the interval between the Gracchi and Caesar, the principal leader of the *populares* was Marius, whose ruthless and tenacious exercise of power revealed the fatal weakness of the constitution in the face of a powerful and determined personality. Sulla, equally ruthless and more revolutionary, put an end to Marius' power by marching on Rome, and instituted constitutional reforms to prevent similar concentration of power in the hands of an individual. But Sulla's safeguards were disregarded as soon as he retired from public life, and the scramble for power was resumed. The principal figures in the scramble, during the 60's and 50's of the first century B.C., were Pompey, Crassus, and Julius Caesar. Pompey had raised himself to eminence by successful campaigns against the rebel Sertorius in Spain, against Spartacus' gladiators in Italy, and against a scourge of pirates that infested the Mediterranean; that these crises could arise, and that recourse had to be taken to a single successful general to confront them, is in itself a sufficient commentary on the condition of the state. In 63 B.C., the year of Cicero's consulship and Catiline's conspiracy, Pompey was on a mission to reorganize Roman rule in the east, and when the senate was slow to grant his reasonable requests for confirmation of his arrangements and rewards for his veterans, it was expected that he would lead his army on Rome to enforce his demands, as Sulla had done. But he did not; he was not revolutionary by nature, but merely ambitious of the distinction of being the Indispensable Man. Instead he joined two other ambitious men in an informal triumvirate which would have enough power to satisfy the ambitions of each in despite of the regular government. One of these men was Crassus, a millionaire who craved the distinction of an important military command, and the other was Julius Caesar.

2

Caesar was born in 102 (or 100) B.C. He was a nephew of the wife of Marius, the leader of the popular party, and as quaestor in 68 he used the occasion of her funeral to deliver a public eulogy of the Julian *gens*. In 63 he advocated leniency to those involved in the Catilinarian conspiracy. With the help of wholesale bribery he became pontifex maximus that same year and praetor the year following. The governorship of Farther Spain, which followed upon his praetorship, first made him aware of his military talents. The triumvirate with Pompey and Crassus gave him the consulship in 59 (his colleague being the patrician nonentity M. Calpurnius Bibaculus) and the government of Gaul for the five years following. It was this post which enabled him to overshadow his rivals and make his bid for supreme power. It gave him great wealth and a superb army devoted to himself, and kept him near enough Rome to keep his finger on the politics of the capital. As Plutarch says (*Caesar*, 20): "During the whole of his campaign in Gaul, unbeknownst to Pompey Caesar was alternately subduing the enemy with the arms of the citizens and captivating and mastering the citizens with the money he got from the enemy." The Gallic campaigns are the subject of Caesar's major literary work.

The arrangement of the triumvirs was renewed in 56, but the death of Crassus in the battle of Carrhae in 53 left the two survivors confronting one another, the death of Julia, who was the daughter of Caesar and the wife of Pompey, having already ruptured the personal bond between the two men. Virtual anarchy in Rome, largely fomented by the rivals, made it inevitable that one of the two must assume extraordinary powers; but because Pompey was willing to do so as the nominal agent of the senate, while Caesar was likely to take a more independent line, senatorial sympathies were with Pompey. The final breach between Caesar and Pompey and the subsequent hostilities are decribed in Caesar's *Civil War*.

Caesar's request that he be permitted to stand for the consulship of 49 *in absentia* (which would alone afford him protection from his enemies) was refused, and he took the revolutionary step of crossing the Rubicon, that is, of appearing under arms in territory where he had no official authority to do so. Pompey withdrew the senatorial forces to Greece; he had a strong army in Spain (which he had been governing through deputies), controlled the seas, and evidently expected to crush Caesar in Italy by a pincer movement from east and west. Caesar first disposed of the Pompeian forces in Spain by a brilliant campaign, stormed Marseilles which had elected to stand neutral, and then went to Greece, where he won a complete victory over the Pompeian forces in the battle of Pharsalus, in August 48.

Caesar still had campaigns to fight in Egypt, Pontus, Africa, and Spain. These are described in three short books, written by subordinates, entitled *Alexandrine War*, *African War*, and *Spanish War;* their contents are indicated at p. 353. He returned to Rome in September 45, and spent the months remaining before the Ides of March of 44 in reorganizing the state and preparing for an expedition against the Parthians who had defeated Crassus.

3

However we may judge the morality of Caesar's rise to power, there can be no question that he used his power, once he had secured it, for the welfare of Rome and of mankind. Alexander before Caesar and Augustus after him were equally self-centered during their rise, and proved to be great benefactors. Caesar was not given time; he treated his defeated opponents with remarkable consideration and did what he could in the direction of reorganizing the economy and administration, leveling classes and raising the political position of the provincials, and safeguarding the frontiers. The fatal weakness of Roman political theory was that it persisted in thinking in terms of the old city-state; it may be argued that Caesar would have attempted to weld the empire into an organic whole, with a strong central authority, to be sure, but with such general participation in the total structure as the peoples of Italy enjoyed. His successor found it prudent to "restore the republic"—to retain autocratic control through a combination of "republican" magistracies which gave him absolute power over army, treasury, and elections, but to disguise his autocracy by preserving republican forms. The anomaly of autocracy without provision for regular succession did in fact plague all subsequent Roman history.

Because Caesar was too cynical or disillusioned or revolutionary to disguise his impatience with forms grown meaningless and dangerous, the Roman *nobiles* were so incensed that they assassinated him. When Tiberius Gracchus introduced popular measures which would have curtailed the privileges of the *nobiles* they accused him of aspiring to kingship and in their righteous indignation lynched him. Later popular leaders were similarly suspected, and Caesar took no pains to avoid the suspicion that he was aspiring to kingship. He seems to have accepted royal and even divine honors. Because Roman *nobiles* were bred to identify their own interests with the interests of Rome we cannot charge the assassins with selfish lack of patriotism, though it is depressing to note that the ringleaders were alive only because Caesar had pardoned them. In their romantic idealism the tyrannicides had thought that once the tyrant was out of the way the republic would automatically spring back to life. Their impracticality and Caesar's realism are proven by the bloody interval which

elapsed before Augustus finally established a permanent
autocracy.

4

Caesar is not only the most competent but also the most
magnetic Roman we know. For his competence his military achievements and his own accounts of them are sufficient testimony. He was imaginative beyond most
Romans, and gay-spirited, as numerous anecdotes in the
biographies of Suetonius and Plutarch testify. The grudg-
ing approval of Cicero, his friendships, his amours, and
the fierce loyalty of his soldiers all bear witness to an
extraordinary personal magnetism. Two paragraphs in
Plutarch's *Life* (17) help explain the devotion of his soldiers:

"Caesar implanted and nurtured high spirit and ambition in his men first by gracious treatment and by
bestowing awards without stint, demonstrating that the
wealth he amassed from his wars was not for his own
pleasure and enjoyment but a carefully guarded trust for
rewarding gallantry, with no larger share for himself
than accrued to the soldiers who merited it, and
secondly by willingly exposing himself to every danger
personally and shrinking from no hardship. His courting
danger was not surprising, in view of his ambition, but
his patient endurance of hardship was astonishing, for he
did not seem robust. His frame was spare, his skin soft
and white, he suffered from migraine and was subject to
epileptic seizures—a malady which first attacked him,
we are told, in Cordova. Yet he did not make delicate
health an excuse for soft living, but on the contrary his
campaigning a remedy for delicate health. He fought his
weakness with exhausting marches, simple diet, spend-

ing night after night in the open, continuous exertion, and so kept his body impregnable. Most of his sleep he got in carriages or sedan chairs, bestowing even his rest on activity. When he rode to garrisons or cities or en- trenchments by day a slave trained to write from dic- tation sat at his side, and a soldier with a sword stood beside him. He drove so rapidly that he completed his first journey from Rome to the Rhone in seven days.

"Riding was easy for him from boyhood; he would twine his arms tight behind his back and race his horse at top speed. In the Gallic campaigns he formed the habit of dictating from horseback, and would keep two—Oppius says even more—stenographers busy si- multaneously. We are told too that Caesar originated the practice of communicating with his staff in writing, for he would not take time for personal interviews when business was urgent, because so many matters required his attention and the city was so large. Here is an instance of his indifference to diet. When Valerius Leo, who was entertaining him in Milan, served asparagus dressed with myrrh instead of olive oil Caesar ate it without ado and rebuked his staff when they grumbled. 'It is enough not to eat what you don't like,' he said, 'to criticize gaucherie is gauche.' Once on a journey when a storm drove his suite into a humble steading, when he found there was only one room and that barely adequate for one person, he told his staff that medals must go to the strongest but necessities to the weakest, and bade Oppius occupy the room while he and the others slept under the door-shed."

5

But for us the most extraordinary facet of this competent Roman is his distinction as a man of letters. As an orator

Quintilian and other good critics ranked him second only to Cicero, but he wrote in many genres, and even in the midst of campaigning. The best ancient summary of Caesar's literary activity is a section in Suetonius' *Life* (56):

"Caesar left *Commentaries* of his own operations in the *Gallic* and the *Civil War* against Pompey. (The authorship of the *Alexandrine, African,* and *Spanish Wars* is uncertain; some ascribe them to Oppius and others to Hirtius, who supplied the final book to the incomplete *Gallic War.*) Of his *Commentaries* Cicero in his *Brutus* remarks [262]: 'The *Commentaries* Caesar wrote are most admirable. They are sinewy, forthright, and charming, stripped of all finery as of a garment. His purpose was to provide materials for others who might wish to write history, but though he might have obliged such scribblers as would prink his matter with curling-irons he has kept sensible people from dealing with the subject.' Hirtius' comment is more emphatic: 'So highly esteemed are the *Commentaries* in everyone's judgment that he seems to have deprived writers of a subject rather than provided them one. But our admiration is higher than other men's; others know how well and meticulously he wrote, but we know how effortlessly and quickly he finished his writing.' Asinius Pollio is of opinion that the *Commentaries* were put together somewhat carelessly and without strict regard for truth, inasmuch as Caesar gave too easy credence to accounts of what others had done and intentionally or out of forgetfulness distorted his own actions; Pollio thinks Caesar meant to correct and rewrite.

"Besides the *Commentaries* Caesar left two books *On Analogy,* two *Against Cato,* and also a poem entitled *The Journey.* The first of these works he wrote while crossing the Alps, on his way back to his army after holding the assizes in Hither Gaul; the second at the time of the battle of Munda; and the last in the course of a twenty-four-day journey from Rome to Farther Spain. Letters he addressed to the senate are also extant . . . as are some written to Cicero and to various friends. . . . He is also reported to have written, as a boy and young man, such things as *Praises of Hercules,* a tragedy called *Oedipus,* and *Collected Apophthegms;* Augustus forbade the publication of these works."

Remarks on the extant fragments of Caesar's lost works will be found at p. 355.

6

Modern critics agree with Cicero's and Hirtius' estimates of the *Commentaries,* but Pollio's exceptions are also well taken. Just as Caesar was the most competent conceivable authority to set forth the details of his campaigns, so was he the most nearly concerned to justify his course of action, and he was less interested in providing information for future historians than in vindicating himself in the eyes of contemporaries. If then the *Gallic War* is a pamphlet in the guise of history, its restraint is as admirable as it is effective; Caesar never raises his voice in partisan recriminations or self-justification but always maintains his third-person objectivity. The conviction of the author's prowess and patriotism grows not out of explicit avowals but out of the total impression of what is implicit in the whole work. His credibility, like his claim to genius, is enhanced by a style at once lucid and precise and elegant, written with the sovereign ease and purity of diction characteristic of the literary aristocrat.

The several books of the *Gallic War* may have been

published separately, each at the end of the year with which it deals, but it is more probable that the whole was written at a single stroke and published in 51. By then it was plain to all that had eyes to see, and surely to Caesar, that a breach with Pompey was inevitable, though the two men were still outwardly friends. In Rome Caesar had many bitter enemies, and if he could influence public opinion he might more easily obtain the second consulship which he needed. It would have defeated his purpose to falsify where his statements might be disproven; he grinds his own ax only in distribution of emphasis and ascription of motives. In his account the Gauls virtually force him to conquer them; the Gauls did in fact seem to offer ample provocation, but we cannot avoid a suspicion that personal ambition had something to do with the conquest. From his account of his dealings with the Usipetes and the Tencteri, no one would suspect that Cato had denounced him vehemently for treacherously violating a truce with those unfortunate tribes. Caesar merely gives his version of the facts, with apparently perfect candor and with no hint that he is refuting a different view.

The geographical disquisitions are regarded by some editors as spurious interpolations. Such an account as that of the Germans at VI:21-28 and especially of the fantastic fauna of the Hercynian forest does seem unworthy of Caesar's intelligence. But such descriptions of exotic regions are characteristic of ancient historiography, and Caesar wished to answer a natural and legitimate curiosity on the part of his readers. The passages in question were doubtless adapted from Greek travel books by secretaries at Caesar's order. Sometimes, as in the passage mentioned, they serve to distract attention from a military failure.

'The third person and the ostensible objectivity as well as the terse elegance of style reappear in the *Civil War*, but it is a more personal book nevertheless. In his distribution of emphasis, his attribution of motives both to himself and to his opponents, in aggrandizing his own merits and depreciating those of his adversaries to the degree of making them the butts of his sarcasm, Caesar's bias is given much more outspoken expression; such passages as I:1-11, III:31-33, and III:82-83 are open propaganda. The satirical thumbnail sketches of the Pompeian leaders, the picture of their brawling rivalry at Pompey's headquarters concerning their shares of Caesar's offices, even the repeated exhibitions of Caesar's military genius and his generous clemency and of Pompey's fecklessness, give the *Civil War* a psychologic interest which the *Gallic War* does not possess. Throughout, even when he is haranguing his troops before battle, Caesar represents himself as a devoted lover of peace who is being forced to take up arms. He is sparing of blood, even his enemies', and repeated examples of his conciliatory disposition and his clemency are given. One editor suggests as a subtitle *On Caesar's Clemency*.

7

We are better informed on Caesar's career than on that of any major political and military figure until the advent of newspapers. To supplement his own and his officers' memoirs we have, in the first place, the massive correspondence of Cicero and a half dozen of his speeches in which Caesar figures. Cicero was himself personally involved with both Caesar and Pompey, and his letters are like the dispatches of a newspaper correspondent. Sallust's *Catilinarian War* and his (or another contemporary's) *Epistle to Caesar* throw light on Caesar's political position. From a later century we have the biographies by Suetonius and Plutarch, both resting on good sources and both rich in anecdotes illustrating Caesar's private life and character. There are full accounts also in Dio Cassius (Books 36-44) and Appian, the former probably based on the later books of Livy which are lost to us. Lucan's epic on the *Civil War*, commonly called *Pharsalia*, is earlier than the others and follows the course of the war carefully.

Modern books on Caesar are numberless. For a reliable narrative, with bibliography, the serious student will turn to Vol. IX of the *Cambridge Ancient History*. The best book on the *Gallic War* for the English reader is the somewhat adulatory *Caesar's Conquest of Gaul* by T. Rice Holmes (2nd ed., 1911). The latest of a long series of popular biographies is Alfred Duggan's *Julius Caesar* (1955).

In the translation which follows geographical terms are given in the ancient form except where the modern equivalent is familiar. Identifications, from Latin to English and the reverse, will be found in the Gazetteer at the end of the volume. Thanks are due to the Columbia University Press for permission to adapt some paragraphs of this Introduction from my *History of Latin Literature*, and to Mrs. Margaret Davidson for valuable secretarial assistance.

MOSES HADAS

THE GALLIC WAR
AND OTHER WRITINGS
BY JULIUS CAESAR

GALLIC WAR

I
58 B.C.

1. The whole of Gaul is divided into three parts; of these one is inhabited by the Belgae, a second by the Aquitani, and the third by a people called Celts in their own language and Gauls in ours. Each differs from the others in language, customs, and laws. The Gauls are separated from the Aquitani by the Garonne, from the Belgae by the Marne and Seine. The most rugged of all are the Belgae, because they are farthest removed from the refinement and civilization of the Province and are less frequently visited by traders introducing wares which serve to slacken virility, and because they are nearest the Germans who live across the Rhine and with whom they are constantly at war. This same factor makes the Helvetii better fighters than other Gauls; they are in virtually daily battle with the Germans, either keeping them out of their own frontiers or carrying war into theirs. The sector occupied by the Gauls, as said above, starts from the Rhone and is bounded by the Garonne, the ocean, and the country of the Belgae; in the direction of the Sequani and Helvetii it touches the Rhine; and its trend is towards the north. The Belgae begin from the farthest frontiers of Gaul and ex-

tend to the lower part of the Rhine; they look to
the north and east. Aquitania extends from the Garonne
to the Pyrenees and the ocean which washes Spain; it
looks to the northwest.

2. Among the Helvetii, the most important and
wealthiest personage was Orgetorix. In the consulship of
Marcus Messalla and Marcus Piso [61 B.C.] ambition for
sovereignty led him to organize a conspiracy of the nobility and persuade the commonality to emigrate in full
force, arguing that their superior valor would easily give
them dominion over the whole of Gaul. They were easy
to persuade because geography confined the Helvetii in
all directions. On one side the broad and deep Rhine
separates the Helvetian country from the Germans; on
another the lofty Jura range lies between the Helvetii
and Sequani; and on the third side Lake Geneva and
the Rhone separate the Helvetii from our Province.
These limitations restricted their movements and made
aggression difficult—a very irksome situation for a bel-
ligerent people. Their territory was 240 miles long and
180 wide, and this they considered disproportionate to
their populousness and their high military reputation.

3. These arguments, reinforced by Orgetorix' prestige,
moved them to undertake preparations for a campaign
—to buy up the greatest quantity of draft-animals and
carts possible, to sow the widest possible extent of land
in order to ensure adequate supplies for the march, and
to establish peace and friendship with neighboring states.
For these preparations they calculated that two years
would suffice, and by official enactment fixed their departure for the third year. The management of the enterprise was delegated to Orgetorix, who undertook a
mission to the states. On his tour he persuaded the Se-
quanian Casticus, whose father Catamantaloedes had

been king over the Sequani for many years and had been
styled Friend of the Roman People by the senate, to
usurp the kingship over his state which his father had
held. Dumnorix the Aeduan, brother to Diviciacus who
then held the chieftaincy over his people and was a favorite of the masses, he persuaded to make a similar
attempt and gave him his daughter in marriage. The enterprise would be extremely easy, he assured them, because he was himself about to secure the sovereignty
over his own Helvetians, who were without doubt the
most powerful element in all Gaul, and he would use his
resources and his army to confirm their royal authority.
On the strength of these arguments they swore mutual
fidelity and expected that when they were kings of three
very powerful and stalwart peoples they would win possession of all Gaul.

4. The Helvetians were apprised of the scheme by an
informer, and compelled Orgetorix to plead his case in
fetters, as was their custom. The stated penalty, if he
were found guilty, was burning. On the day fixed for the
trial he brought into court all his retainers from all quarters, to the number of ten thousand, and also assembled
all his dependents and debtors, of whom he had a large
number. Through their presence he avoided standing
trial. This incensed the officials, who tried to impose
authority by force of arms. The magistrates were busy
collecting a large body of men from the countryside
when Orgetorix died; there is some suspicion that, as the
Helvetii think, he took his own life.

5. But despite his death the Helvetii persisted in their
determination to migrate. When they deemed their
preparations for the enterprise complete, they set fire to
all their strongholds, twelve in number, about 400
villages, and their other private buildings, and burned

all the grain except the three months' supply of meal
each man was ordered to take from home. The object
was to make them readier to undergo any danger by
eliminating hope of return. They persuaded their neighbors the Rauraci, Tulingi, and Latobrigi to join in their
scheme, burn their strongholds and villages, and emigrate with them. They also joined to their partnership
the Boii, who had lived across the Rhine but had crossed
into Noricum and taken Noreia.

6. There were only two routes which they could take.
The one through the Sequani, between the Jura range
and the Rhone, was so narrow and difficult that carts
could scarcely pass single file and a handful of men on
the high mountain overhanging it could easily prevent
movement. The other, through our Province, was much
easier and more convenient. The Rhone flows between
the Helvetii and Allobroges (who had lately been subdued) and is fordable in a number of places. Geneva
is the last town of the Allobroges and the nearest to the
Helvetii, and from it a bridge connects with the Helvetii.
The Helvetii thought they could either persuade the
Allobroges, who did not yet seem wholly reconciled to
Rome, to allow them passage through their country, or
else compel them to. When everything was ready, they
named a day for assembling at the banks of the Rhone;
the day was 28 March in the consulship of Lucius Piso
and Aulus Gabinius [58 B.C.].

7. When Caesar was informed that the Helvetii were
attempting a march through our Province, he left the
capital promptly, pushed on to Farther Gaul by the
longest stages possible, and arrived at Geneva. He requisitioned the largest possible number of troops from
the whole Province (there was only one legion in
Farther Gaul), and ordered the bridge at Geneva de-

stroyed. When the Helvetians were informed of Caesar's arrival, they sent him an embassy of their notables under the headship of Nammeius and Verucloetius, to declare their intention of marching through the Province, without doing any injury, because they had no other route, and to ask his permission to do so. Caesar was not minded to grant concessions to the Helvetii when he remembered that they had killed the consul Lucius Cassius and sent his defeated army under the yoke [107 B.C.], nor did he believe that a truculent people would refrain from mischief and violence if they were allowed to march through the Province. Nevertheless, to gain time for the soldiers he had requisitioned to muster, he told the embassy that he would require an interval for deliberation: they could come back on 13 April if they wished.

8. Meanwhile he used the legion he had with him and the soldiers from the Province who had assembled to build a wall sixteen feet high and a trench over the nineteen miles from Lake Geneva, which flows into the Rhone, to the Jura, which separates the Sequani from the Helvetii. When this was finished he built redoubts and posted pickets to prevent any attempt at crossing in defiance of his wish. When the embassy returned on the day appointed he said that he could not, following the established custom of the Roman people, grant anyone passage through the Province, and he made it plain that he would stop anyone who attempted to use force. Their hopes dashed, the Helvetii lashed boats together, made many rafts, forded the Rhone where it was shallow, sometimes by day and oftener by night, and tried to break through. But they were foiled by the earthworks, the quick concentration of soldiers, and showers of missiles, and abandoned the attempt.

9. The one route left was through the Sequani, but this was so narrow that it was impracticable unless the Sequani allowed them passage. They could not themselves persuade the Sequani to do so, and sent a deputation to the Aeduan Dumnorix in the hope that they could obtain permission through his intercession. Dumnorix had great influence with the Sequani because of his popularity and generosity, and he was also friendly to the Helvetians because he had married Orgetorix' daughter, who belonged to that state; moreover his ambition for rule gave him an interest in revolution and a desire to attach as many states as possible by doing them favors. He therefore undertook the mission and obtained permission of the Sequani for the Helvetii to pass through their country. He arranged an exchange of hostages, to oblige the Sequani not to obstruct the passage of the Helvetii, and the Helvetii to do no mischief or injury in their passage.

10. Caesar received intelligence of the Helvetii's intention to pass through the territory of the Sequani and Aedui into that of the Santones. This is not far from Toulouse, a state in our Province, and he realized the danger which a warlike people hostile to Rome would bring to the open and fertile districts of the Province if they adjoined it. Accordingly he put his legate Titus Labienus in charge of the fortifications he had built and himself hurried to Italy by forced marches. There he recruited two legions and brought out of their cantonments three which had been wintering near Aquileia. With these five legions he pushed on to Farther Gaul over the Alps. There, from their mountain strongpoints, the Ceutrones, Graeoceli, and Caturiges tried to stop the army's march but were repulsed in several engagements. In seven days Caesar moved from Ocelum,

the farthest point in Hither Gaul, to the Vocontii in Farther Gaul. From there he led his army to the territory of the Allobroges, and thence to that of the Segusiavi, the first people beyond the Province, across the Rhone.

11. By this time the Helvetii had passed the defiles through the territory of the Sequani and had reached that of the Aedui, whose farms they were ravaging. Unable to defend themselves and their property, the Aedui sent representatives to Caesar to ask for help. They had always been loyal to the Roman people, they said, and did not deserve to have their fields ravaged, their children carried off to slavery, and their towns sacked almost under the eyes of a Roman army. At the same time the Ambarri, kith and kin of the Aedui, told Caesar that their fields had been devastated and they could hardly defend their towns from enemy attack. Likewise the Allobroges who had villages and property across the Rhone fled to Caesar and showed him they had nothing left but their bare soil. In view of this situation Caesar decided to act before the Helvetii had dissipated all the property of the allies and reached the Santones.

12. The Saône flows through the Aedui and Sequani into the Rhone, and is so incredibly sluggish that the eye cannot discern the direction of its current. This the Helvetii were in process of crossing on rafts and boats lashed together. Upon his scouts' intelligence that three parts of the Helvetian host had already crossed and the fourth was still on the near side of the river, Caesar quitted his camp with three legions, a little after midnight, and reached the portion which had not yet crossed. He surprised them when they were laden with baggage and killed a great number; the remainder fled precipitately and hid in neighboring forests. The canton involved was the Tigurine, one of the four into which

the Helvetian state is divided. It was this canton which
had marched forth, in the memory of our fathers, and
killed the consul Lucius Cassius and sent his army under
the yoke. Whether by chance, then, or by the design of
the immortal gods, the portion of the Helvetian state
which had inflicted so signal a disaster upon the Roman
people was the first to receive full requital. In this case
Caesar exacted personal as well as public vengeance, for
in the battle in which they killed Cassius, the Tigurini
had also killed the legate Lucius Piso, grandfather of
Caesar's father-in-law Lucius Piso.

13. Following this battle Caesar bridged the Saône
and led his army across to take the offensive against the
rest of the Helvetian forces. When they saw that he accomplished in a single day a crossing that had taken
them fully twenty they were alarmed at his approach
and sent him a deputation headed by Divico, who had
commanded the Helvetians in the campaign against Cassius. His argument was as follows: If the Roman people
would make peace with the Helvetians they would go to
whatever district Caesar determined and settle there,
but if the Romans persisted in their hostilities they had
better remember their earlier reverse and the traditional
prowess of the Helvetians. Caesar had indeed surprised
a single canton when their countrymen who had already
crossed the river could not support them, but he must
not on that account exaggerate his own prowess or despise theirs. The tradition in which they had been
schooled by their forebears was to fight like men and not
rely on cunning or stratagems. Caesar must therefore
take no step that would make the ground they stood on
the site of a Roman disaster and the annihilation of a
Roman army whose name would go down in history.

14. And this was Caesar's response: He remembered

well the circumstances which the Helvetian representatives referred to and could therefore speak without hesitation. The conduct of the Helvetians had been outrageous because the Romans had done nothing to provoke it. If they had been conscious of any wrong on their part it would have been simple for them to take precautions; they had been overreached only because they knew they had done nothing to make them apprehensive, and thought there was no need for baseless apprehension. And even if he chose to forget the old affront, could Caesar put their fresh outrages from his mind— their attempt to force a passage through the Province against his will and their harassment of the Aedui, Ambarri, and Allobroges? Their insolent boasting of their victory, their surprise that Caesar had suffered their outrages so long with impunity, pointed to a single conclusion: To those whom the immortal gods meant to avenge for their crimes they regularly allowed a period of prosperity and continuing impunity, to make the reversal of their fortune more painful. Nevertheless, if the Helvetii would give hostages to assure him that they would perform their promises, and if they would give satisfaction to the Aedui and their allies for the damages they had done them, and likewise to the Allobroges, he would make peace with them. Divico replied that it was the established practice of the Helvetians to receive hostages, not give them, as the Roman people could testify, and with this reply he departed.

15. Next day the Helvetii struck camp. Caesar did likewise and sent all his cavalry, 4,000 men whom he had raised from the whole Province, the Aedui, and their allies, to reconnoiter the enemy's march. In their excessive eagerness to harass the enemy's rear, they engaged the Helvetian cavalry on unfavorable ground and suf-

fered a few casualties. The Helvetians, elated at having
repulsed so large a body of cavalry with but 500 men,
began to make halts, when their rear guard would
attempt to provoke a battle. Caesar kept his men from
fighting, satisfied for the present with keeping the enemy
from pillaging, foraging, and ravaging. The march continued for some fifteen days, with no more than five or
six miles between the rear of the enemy column and the
van of ours.

16. Meanwhile Caesar continually pressed the Aedui
for the grain which they had formally engaged to supply.
Gaul, as has been noted, lies in the north, and the cold
not only retarded the ripening of crops but there was not
even enough fodder. The grain Caesar had brought up
the Saône on barges was not available for use because
the Helvetii had veered away from the river and Caesar
was determined to keep close to them. The Aedui
dragged the business on—the grain was being collected,
they said, it was being hauled up, it was very near.
When Caesar realized that they were temporizing, and
the day for issuing the soldiers their rations was approaching, he summoned the Aeduan notables, of whom
he had a goodly number in his camp. Among them were
Diviciacus and Liscus, who was their highest magistrate
—the Aeduan title is Vergobret; he is elected annually
and holds power of life and death over his people. Caesar took them to task for not helping out at so critical
a juncture when the enemy was so near and there was no
grain to buy or take from the fields. It was largely
at their prayers that he had undertaken the war, and
their failure was therefore particularly reprehensible.

17. Stung by Caesar's upbraiding, Liscus at long last
disclosed a fact he had previously dissembled. There
were certain influential persons whose prestige among

the masses gave them as individuals higher power than
the magistrates themselves. Their wickedly subversive
agitation deterred the multitude from delivering their
due quotas of grain. It was better, they argued, if the
Aedui could not secure the primacy in Gaul, to submit
to Gallic rather than Roman suzerainty, for there could
be no doubt that if the Romans defeated the Helvetii
they would enslave the Aedui along with the rest of
Gaul. It was these same persons who communicated all
our plans and all that went on in the camp to the Helvetii, and Liscus could do nothing to stop them. He realized the danger he was exposing himself to in making
these revelations to Caesar, as he was compelled to do;
that was why he had kept silent as long as he could.

18. Caesar sensed that Liscus' remarks referred to Diviciacus' brother Dumnorix, but because he did not wish
to bring his suspicions up before so many people,
he promptly dismissed the council but retained Liscus
and questioned him privately about his remarks in the
meeting. Liscus was outspoken and explicit, and when
Caesar questioned others individually his suspicions were
confirmed. The culprit was Dumnorix, a bold character
whose open-handedness made him popular with the
masses and an ambitious revolutionary. For many years
he had contracted for the Aeduan customs and other
taxes at a low figure because no one dared oppose his
bid. This multiplied his fortune and enabled him to bribe
on a lavish scale. He maintained at his own expense and
always kept about his person a large force of cavalry,
and his influence spread beyond his own to neighboring
states. To extend his power he had married his mother
to the noblest and most powerful of the Bituriges, had
himself married a Helvetian wife, and had arranged
marriages for his half-sister and other female relatives in

other states. His connection with the Helvetii made him a strong partisan of their cause, and he hated Caesar and the Romans on his own account because their coming had diminished his power and restored his brother Diviciacus to his former influence and dignity. If the Romans should meet with adversity he cherished high hopes of securing the throne through Helvetian support. Roman rule thwarted not only his hope of kingship but even of retaining the popularity he possessed. Caesar also found, in his investigation, that in the cavalry reverse suffered a few days before it was Dumnorix and his squadron (he was in command of the cavalry the Aedui had sent to support Caesar) who had started the retreat; it was their flight which had spread panic in the rest of the cavalry.

19. To top these damning revelations there was a series of indisputable facts: Dumnorix had brought the Helvetii through the territory of the Sequani, had procured the interchange of hostages, had done this not only without Caesar's and his own people's permission but even without their knowledge, and had now been accused by the highest Aeduan authority. Caesar considered the grounds sufficient for punishing Dumnorix himself or ordering his state to do so. But there was a strong objection. Caesar had grown convinced that Dumnorix' brother Diviciacus was devoted to the Roman cause, loyal to himself, and a man of singular fidelity, justice, and moderation; and he was apprehensive of offending Diviciacus by punishing his brother. Before taking further steps, therefore, he summoned Diviciacus, dismissed the regular interpreters, and talked with him through Gaius Valerius Procillus, a leading personage in the Province and an intimate friend in whom he had the fullest confidence in all matters. Caesar reminded

Diviciacus of what had been said about Dumnorix in the Gallic council in his own presence and told him what individuals had said about him separately. He begged and urged him not to be offended if he should either deal with the case himself and pass sentence or bid the state do so.

20. With a flood of tears Diviciacus embraced Caesar and began to implore him not to pass a severe judgment upon his brother. The allegations were true, he admitted, and no one was sorrier than himself. When his own influence was supreme at home and in the rest of Gaul, and his brother's, because of his youth, very low, it was he that made his brother great, and his brother had exploited his resources and connections not only to undermine Diviciacus' influence but very nearly to destroy him. But Diviciacus still felt the force of brotherly affection and public opinion. If Dumnorix should come to grief at Caesar's hands while Diviciacus ranked as Caesar's friend, no one would believe that Diviciacus had not consented to the step, and in consequence all Gaul would be alienated from him. While Diviciacus was beseeching Caesar, volubly and tearfully, Caesar grasped his right hand to console him and bade him say no more: so highly did he value his good will that he would yield to his urgent request and condone Dumnorix' political offense and his own grievances. Then Caesar summoned Dumnorix, with Diviciacus present, itemized the derelictions based on his own investigations and the complaints of Dumnorix' countrymen, admonished him to avoid suspicious conduct in future, and said that he would overlook the past for his brother's sake. Caesar then assigned agents to keep Dumnorix under observation and report on his movements and associations.

21. That same day his patrols informed Caesar that

the enemy had encamped under a height eight miles
from the Roman camp, and he sent a party to reconnoiter the hill and ascertain the difficulty of an ascent
from the rear. The report was that the ascent was easy.
Caesar discussed his plan with his first deputy Titus
Labienus and ordered him to ascend the height a little
after midnight with two legions and the guides who had
scouted the route. About two in the morning he pushed
on towards the enemy on the road they had themselves
taken, sending all his cavalry ahead. With these patrols
he sent Publius Considius, who had served under Sulla
and then under Crassus and was reputed to be a very
competent officer.

22. At dawn Labienus was in possession of the height
and Caesar only a mile and a half from the enemy camp
and, as he subsequently ascertained from prisoners,
neither his nor Labienus' position was known to the
enemy. At this moment Considius rode up at a gallop
and said that the hill Labienus was to occupy was in
possession of the enemy; he had recognized the Gallic
arms and standards. Caesar withdrew his forces to the
nearest hill and formed his line, and Labienus, who had
been instructed not to engage until he saw Caesar's
troops near the enemy camp so as to synchronize the
attack, held off after he had seized the hill and waited
for the main body. Late in the day Caesar's patrols reported that his own men were holding the hill and that
the Helvetii had moved off; Considius had panicked and
given an eye-witness account of something he had not
seen. That day Caesar followed the enemy at the usual
interval and pitched camp three miles from theirs.

23. In just two days rations were due to be issued to
the army, and as he was only eighteen miles from
Bibracte, the largest and richest town of the Aedui, he

thought his commissary should be secured and turned from the Helvetians' route to make for Bibracte. Deserters from Lucius Aemilius, commander of a Gallic troop of horse, reported the move to the enemy. The Helvetii thought the Romans had veered off because they were afraid, on the basis of their failure to engage the day before when they had advantage of position, or perhaps they thought they could cut the Romans off from their grain stocks. In any case they altered their plan, reversed their march, and began to pursue and harass our rear.

24. When he became aware of the situation, Caesar withdrew his forces to the nearest hill and sent his cavalry to meet the enemy onset. Halfway up the hill, meanwhile, he deployed the four veteran legions in a triple line and posted the two legions newly recruited in Nearer Gaul and all the auxiliaries on the summit. The whole hill was filled with men. All the packs he ordered stacked in one place, which was entrenched by the men in the top line. The Helvetii came up with all their wagons. They parked their baggage in one spot, repulsed our cavalry with their dense mass, and formed a phalanx to move against our front line.

25. Caesar removed his own and then the others' horses from sight so as to equalize the danger and banish any thought of flight, harangued his men, and joined battle. Hurling their pikes from higher ground, the soldiers easily broke the enemy phalanx and charged its members with drawn swords. The Gauls were greatly hampered by the fact that our pikes pierced a number of their shields and locked them together. The iron shanks of the heads bent so that they could not pull the shields loose or use their left arms freely. After thrashing their arms about they preferred to drop their shields al-

together and fight with bodies uncovered. At last they
were worn down by wounds, began to give ground, and
withdraw to a hill a mile off. They had gained the hill
and our men were pressing after them when the Boii and
Tulingi, about 15,000 strong, who had served as a rear
guard to close the enemy column, attacked our exposed
right flank and began to take it from the rear. Upon seeing this the Helvetians who had retired to the hill
pressed forward to launch a fresh attack. The Romans
reversed standards to form two divisions: the first two
lines to oppose the enemy which had been beaten and
driven off, the third to meet the newcomers.

26. The battle on two fronts was long and hard
fought. When they could no longer withstand our pressure, one division retired up the hill as they had begun to
do, and the other to their wagons and baggage. And in
good order, for though the battle had gone on from early
afternoon till evening, no one saw an enemy turn his
back. At the baggage too the fighting went on till late in
the night, for the enemy had made a stockade of their
wagons and from their elevation hurled weapons at our
men as they came up. Some threw pikes and darts from
between the cart wheels and wounded our men. After
a long fight our men got possession of their camp and
baggage. Orgetorix' daughter and one of his sons were
taken prisoner. About 130,000 survived the battle and
marched without stopping all that night. Three days
later they reached the territory of the Lingones; our men
were unable to pursue, for they remained for three days
to tend the wounded and bury the dead. Caesar sent
messengers and dispatches to the Lingones forbidding
them to assist the Helvetii with grain or otherwise: if
they did so he would make no distinction between them

and the Helvetii. After an interval of three days he resumed his pursuit in full force.

27. The Helvetii now had nothing and were compelled to send representatives to Caesar to capitulate. These encountered him on the march, prostrated themselves at his feet, and with tearful importunities begged for peace. Caesar directed them to wait for him where they were, and they obeyed. Upon his arrival he required them to surrender hostages, their weapons, and the slaves who had deserted to them. While these were being searched out and brought together night fell, and about 6,000 men of the canton called Verbigeni left the camp. They may have been afraid that they would be executed when they had given up their arms, or they may have thought their flight would be covered up by the surrender of so great a multitude or go unnoticed altogether. In the hope of saving themselves they pushed on to the German frontiers on the Rhine.

28. When Caesar learned of this he ordered the peoples through whose territory they had gone to round them up and bring them back if they wished to be clear of complicity. They were brought back, and Caesar treated them as enemies; but all the rest he allowed to surrender when they had delivered hostages, weapons, and deserters. The Helvetii, Tulingi, and Latobrigi he ordered to return to their own country which they had left, and since all their grain was lost and they had not the wherewithal to prevent starvation, he directed the Allobroges to help them out with grain; they themselves had to rebuild the towns and villages they had burned down. Caesar's motive was not to leave the country the Helvetii had abandoned unoccupied, for its fertility might tempt the Germans across the Rhine to move in to

the Helvetian lands and become neighbors of the
Province of Gaul and the Allobroges. Upon the petition
of the Aedui he allowed the Boii, whose outstanding
courage was generally acknowledged, to settle in their
country. The Aedui assigned them lands and subsequently admitted them to equal rights and privileges
with themselves.

29. In the Helvetian camp there were found and
brought to Caesar rosters written in Greek characters
giving the names and numbers of those who had emi-
grated and of those able to bear arms, with separate lists
of boys, old men, and women. The totals amounted to
263,000 Helvetii, 36,000 Tulingi, 14,000 Latobrigi, 23,-
000 Rauraci, 22,000 Boii. Those capable of bearing arms
numbered 92,000, and the grand total was 368,000. Pursuant to Caesar's orders a census was taken of those who
returned home, and the number was found to be 110,000.

30. Upon the completion of the Helvetian campaign
the chieftains representing virtually all the Gallic states
came to thank Caesar. They realized, they said, that he
had requited long-standing Helvetian affronts to the Roman people, but Caesar's success had benefited Gaul as
well as the Roman people, because the Helvetians had
migrated, though they were prospering in their own
country, to make aggressive war upon all Gaul and usurp
sovereignty over it, and then out of the wide choice before them choose the most fertile and convenient loca-
tion for their own abode and make the remainder
tributary. The chieftains petitioned Caesar for permission to convoke a council of all Gaul on a given day, on
the grounds that they wished to obtain unanimous consent for certain requests they wanted to make of Caesar.
Permission given, they fixed a day for the council and ex-

changed oaths that none should divulge their proceedings except to persons authorized by the council.

31. Upon the dissolution of their council the same chieftains who had foregathered with Caesar before returned and asked for the privilege of a secret and secluded conference on matters of import to their own and the general welfare. The privilege granted, they prostrated themselves at Caesar's feet in tears and told him that it was of as great moment to them that the information they gave him should not be divulged as it was that he should act favorably upon it, because if it were divulged they would be subject to dire vengeance. Their spokesman was Diviciacus. "Gaul as a whole," he said, "is divided into two factions, headed respectively by the Aedui and the Arverni. The two had bitterly contested the supremacy for many years, until the Arverni and Sequani hired the Germans. At first some 15,000 of the savage barbarians crossed the Rhine, but when they had fallen in love with Gallic farming and civilization and abundance they brought more over, until now there are 120,000 of them in Gaul. The Aedui and their dependents have fought them repeatedly, but we have been disastrously defeated and have lost all our nobility, all our senate, all our knighthood. It is these disastrous defeats that have shattered a power which our courage and our alliance with Rome once made paramount in Gaul. We have been compelled to surrender our leading personages to the Sequani as hostages and to engage our commonwealth on oath not to ask our hostages back or to solicit assistance from Rome but remain submissive forever to their sovereign dictates. I alone of the whole Aeduan state could not be brought to swear the oath or surrender my children as

hostages. That is why I fled to Rome and went to ask help of the senate; I was the only one not bound by oaths and hostages. But the Sequani have fared worse than the vanquished Aedui. The German king Ariovistus has settled in their territory and occupied a third part of the lands, which are the best in all Gaul. Now he is asking them to cede another third because a few months ago 24,000 Harudes joined him, and he must provide a place for them to settle in. In a few years all the Gauls will be expelled, and all the Germans come over across the Rhine, for there is no comparison between German soil and Gallic or between their victuals and ours. The single victory Ariovistus won over the Gallic forces in a battle at Magetobriga has made him a cruel and arrogant tyrant. He demands the children of all the noblemen as hostages and inflicts every species of torture upon them if they do not heed his every nod and beck. He is a passionate and headstrong savage and his tyranny has grown intolerable. Unless Caesar and the Roman people come to our aid we shall all have to follow the example of the Helvetians—emigrate, seek new lands to settle in far from the Germans, and try what luck will bring. If Ariovistus gets wind of this he will certainly wreak the ultimate vengeance upon all the hostages in his keeping. You, Caesar, can prevent a larger horde of Germans from crossing the Rhine, by your and your army's prestige, by your recent victory, by the name of Rome; only you can protect all Gaul from Ariovistus' oppression."

32. Upon the conclusion of this address all present burst into tears and begged Caesar's help. Caesar noticed that the Sequani alone failed to join in but gloomily stared at the ground with bowed heads. Caesar wondered what the reason might be, but they made no answer when he asked but kept their gloomy silence,

When repeated questioning could elicit no response the same Aeduan Diviciacus spoke up: "The Sequani are in a more wretched and difficult situation than the rest; even alone and in secret they dare not complain or beg for help and they shudder at Ariovistus' savagery though he is far away as though he were present in the flesh. The others have a chance of running away, but the Sequani have Ariovistus inside their country and all their towns are in his possession; they must put up with all his torments."

33. On learning what their situation was, Caesar heartened the Gauls and promised that he would give the matter his attention; he was very hopeful, he said, that his good offices and influence would prevail on Ariovistus to desist from his outrages. Then he adjourned the meeting. There were additional urgent considerations which made it advisable for Caesar to face and deal with the problem. He could see, in the first place, that the Aedui, whom the senate had repeatedly addressed as Brothers and Kinsmen, were held in bondage to German tyranny, and he knew that their hostages were in the power of Ariovistus and the Sequani. In view of the stature of the Roman Empire, this was very discreditable to himself and the commonwealth. He saw, furthermore, that the Germans were gradually forming a habit of crossing the Rhine and that the presence of large numbers of them in Gaul was prejudicial to Roman interests. And when they had occupied all Gaul he did not think that men so barbarous and uncontrolled would hesitate to march into the Province, as the Cimbri and Teutoni before them had done, and thence push on into Italy, especially since only the Rhone separated the Sequani from our Province. These contingencies only prompt action could obviate, he thought, and as for

Ariovistus himself, his high airs and the arrogant posture
he assumed could not be tolerated.

34. His decision, then, was to send representatives to
ask Ariovistus to designate some halfway point for a
conference, saying that he wished to discuss state matters of the highest moment to both parties. Ariovistus
answered the deputation that if he needed anything of
Caesar he would have come to him, and if Caesar wished
anything he must come to him. He would not venture
into the area of Gaul which Caesar held, furthermore,
without an army, and it would involve a great bother
and an extensive commissariat to concentrate an army.
He wondered anyhow, he said, what business Caesar or
the Roman people had in the part of Gaul which was his
by right of conquest.

35. Upon receipt of this response Caesar again sent
envoys to Ariovistus with the following message: Ariovistus had been treated with great courtesy by Caesar
and the Roman people, for it was in Caesar's consulship
that the senate had styled him King and Friend. His requital to Caesar and the Roman people was a rejection
of an invitation to a conference and refusal to consider
and discuss matters of mutual interest. These now were
Caesar's demands: First, Ariovistus must bring no further body of men across the Rhine into Gaul; second, he
must restore the Aeduan hostages he held and allow the
Sequani, with his consent, to restore those they held; further, he must not molest the Aedui nor make war upon
them and their allies. If he complied, Caesar and the Roman people would maintain permanent friendly relations
with him; if not, then in pursuance of a senatorial decree
dated in the consulship of Marcus Messalla and Marcus
Piso to the effect that the governor of Gaul should protect the Aedui and other friends of the Roman people

consistently with the interests of the state, Caesar would not overlook the wrongs inflicted upon the Aedui.

36. Ariovistus' response was as follows: By the rights of war the victors dictate their own terms to the vanquished. So the Roman people followed the principle of dictating to conquered peoples at its own discretion and not according to the mandates of a third party. If Ariovistus did not prescribe limits within which the Romans should exercise their right, the Romans should not interfere in his rights. The Aedui had risked war and been defeated, and had become tributary to him; Caesar was damaging his interest, for his march was reducing Ariovistus' income. He would not restore their hostages to the Aedui, nor would he make war upon them and their allies without cause if they stood by their agreement and paid their annual tribute. If they did not, the title Brethren of the Roman People would do them little good. Caesar had said that he would not overlook the injuries inflicted upon the Aedui: no man has fought Ariovistus and escaped ruin. Caesar might come on whenever he liked; he would learn the prowess of the invincible Germans, who were past masters of war and had not sheltered under a roof for fourteen years.

37. As this message was being delivered to Caesar, there came deputies of the Aedui and the Treveri. The Aedui complained that the Harudes who had newly been brought into Gaul were ravaging their field; even the surrender of additional hostages had failed to purchase peace of Ariovistus. The Treveri complained that a hundred cantons of Suebi had halted at the Rhine and were attempting a crossing; their leaders were the brothers Nasua and Cimberius. At this Caesar was gravely alarmed. Time was of the essence, for if this new band of Suebi joined Ariovistus' veteran force they

would not be easy to oppose. Accordingly Caesar secured his commissary with all possible speed and
pushed on towards Ariovistus by forced marches.

38. When he had marched for three days word came
that Ariovistus was hurrying on in full force to seize
Besançon, the largest town of the Sequani, and had already gone three days' march beyond his frontier. This
must be prevented, Caesar thought, at all costs. The town
was abundantly stocked with every kind of war material,
and its strong natural defenses made it an ideal seat for
extensive military operations. The river surrounds it in
an almost complete circle; the arc not protected by the
river is only 1,600 feet and is closed by a high hill whose
roots touch the banks of the river. A circuit wall makes a
citadel of the hill and joins it to the town. It was to this
place that Caesar pushed on, marching night and day; he
seized it and posted a garrison in it.

39. During the wait for provisions and other supplies
at Besançon, a violent panic suddenly shook the sanity
of the whole army and demoralized it. It arose from the
queries of our men and the remarks of Gauls and traders
who declared that the Germans were huge men and un-
believably brave and skillful fighters; often when they encountered them, they said, they could not endure the expression on their faces or their piercing eyes. The panic
started with tribunes, auxiliary officers, and others who
had followed Caesar from the capital for political pre-
ferment and had little military experience. One after
another asked for furloughs, alleging important reasons
that required them to leave. Some were shamed into
staying to avoid the imputation of cowardice. But they
could not put on a brave front or even hold their tears,
but hid in their tents to bemoan their fate or joined their
intimates to commiserate the general doom. All over the

camp wills were being drawn up. Gradually even the
experienced campaigners, soldiers, centurions, and cavalry commanders, were affected by the gloomy tenor of
this talk. Some who were unwilling to betray their cowardice declared that it was not the enemy they were
afraid of but the narrow roads and wide forests which
lay between them and Ariovistus, or the failure of the
transport. Some even announced to Caesar that when
he gave orders to strike camp and advance the soldiers
would not heed the command but stand rooted for fear.

40. Caesar took cognizance of the situation and convoked a meeting at which centurions of all grades were
present. He upbraided them roundly for presuming that
it was their business to question or debate their general's
objectives or designs. When Caesar was consul Ariovistus
had been very eager to court the friendship of the Roman people; why should anyone suppose that he would
now rashly deviate from his obligations? For himself Caesar was convinced that when Ariovistus studied his demands and realized how fair the terms were he would
not repudiate his tie with Caesar and the Roman people.
But even if mad passion goaded him to war, what was
there to fear, and why should they distrust their own
courage and Caesar's competence? Rome had taken this
enemy's measure within our fathers' memory, when the
defeat of the Cimbri and Teutoni [102 B.C.] had
reflected no less glory on the army than on its general;
and more recently in the slave uprising [73-71 B.C.],
though there they were helped by the practice and training we had given them. That war, indeed, is a demon-
stration of the value of steadfastness: the men the soldiers had dreaded without reason when they were unarmed they subsequently defeated when they were
armed and flushed with victory. Finally, Caesar said,

these were the same men the Helvetii had repeatedly encountered, not only in their own but in the Germans'
country, and had generally defeated; and yet the Helvetii had proven no match for our army. What then of
the defeat and rout of the Gauls? If that case were ex-
amined it would be found that the Gauls were tired out
by the long campaign, because Ariovistus hid in his
camp in the marshes and offered no chance for an engagement, and then when the Gauls had given up hope
of a battle and were dispersing Ariovistus attacked and
won by stratagem rather than courage. Against naïve
natives there was room for a stratagem, but not even
Ariovistus could expect that our army would be taken in
by it. Those who dissembled their panic as concern over
the commissary and the narrow roads were guilty of
presumption, for they apparently either mistrusted the
general's competence or meant to teach him his job. The
business was receiving his attention; Sequani, Leuci,
and Lingones were supplying grain, and the crops were
ripe in the fields. Of the roads they would themselves
shortly be in position to judge. The disobedience that
was threatened, the refusal to march when ordered, both-
ered him not at all. Mutinies rise only against generals
who have blundered and failed or who had been guilty
of criminal and proven avarice. Caesar's whole life testified to his integrity, and the Helvetian campaign proved
his success. Accordingly the move he would have postponed to a later day he would execute at once; camp
would be struck the following day in the last quarter of
the night, so that Caesar might ascertain at once whether
honor and duty or cowardice was the stronger. If no one
else would follow he would march with the Tenth Legion
alone, about which he had no doubts, and it would serve
as his official escort. Caesar had always shown special

favor to the Tenth, and had complete confidence in its soldierliness.

41. This speech effected a remarkable change of morale. The greatest readiness and ardor for active duty was manifested, and the Tenth Legion took the lead in thanking Caesar, through their tribunes, for his high opinion of them and in declaring their complete readiness for action. Then the other legions delegated their tribunes and senior centurions to satisfy Caesar that they had never doubted or been afraid and had recognized that it was the general's part, not theirs, to direct operations. Their apologies were accepted, and from Diviciacus, the one Gaul Caesar fully trusted, he discovered a route through open country, though it involved a detour of more than fifty miles. In the fourth watch he started the march, as he said he would do, and after seven days of continuous marching was notified by his patrols that Ariovistus' forces were twenty-four miles off.

42. Upon learning of Caesar's approach, Ariovistus sent representatives to say that since Caesar had come near enough for a parley to be held without danger to himself he would now not oppose Caesar's previous request for an interview. Caesar did not spurn his terms, for the unsolicited offer to do what he had previously refused to do on request suggested that he had recovered his sanity, and he hoped that when Ariovistus learned his demands he would abandon his stubbornness in consideration of the great favors conferred upon him by Caesar and the Roman people. The interview was fixed for four days later, but in the meanwhile there were frequent interchanges of representatives. Ariovistus insisted that Caesar bring no infantry to the parley, for fear he might be overreached by treachery; he would come only if each party would bring a cavalry escort. Caesar did

not wish the excuse to stand in the way of the conference,
but neither was he willing to trust his life to Gallic troop-
ers. The best plan, he decided, was to mount the legionary soldiers of the Tenth on the Gallic cavalry horses; he
had complete confidence that these men would provide
perfectly loyal protection in case of need. As the change
was being made a soldier of the Tenth passed a witty remark: "Caesar is better than his promise; he said he
would make the Tenth his official escort, and now he's
knighting us."

43. For the conference they repaired, as had been
agreed, to a large plain with an earthen knoll about equi-
distant from Caesar's and Ariovistus' camps. Caesar
posted the mounted legion he had brought 200 paces
from the knoll, and Ariovistus' cavalry halted at an equal
distance. Ariovistus demanded that they confer on horseback, each with an escort of ten men. When they reached
the spot Caesar began by mentioning the favors he and
the senate had conferred upon Ariovistus: he had been
styled King and Friend by the senate and had received
magnificent gifts. Such privileges, Caesar pointed out,
were conferred very rarely, and in recognition of outstanding services; Ariovistus had had no right to approach the senate and no claim upon it, but had obtained his distinctions by the free grace of Caesar and
the senate. Caesar proceeded to show that Roman ties
with the Aedui were well-based and of long standing.
Frequent senatorial decrees had been passed to honor
them, and they had always been the paramount power
in Gaul, even before they sued for our friendship. It was
the settled principle of the Roman people that their allies
and friends should not only suffer no loss but be enhanced in influence and dignity and honor; how then
could it be tolerable for them to be despoiled of what

they already possessed when they entered into friendship with the Roman people? Next Caesar made the same demands as he had transmitted through his envoys: Ariovistus must not make war on the Aedui or their allies; he must return the hostages; if he could send no part of the Germans back home, he must allow no more to cross the Rhine.

44. To Caesar's demands Ariovistus' reply was brief, but he enlarged on his own virtues. He had crossed the Rhine, he said, not on his own initiative but at the urgent summons of the Gauls, and it was not without great inducements and great expectations that he had left home and kin. The lands he occupied had been granted him by the Gauls themselves, and it was with their consent that they gave him hostages; their tribute he collected by right of war, according to the usage of conquerors and conquered. He had not made war upon the Gauls, he said, but they on him; all their states had gathered to attack him and had pitched camp against him, and he had beaten and crushed all their forces in a single battle. If they wished to try again he was ready to fight it out again; but if they wished to enjoy peace it was unreasonable to demur at the tribute which they had been paying voluntarily. Friendship with the Roman people should be a distinction and a safeguard, not a liability, and that was why he had solicited it. If friendship with Rome meant the loss of tribute and the withdrawal of his subjects, he would reject that friendship as heartily as he had solicited it. His importation of a horde of Germans into Gaul was a measure of defense, not aggression; the proof he cited was that he had himself come only on invitation, and that his war had been defensive, not offensive. He had entered Gaul ahead of the Romans; no Roman army had previously advanced beyond its

Gallic Province. What did Caesar mean by invading his domains? This part of Gaul was his as much as the other was ours. It was as improper for us to interfere in his domain as it would be for him to raid the Roman Province. Caesar had called the Aedui Brethren, but Ariovistus was not so ignorant or naïve as not to know that in the recent Allobrogian war the Romans had given the Aedui no assistance, nor had the Aedui benefited by Roman help in their conflicts with himself and the Sequani. He was bound to suspect that Caesar's "friendship" was a pretext for keeping an army in Gaul in order to ruin him. And if he did not go and take his army out of the district, he would consider him not a friend but an enemy. If he killed Caesar he would be obliging many important personages in Rome; this he knew from the emissaries they had sent; he was in position to purchase their grateful friendship by Caesar's death. But if Caesar did withdraw and leave Ariovistus in free possession of Gaul, he would recompense him very handsomely and also carry out any military operations he wished with no effort or danger on Caesar's part.

45. Caesar spoke at length to the proposition that it was impossible to withdraw from the business in hand. It was contrary to his own and Roman practice, he said, to abandon highly deserving allies, nor could he acknowledge that Ariovistus had a better claim to Gaul than had Rome. The Arverni and Ruteni had been conquered by Quintus Fabius Maximus, but the Roman people had pardoned them and neither reduced them to a province nor subjected them to tribute. If priority was the criterion, the Roman claim to sovereignty over Gaul was unimpeachable; if the judgment of the senate was to be respected, Gaul should be free, for though it was vanquished in war, the senate had granted it autonomy.

46. The debate was still in progress when Caesar received word that Ariovistus' horsemen were moving towards the knoll and riding up to our troops to throw stones and darts at them. Caesar put an end to his speech and rejoined his men, whom he gave strict orders not to return the fire. A battle between the elite legionaries and cavalry involved no risk whatever, but he thought an engagement should be avoided, for if the enemy were defeated they might allege that they had been treacherously surrounded during a parley. Word of Ariovistus' arrogant attitude spread among the rank and file, and when they heard how insolently he had interdicted all Gaul to the Romans, how his horsemen had attacked ours, and how this action had broken off the parley, the army was inspired with even keener appetite for battle.

47. Two days later Ariovistus sent representatives to tell Caesar that he wished to resume the discussions which had been begun but left unfinished: Caesar should again appoint a day for a meeting, or if this did not suit him, send one of his officers as a deputy. Caesar saw no occasion for a conference, particularly since the Germans could not be prevented from firing missiles at our men the day before. To send one of his own staff and expose him to savages, he thought, would be very dangerous. The best course appeared to be to send Gaius Valerius Procillus, son of Gaius Valerius Caburus, a young man of high gallantry and courtesy whose father had been enfranchised by Gaius Valerius Flaccus. Procillus was loyal and knew Gallic, which Ariovistus had learned from long association, and the Germans had no motive to misuse him. With him he sent Marcus Mettius, who had ties of hospitality with Ariovistus. Their orders were to learn Ariovistus' views and report to Caesar. As soon as Ariovistus caught sight of them in his camp he

shouted out: "What are you coming here for? To spy?"
When they tried to speak he prevented them and threw
them in chains.

48. That same day Ariovistus moved his camp forward to the foot of a hill six miles from Caesar's camp.
The next day he marched his troops past Caesar's camp
and encamped two miles beyond, with the design of cutting off the convoys of food which were being brought
up by the Sequani and Aedui. For five successive days
Caesar deployed his forces in battle order in front of his
camp to give Ariovistus a chance to fight if he wished to
take it; all this while Ariovistus kept his army in camp
but fought daily cavalry battles. The mode of fighting
to which the Germans were trained was the following.
There were 6,000 cavalry and the same number of nim-
ble and rugged foot soldiers, individually chosen out of
the whole army by individual cavalrymen for their own
protection. These men accompanied the cavalry in action, covered their retreat, intervened if the fighting was
stiff, and surrounded and protected any trooper who
had been seriously wounded or unseated. Training had
given them such speed that in a prolonged advance or
rapid retreat they could keep up with the horses by holding onto their manes.

49. When Caesar realized that Ariovistus meant to
keep to his camp he decided to regain access to his convoys. He chose a suitable camp site some 600 paces beyond where the Germans were encamped and marched
to the new position in triple column. He directed the
first two lines to stand under arms and the third to build
the camp. To this site, which, as has been noted, was
600 paces away, Ariovistus sent some 16,000 light-armed
men and all his cavalry to frighten our people and keep

them from working. Caesar nevertheless persisted in his design, and directed the two lines to repel the enemy and the third to finish its work. When the camp was completed he left two legions and part of the auxiliaries there and brought the remaining four back to the larger camp.

50. The next day Caesar resumed his practice of offering the enemy a chance to fight; he led his forces out of both camps to a point a little forward of the larger and there formed up. When he realized that Ariovistus would not advance even so, he withdrew to camp about noon. Then at last Ariovistus sent part of his forces to attack the lesser camp. Both sides fought briskly until evening, and after he had inflicted and suffered many casualties Ariovistus retired to camp at sunset. When Caesar inquired of his prisoners why Ariovistus had not joined battle, he discovered the reason was that German custom required that their matrons must declare on the basis of lots and divinations whether or not it was advantageous to give battle, and the matrons had stated that the Germans were not fated to win if they fought before the new moon.

51. On the following day Caesar left what appeared to be an adequate garrison in each camp; posted all the auxiliaries in front of the lesser camp in sight of the enemy, mainly for show, because his legionaries were numerically inferior to the enemy; and himself advanced against the enemy camp in triple line. Now the Germans had to lead their forces out of camp perforce, and they posted them at intervals by tribes—Harudes, Marcomani, Triboci, Vangiones, Nemetes, Sedusii, Suebi. To leave no hope of flight they surrounded their line with carts and wagons, in which they placed their

women. As the men advanced, the women stretched their hands out and tearfully implored them not to deliver them into Roman slavery.

52. Caesar put his staff officers in command of the individual legions, so that each man would have a witness to his gallantry, and himself engaged in the right wing because he had observed that the confronting sector of the enemy was the weakest. Upon the signal our men charged with spirit, and the enemy dashed forward so suddenly and speedily that there was no room to hurl javelins. Our men dropped their javelins and took to their swords for hand-to-hand fighting. The Germans followed their usual tactic of forming into a phalanx to receive the sword charge. Many of our men went to the length of leaping upon the phalanx, wrested shields from enemy arms, and wounded them from above. On the left wing the enemy line was beaten back and turned to flight, but on the right their weight of numbers pressed our line hard. Young Publius Crassus, who commanded the cavalry, was more mobile than the officers busy in the line, and when he saw where our men were in difficulties he sent the third line to their support.

53. The situation was thus restored, and all the enemy turned tail; nor did they cease running before they reached the Rhine, some five miles away. There a handful had enough confidence in their strength to try to swim across, or found skiffs in which they reached safety. Among these was Ariovistus, who fled in a boat he found moored to the bank; all the others our cavalry rounded up and killed. Ariovistus had two wives, one a Sueban he had brought from home, and the other the sister of King Voccio of Noricum, who had sent her to be married to Ariovistus in Gaul. Both wives died in the rout. Of his two daughters, one was killed and the other cap-

tured. As Caesar was pursuing the enemy with the cavalry he came upon Gaius Valerius Procillus, shackled in
three chains and dragged along by his keepers in the
rout. To see this eminent Gaul and his own intimate
friend snatched from the enemy's hands and restored to
himself afforded Caesar no less pleasure than the victory
itself. Fortune had not detracted from his satisfaction
and gratification by a disaster to Procillus. Procillus said
that lots had been cast in his own presence to determine
whether he should be burned to death at once or kept
for another time, and that thanks to the lots he had been
saved. Marcus Mettius was also found and brought back
to Caesar.

54. When the outcome of this battle was reported
across the Rhine, the Suebi who had reached its banks
started to return home, but the Rhineland tribes sensed
their panic and pursued and killed a large number. Having finished two important campaigns in a single summer Caesar withdrew his army to winter cantonments
among the Sequani somewhat earlier than the season
required. He left Labienus in charge of the cantonments
and himself set out for Cisalpine Gaul to hold the assizes.

II 57 B.C.

1. While Caesar was wintering in Cisalpine Gaul, as was
stated above, he was made aware of persistent rumors,
which were confirmed by Labienus' dispatches, that all
the Belgians (we have said that they occupied a third
of Gaul) were conspiring against Rome and interchang-

ing hostages. The motives alleged were the following:
first, they apprehended that when all Celtic Gaul was
subdued they would be the next objective of our armies;
and second, they were being put under pressure by certain Gauls. Some had resented the continued sojourn of
the Germans in Gaul, and now were irritated by the Roman army wintering and establishing itself there. Others
hankered for a change of rule out of sheer instability of
temperament. In Gaul authority is commonly usurped
by powerful individuals who possess resources for hiring
mercenaries, and under our administration their ambition had less scope.

2. Actuated by these messengers and dispatches, Caesar raised two new legions in Cisalpine Gaul, and at the
opening of the summer directed his legate Quintius
Pedius to lead them into Farther Gaul. He himself joined
the army as soon as forage was available, and charged
the Senones and other neighbors of the Belgae to discover what the Belgae were about and keep him informed. Unanimously they reported that forces were being mustered and concentrated, and this determined
Caesar to proceed against them without delay. He arranged for his commissariat, struck camp, and in about
a fortnight reached the Belgic frontier.

3. His speed was greater than anyone had anticipated,
and upon his unexpected arrival the Remi, the Belgic
tribe nearest Gaul, sent their leading men, Iccius and
Andecumborius, to tell Caesar that they would put their
persons and property under the protection and at the
disposal of the Roman people. They had not, they maintained, been in collusion with the rest of the Belgae in
the conspiracy against Rome, and they were ready to
give hostages, obey orders, receive Romans into their
strongholds, and provide food and other supplies. All

other Belgians, they said, were under arms, and had been joined by the Germans who lived this side the Rhine. Passions had risen to such a pitch that they could not prevail even upon the Senones, their own close kin who shared their laws and ordinances and were under the same government and executive, not to fall in with the subversives.

4. Caesar interrogated the emissaries to ascertain the identity, extent, and potential of the opposition, and discovered that most of the Remi were descended from Germans who had crossed the Rhine in the remote past to settle in a more fertile country. They had driven the Gallic natives out, and when, in our fathers' memory, the whole of Gaul was devastated, they were the only people who barred the Cimbri and Teutoni from invading their country. Their prowess on this occasion gave them high prestige, and they prided themselves on their military might. On the question of numbers the Remi declared that they had exact information; they were related by blood and marriage, and so had learned how large a contingent each chief had promised for the impending war in the common council of the Belgae. Courage, prestige, and numbers gave preëminence to the Bellovaci; they could put 100,000 men into the field, had promised 60,000 picked troops, and claimed supreme command. The immediate neighbors of the Remi, the Suessiones, possessed extensive and fertile lands. In recent times their king had been Diviciacus, the most powerful individual in Gaul, with sovereignty over much of the Belgic territory and even Britain. Now their king was Galba; he was a just and prudent man, and had been entrusted with the supreme command by universal consent. Galba controlled twelve towns and promised 50,000 armed men. An equal number was prom-

ised by the Nervii, who were reputed the fiercest of all
and were farthest distant. The Atrebates promised 15,000,
the Ambiani 10,000, the Morini 25,000, the Menapii
7,000, the Caleti 10,000, and Veliocasses and the Viromandui 10,000, the Aduatici 19,000. The Condrusi, Eburones, Caeroesi, Paemani, all indifferently styled "German,"
had promised, the Remi believed, about 40,000.

5. Caesar heartened the Remi and in a gracious speech
bade their senate assemble in his presence and the children of their principal personages brought him as hostages. These things they did with good will. In an earnest
appeal to Diviciacus the Aeduan, Caesar explained how
important it was to Rome and indeed to the welfare of
both parties for the enemy forces to be divided, to eliminate the necessity of confronting so large a host at once.
This could be accomplished if the Aedui would invade
the Bellovaci and begin to ravage their fields. With this
injunction Caesar dismissed Diviciacus.

When Caesar found that the Belgic forces had mobilized and were marching against him, and was informed
by his reconnaissance and the Remi that they were not
far off, he pushed rapidly across the Aisne, which flows
through the farther stretches of the Remi, and there
pitched camp. This strategy protected one side of the
camp by the river bank, sheltered the country to his
rear, and enabled the Remi and other native states to
bring in supplies without danger. At the bridge which
spanned the river he posted a guard, and on the farther
bank he left his legate Quintus Titurius Sabinus with six
cohorts. For his camp he ordered a rampart twelve feet
high and a trench eighteen feet wide.

6. Eight miles from the camp was a town of the Remi
called Bibrax. The oncoming Belgae assaulted it vigorously, and the defenders could scarcely hold out the day.

The Belgian mode of attack is the same as the Gallic. They surround the wall with a great host, throw stones until it is cleared of defenders, hold shields over their heads to form a "tortoise," and move up to the gates and undermine the wall. This time the operation was easy, for with such huge numbers throwing stones, no defender could keep his footing on the wall. When night stopped the assault, the Reman Iccius, an aristocrat and a favorite among the people, one of the emissaries who had capitulated to Caesar and was now in command at Bibrax, sent Caesar word that unless he received reinforcements he would be unable to hold his position.

7. Using Iccius' couriers as guides, about midnight Caesar sent Numidian and Cretan archers and Balearic slingers to relieve the townsfolk of Bibrax. Their arrival brought the defenders hope, and inspired them to take the offensive. The enemy abandoned their effort to take the city and after a short halt ravaged the fields of the Remi, burned all the villages and farms they could reach, pushed on towards Caesar's camp in full force, and encamped less than two miles away. Smoke from watch-fires indicated that their camp covered a stretch of eight miles.

8. Because of their huge numbers and extraordinary reputation, Caesar at first decided to avoid battle; but he did probe the enemy's courage and our men's gallantry in daily cavalry skirmishes, and found our men fully their equal. The ground in front of our camp was exactly suited to deploying a battle line. Before the slight eminence on which the camp stood was a bare field of just the size to hold a formation; on either side there was a sharp drop, but the front merged with the plain by an easy grade. At either side of this field Caesar dug a trench about 400 feet long at right angles to the line he would

form, and at the ends of the trench he erected redoubts
in which he posted artillery to prevent the enemy from
exploiting their numerical superiority to attack his men
in the flank and surround them. This done, he left the
two newly recruited legions in camp as a reserve in case
of need and deployed the remaining six in battle formation in front of the camp. The enemy likewise marched
out of their camp and formed up in line.

9. Between the two armies was a small stretch of
marsh. The enemy waited to see whether our men would
cross it, and our men stood ready to attack them at a
disadvantage if they should attempt to cross first. In the
meantime a cavalry skirmish was in progress between
the two lines. Here our men had the better of it, but
since neither side would cross the marsh first, Caesar
returned to his camp. Immediately the enemy pushed
on to the Aisne, which, as has been noted, was at the
rear of our camp. There they found a ford and attempted
to throw part of their forces across, with the design of
storming the fort commanded by Quintus Titurius and
destroying the bridge if they could, and if they could
not, of ravaging the fields of the Remi, which were very
useful for our campaign, and so cutting off our supplies.

10. Titurius notified Caesar, who marched all his
cavalry, light-armed Numidians, slingers and archers,
across the river, and pushed on to meet the enemy. The
fighting was intense. Our men attacked as the enemy
struggled in the water and killed a large number of
them; others, who boldly tried to pass over the bodies of
the fallen, they repulsed with showers of missiles; those
who had got across, the cavalry rounded up and killed.
The enemy realized that their expectation of storming
the town and crossing the river had been illusory; they
saw that our men would not advance to unfavorable

ground to fight, and their own commissary was beginning to fail. They convoked a council and decided the
best course was for all to return home and then rally from
all quarters to defend whichever country the Romans
would invade first; it was better to fight in their own
than in strange territory, and they would have the advantage of home-grown supplies. Among the motives
for this decision was the realization that Diviciacus and
the Aedui were approaching the country of the Bellovaci; their contingent could not be persuaded to remain and not go to help their own people.

11. Pursuant to this decision they decamped in the
second watch, with great clatter and tumult. There was
no system and no discipline; in haste to get home each
man made for the head of the line, so that their departure looked like a rout. Caesar was informed of this by
his patrols, but since he did not know why they were
leaving he was afraid of an ambush, and left infantry
and cavalry within their entrenchments. At dawn, when
the facts had been confirmed by reconnaissance, he sent
all his cavalry ahead, under command of the legates
Quintus Pedius and Lucius Aurunculeius Cotta, to retard their rear guard, and ordered the legate Titus Labienus to follow with three legions. These forces attacked
the enemy rear, following them for many miles, and cut
large numbers down as they fled. While the rear of their
column halted when overtaken and met our attack,
those in the van thought they were in no danger, and
since there was neither need nor discipline to hold them
back, they broke ranks as soon as they heard the shouting and ran for safety. Without danger to themselves,
then, our men killed as many as daylight allowed; at sunset they desisted and returned to camp according to instructions.

12. The next day, when the enemy recovered from
their panic rout, Caesar marched into the territory of
the Suessiones, who adjoined the Remi, and drove on
to the town of Noviodunum by a forced march. This he
tried to storm without preparation, for he heard that it
was undefended; but though the defenders were few
he was unable to take it because of the width of its
trench and the height of its wall. He entrenched a
camp, therefore, and began to prepare sheds and other
requisites for assault. On the following night, while these
preparations were in progress, the horde of Suessiones
who had been in the rout gathered near the city. The
speed with which our sheds were brought up to the city,
a ramp heaped up, towers built—operations such as the
Gauls had never before seen or heard of—moved them
to send emissaries to capitulate to Caesar. The Remi in-
terceded for them, and their lives were spared.

13. The leading men, including the two sons of King
Galba, were delivered to Caesar as hostages, and all the
weapons in the city were handed over, whereupon Caesar accepted the surrender of the Suessiones and marched
his army against the Bellovaci.

The Bellovaci, with their chattels, had betaken themselves to Bratuspantium, and when Caesar and his army
were within five miles all the older men came out of the
town with arms outstretched and made sounds to signify
that they would entrust themselves to his good faith
and power and that they were not in arms against the
Roman people. Similarly, when he neared the town and
pitched camp, the women and children on the wall
opened their arms out in their own fashion and begged
the Romans for peace.

14. Diviciacus too—on the departure of the Belgae
he had disbanded the Aeduan force and returned to Cae-

sar—spoke on behalf of the Bellovaci. "The Bellovaci," he said, "have always been friendly dependents of the Aeduan state. Their own chiefs had instigated them to defection and to hostility against Rome by asserting that the Aedui had been enslaved by Caesar and humbled by contemptuous treatment. Their ringleaders have realized what a disaster they brought upon the state and have fled to Britain. Not the Bellovaci alone but the Aedui also on their behalf beg you to show your characteristic gentleness and mercy. By so doing you will enhance Aeduan prestige among all the Belgae, whose troops and resources we count on in case of war."

15. Caesar said that out of respect for Diviciacus and the Aedui he would spare the Bellovaci and take them under his protection, but as they were very populous and prominent among the Belgae he required 600 hostages. These were delivered, and all the weapons in the town were taken up. Next Caesar marched against the Ambiani, who promptly surrendered themselves and their property. Their territory adjoined the Nervii; inquiries concerning the character and customs of this people elicited the following information: Traders were not admitted, they did not allow the importation of wine or other wares which they thought would soften their spirits or diminish their valor, they were fierce and brave, and they despised and reviled other Belgae for treading their traditional valor underfoot. For themselves they vowed they would never send emissaries to Caesar or accept peace on any terms.

16. After he had marched through their territory for three days Caesar learned from prisoners that the Nervii had taken a position across the Sambre, not more than ten miles from his camp, that they had been joined by their neighbors the Atrebates and Viromandui, whom

they had persuaded to share the fortunes of war, and
were awaiting the coming of the Romans. In addition
they were expecting the forces of the Aduatici, which
were en route. The women and other non-combatants
they had removed to a retreat in the swamps, inaccessible
to an army.

17. Upon receiving this information Caesar sent scouts
and centurions ahead to choose a spot suitable for a
camp. Accompanying Caesar's march were a number of
Belgae and other Gauls who had surrendered, and some
of these, as was later learned from prisoners, took careful note of our marching order and at night made their
way to the Nervii and explained it to them. The massed
baggage, they said, moved between individual legions;
when the first legion reached camp and the rest were a
long way off it would be very easy to attack while the
men still had their packs on, and when this legion was
beaten and the baggage plundered the rest would not
have courage to resist. The suggestion proffered by
these informants was favored by the traditional practice
of the Nervii. Since they were weak in cavalry (to this
day they neglect that branch and keep their whole
strength in infantry) their device for checking raids by
their neighbor's cavalry was to notch saplings, bend them
over, weave brush and briars in with the horizontal
trunks and branches, and so contrive a wall-like rampart
which not only obstructed entry but could not even be
seen through. This device was now being used to block
our column, and the Nervii were therefore inclined to
adopt the suggestion proposed.

18. The terrain which our people had chosen for a
camp was as follows. A hill sloped down evenly to the
Sambre, which has been mentioned. From the river there
rose another hill, of the same grade, opposite to and fac-

ing the first. The lower part was an open space of about 200 paces, but the upper part was wooded, so that it was not easy to see through. Inside the wood the enemy lay hidden; a few cavalry posts could be seen in the open space along the river. The depth of the river was about three feet.

19. Caesar had sent his cavalry ahead and was following with all his forces; but the arrangement of his column was different from what the Belgae had reported to the Nervii. Caesar followed his usual practice when approaching an enemy and advanced with six legions light-armed; behind them was the baggage of the whole army, and then the two legions most recently recruited closed the line and formed a guard for the baggage. Our cavalry, with slingers and archers, crossed the river and engaged the enemy cavalry. The latter repeatedly fell back upon their comrades in the woods only to charge again, and our men dared not pursue beyond the stretch of open ground; but in the meanwhile the six legions who arrived first began to entrench the camp which had been measured out. In the woods the enemy had formed their line and heartened one another, and as soon as our baggage train came into sight—the moment they had agreed upon for their attack—they suddenly dashed out in full force and charged our cavalry. These they defeated and scattered easily, and with incredible speed ran down to the river; almost at the same instant they were at the woods, in the river, and at close quarters with our men. At the same speed they pushed up hill to our camp and the men busy entrenching it.

20. Everything was to do at once—the flag which was the general call to arms hoisted, the trumpet sounded, working parties recalled, the parties gone afield to fetch material fetched back, the line to form, the

troops to harangue, the battle signal to give. Many of these duties could not be discharged for want of time and the pressure of the enemy, but two factors alleviated the difficult situation: the knowledge and discipline of the troops, who were seasoned campaigners and needed no one to explain what was to be done, and Caesar's injunction to his deputies not to leave their several legions and their assigned work before the camp was fortified. These did not await Caesar's orders, in view of the nearness and speed of the enemy, but took the necessary measures on their own responsibility.

21. The essential orders Caesar gave, and then ran down, as chance directed, to encourage the soldiers. He encountered the Tenth Legion and addressed them briefly, charging them to remember their traditional prowess, to keep cool, and to withstand the enemy onset with fortitude; and then, since the enemy were within range, he gave the signal for action. When he moved off to give similar encouragement in another part of the field, he found the men already fighting. Time was so scant and the enemy so zealous that there was no time to put on helmets or pull covers from shields, let alone to put insignia on. Wherever a man found himself as he came from his work, whatever standard he saw first, there he took his stand, not to waste fighting time in looking for his own unit.

22. The terrain, the slope of the hill, and the exigencies of the moment, rather than ordinary tactical rules, governed the position of our army. Disparate legions resisted the enemy at different points. The view was obstructed, as has previously been noted, by thick hedges; this made it impossible for reserves to be posted with any assurance or to foresee what would be wanted in various quarters or for the whole operation to be

directed by a single individual. With conditions so adverse it followed that the outcome was various.

23. The men of the Ninth and Tenth Legions were posted on the left, where, as it happened, the Atrebates had charged. They discharged their javelins, and from the higher ground quickly drove the enemy, who were breathless from their charge and weakened by wounds, into the river; when they attempted to cross, our men pursued them with drawn swords and killed many who were hampered by the water. They themselves crossed the river without hesitation, and though the ground was against them, again attacked the enemy when they turned to resist and routed them. Similarly, in another part of the field, the Eleventh and Eighth routed the Viromandui, with whom they engaged and fought from the higher ground down to the very banks of the river. But this denuded the camp in front and left (on the right there was the Twelfth and then at no great distance the Seventh) and to the unprotected section all the Nervii in a mass, under command of their general Boduognatus, pushed forward. Part of the mass began to surround the legions on their exposed flank and part to make for the higher ground of the camp.

24. I have mentioned that our cavalry and attached light-armed infantry had been beaten back by the initial onset. Now as they were retreating into the camp they came full upon the enemy and again took to flight in another direction. The sutlers at the rear gate of the camp on the crest of the hill had seen our victorious troops cross the river, and left the camp to pick up booty; when they looked back and saw the enemy in the camp they fled precipitately. At the same time a noisy clamor arose from the men bringing up the baggage

train and they scattered in all directions in a panic. The
Treveri had sent a body of their horse, who enjoyed an
extraordinary reputation for courage among the Gauls,
to join Caesar as auxiliaries. When they saw our camp
filled with large numbers of the enemy, our legions hard
pressed and almost encircled, sutlers, horsemen, slingers,
Numidians separated and scattered and fleeing in all directions, they thought our situation hopeless and rode
off home, where they reported to their people that the
Romans had been driven out and beaten and that the
enemy had captured their camp and baggage.

25. After haranguing the Tenth Legion, Caesar started
for the right wing where he saw his men under great
pressure. The standards of the Twelfth were huddled in
one place and the soldiers so cramped that their fighting
was hampered. All the centurions of the fourth cohort
were cut down, the standard-bearer was killed and the
standard lost, and almost all the centurions of the other
cohorts were killed or wounded: among the casualties
was Publius Sextius Bacalus, a first centurion and a gallant soldier, who was so badly wounded in a number of
places that he could not keep his feet. The others were
grown lethargic, and some in the rear gave up the fight
and got out of range. The enemy did not remit their
pressure from below and were pressing in from either
flank. Caesar saw that the situation was critical, and
there was no reserve to throw in. He snatched a shield
from a soldier in the rear—he had not brought one himself—and moved to the front line; he called upon the
centurions by name, encouraged the men to advance,
and directed them to open their lines out to give freer
play to their swords. His coming inspired the men with
hope and gave them new heart. Even in a desperate

situation each man was anxious to do his utmost when his general was looking on, and the enemy's onset was somewhat slowed down.

26. When Caesar saw that the Seventh Legion, which had taken a stand nearby, was similarly hard pressed by the enemy, he instructed the tribunes to bring their legions up gradually and then whirl to face the enemy on all sides. When this was done the men could support one another and were not afraid of being taken in the rear, and they began to resist more vigorously and attack more bravely. Meanwhile the two legions marching at the rear of the baggage train had heard the news and quickened their pace, and were now visible to the enemy at the top of the hill. Furthermore Titus Labienus, who had taken the enemy's camp, could see what was going on in ours from his higher position, and sent the Tenth Legion to support our men. When the flight of the cavalry and sutlers apprised them of the situation and of the imminent danger to camp, legions, and general, they put forth their best speed.

27. So transformed was the situation by their arrival that even those of our men who lay foredone with wounds propped themselves on their shields and fought anew. Next the sutlers noticed that the enemy were frightened, and unarmed as they were charged against armed men. And finally the cavalry fought all over the field in an effort to outdo the infantry and erase the shame of their flight. But even in their despair the enemy showed such gallantry that when their front line had fallen the next stood upon their bodies to carry on the fight, and when these too were struck down the survivors stood upon the heaped up bodies and discharged their missiles as from a mound or caught and returned our javelins. We must not dismiss as futile the gallantry of

men who dared cross a very wide river, climb very steep
banks, attack from an unfavorable position: it was their
heroism which had made such difficult things easy.

28. This battle almost annihilated the race and name
of the Nervii. The older men along with the women and
children had been placed for safety, as I have said, in
swamps and marshes; when they received news of the
battle they thought there was nothing to stop the victors,
nothing to protect the vanquished, and all the survivors
agreed to send emissaries to surrender to Caesar. In re-
counting the disaster to their state they declared that
their senate was reduced from 600 to three and their
men capable of bearing arms from 60,000 to barely 500.
To demonstrate his compassion for unfortunates and
suppliants Caesar was very careful to preserve them. He
bade them retain their territory and their towns and
ordered the neighboring peoples not to injure or molest
them and to keep their subject peoples from doing so.

29. The Aduatici, of whom I have written above,
were coming to support the Nervii in full force, but
when they heard of the battle they shifted their direction
and returned home. They abandoned all their towns
and strongholds and removed their property to a single
fortress whose terrain made it extremely strong. Steep
cliffs surrounded it on all sides, leaving only one
approach of an easy grade not more than 200 feet wide.
This place they had fortified with a double wall of great
height, and on the wall they were placing heavy
boulders and beams sharpened to a point. The Aduatici
were descended from the Cimbri and the Teutoni who,
when they invaded our province and Italy [45 years be-
fore], left such baggage as they could not drive or carry
on this side of the Rhine with 6,000 of their men
to guard it. When their main body was destroyed this

band was for many years harassed by war with their neighbors, defensive and offensive. Finally peace was made, by general agreement, and they chose this district to live in.

30. When our army first arrived at the stronghold of the Aduatici they made frequent sorties and engaged our men in minor skirmishes. Later, when they were encompassed by a rampart of 15,000 feet with numerous redoubts, they stayed inside the stronghold. When our sheds were built and a ramp piled up and they saw our tower rising at a distance, they laughed and jeered at us from the wall for erecting so large an engine at so great a distance: where would such manikins (the Gauls are big and make fun of our shorter build) hope to find hands or strength to set so ponderous a tower on the wall?

31. But when they saw that it moved and was approaching the walls, they were dismayed by the novel and unnatural spectacle and sent emissaries to Caesar to sue for peace. Their speech was somewhat as follows: The Romans must surely enjoy divine assistance in their warfare; how else could they move such tall engines with such speed? They therefore surrendered themselves and their property to the power of the Romans, but would beg for one indulgence. If, in keeping with the compassion and kindness of which they had heard from others, Caesar would resolve to spare the Aduatici, they prayed that he would not deprive them of their arms. Their neighbors were almost all hostile and envious of their prowess; if they surrendered their arms they would be defenseless against them, and in that case would prefer to suffer any fate at the hands of the Roman people than to be tortured and killed by men among whom they were used to be masters.

32. To this Caesar replied that he would spare the Aduatici, in keeping with his practice, not their deserts, if they surrendered before the ram touched the wall; without the delivery of their arms there would be no terms. He would do, he said, what he had done in the case of the Nervii—bid their neighbors not to molest a people that had capitulated to Rome. This the emissaries reported to their people, who declared that they would obey Caesar's orders. So great a quantity of arms was pitched from the wall into the trench in front of the stronghold that the heaps were almost level with the height of the wall and the ramp; nevertheless, as was subsequently discovered, about a third was kept back and hidden in the town. That day the gates were opened and they enjoyed peace.

33. Towards evening Caesar ordered the gates shut and the soldiers to leave the town, to prevent any injury to the townsfolk on the part of the soldiers during the night. The Aduatici, as it proved, had formed a plan in the belief that after the capitulation our guard posts would be withdrawn or negligently kept. Equipped partly with the weapons they had kept back, and partly with shields of bark or plaited osiers which, as the exigencies of time permitted, they covered with hide, about midnight they made a sudden sortie in full force where the ascent to the entrenchments seemed least steep. Notice was quickly signaled by flares, as Caesar had previously ordered, and troops from nearby redoubts proceeded to the danger point. The fight was as fierce as could be expected when brave men reduced to desperation struggled against men who could fire missiles from rampart and towers and when their sole hope of salvation lay in their courage. About 4,000 were killed and the rest thrown back into the town. On the following

day, the gates, which were now without defenders, were broken open, and our soldiers were sent in. Caesar sold the booty of the town in a single lot; the purchasers reported a total of 53,000 persons.

34. At this same time Publius Crassus, who had been dispatched with a single legion against the Veneti, Venelli, Osismi, Curiosolitae, Esubii, Aulerci, and Redones—maritime states on the Atlantic—reported that all of them had been brought under the dominion of the Roman people.

35. These operations ended resistance throughout Gaul, and the natives were so impressed by reports of them that the tribes who lived across the Rhine sent emissaries to Caesar with promises to deliver hostages and fulfill his commands. These Caesar bade return to him at the beginning of the following summer, for he himself was eager to get to Italy and Illyricum. He quartered his legions for the winter among the Carnutes, the Andes, the Turones, and the states nearest the scene of the recent campaign, and himself set out for Italy. On receipt of Caesar's dispatches a thanksgiving of fifteen days was decreed for his achievements; this was an unprecedented honor.

III 56 B.C.

1. As Caesar was starting for Italy he sent Servius Galba with the Twelfth Legion and a detachment of cavalry to the territory of the Nantuates, Veragri, and Seduni, which extends from the frontiers of the Allobroges to

Lake Geneva, from the Rhone to the crest of the Alps.
His motive was to open the route through the Alps,
which merchants had been able to travel only with great
danger and exorbitant tolls. He authorized Galba to
quarter the legion in this area for the winter if he
thought it advisable. Galba fought a number of successful engagements and stormed several of their strongholds, whereupon he was approached by deputations
from all sides, who delivered hostages and capitulated.
Galba then decided to station two cohorts among the
Nantuates and himself to winter with the remaining cohorts of his legion in a town of the Veragri called Octodurus. The town lay in a small level valley surrounded
by towering mountains, and was bisected by a river.
One part Galba permitted the Gauls to winter in, and
the other, from which the Gauls were evacuated, he assigned to his cohorts; this sector he fortified with a rampart and trench.

2. Several days had been passed in the cantonment
and Galba had ordered grain brought in, when he was
informed by his reconnaissance that the Gauls had
abandoned their sector of the town during the night and
that the overhanging mountains were swarming with a
huge host of Seduni and Veragri. Several factors had
contributed to the Gauls' sudden decision to renew hostilities and overpower the legion. In the first place, they
were contemptuous of its thinness; two cohorts had been
withdrawn, and many individuals had been sent off to
procure supplies. Secondly, the terrain favored them;
they could shoot and charge from higher ground down
into the valley, and believed their first attack would be
irresistible. Again, they resented their children being
taken from them under the title of hostages, and were
convinced it was not merely to safeguard communica-

tions that the Romans were attempting to occupy the crest of the Alps, but in order to annex the districts adjacent to their province as a permanent holding.

3. Upon receipt of this intelligence Galba speedily convoked a council of war to canvass opinions. The construction and fortification of the winter camp were still incomplete, nor had provision yet been made for grain and other supplies. Galba had thought the danger of war was past when the natives capitulated and yielded hostages. In view of the great and unexpected crisis, when an armed multitude could be seen swarming over almost all the higher ground and roadblocks made reinforcement of men and supplies impossible, some in the council almost despaired and proposed that the baggage should be abandoned, a sortie ventured, and an effort made to reach safety by the same route by which they had come. But the majority decided to reserve this recourse to the last and meanwhile to await developments and defend the camp.

4. After a pause barely sufficient to complete the dispositions and arrangements resolved upon, the enemy rushed down from all sides upon a given signal and hurled stones and javelins against the rampart. At first, while our men were fresh, they resisted stoutly; their every missile from the rampart's elevation found its mark, and when any part of the camp was inadequately manned and in trouble they brought speedy relief. But they were at a disadvantage: when the enemy were wearied by the prolonged fighting they retired from the battle and fresh men took their place, whereas their small numbers forbade our men to do likewise. Not only could the weary not retire from the fight, but not even a wounded man could leave his post to recruit his strength.

5. After six hours of incessant fighting ammunition as

well as energy began to fail. As our men faltered, the
enemy pressed on more vigorously and were beginning
to pull down the rampart and fill up the trench. When
the situation reached the critical point Publius Sextius
Baculus, the senior centurion of whom we mentioned
that he received several severe wounds in the battle with
the Nervii, and the tribune Gaius Volusenus, a brave
and intelligent officer, ran to Galba and pointed out that
their sole hope of salvation was to try the last resource
of attempting a sortie. Galba accordingly assembled the
centurions and quickly notified the troops that they were
to leave off fighting for a little and only parry the enemy
missiles, take a rest, and upon a given signal charge out
of the camp and place their whole hope of survival in
their courage.

6. The men did as they were bidden. Suddenly they
charged from all the gates and gave the enemy no
chance to realize what was happening or to close ranks.
The tables were turned; the men who had expected to
take our camp were surrounded and killed. Of the
30,000 natives known to have attacked the camp more
than a third were killed and the remainder routed in
panic and not suffered to rally even on the heights.
When all the enemy forces were dispersed and their
dead stripped, our men returned to their own entrenched camp. Galba did not wish to tempt fortune
again, after this battle: he realized that his situation was
very different from the design with which he had come,
and the shortage of grain and supplies was disturbing.
On the next day, accordingly, he burned all the buildings
in the village and hurried his return to the Province.
With no enemy to hinder or delay his march, he brought
his legion safe through the country of the Nantuates into
that of the Allobroges, where he passed the winter.

7. These successful operations gave Caesar every reason to suppose that Gaul was subdued: the Belgae were overpowered, the Germans driven out, and the Seduni in the Alps beaten. At the beginning of winter, therefore, he started for Illyricum, desiring to visit the peoples there and learn the country. But suddenly war broke out in Gaul. The cause was the following. Young Publius Crassus and the Seventh Legion were wintering in the country of the Andes, near the ocean. Because of a shortage of grain in that area Crassus dispatched a number of prefects and military tribunes to the neighboring states to procure a supply; Titus Terrasidius was sent to the Esubii, Marcus Trebius Gallus to the Curiosolites, and Quintus Velanius and Titus Silius to the Veneti.

8. The Veneti were dominant in that whole maritime district because they had many ships which they regularly sailed to Britain and they surpass the rest in knowledge and experience of seafaring. Controlling the few scattered harbors along the violent open sea, they exacted tribute from virtually all who sailed these waters. The Veneti took the initiative by detaining Silius and Velanius; they thought this would enable them to recover their own hostages whom they had surrendered to Crassus. Their neighbors emulated the Veneti (Gallic decisions are hasty and sudden) and detained Trebius and Terrasidius for the same reason. Through representatives quickly dispatched among their peoples the chiefs pledged themselves to take no action without previous agreement and to share whatever outcome fortune would bring. They called upon other tribes to abide in the freedom they had inherited from their ancestors rather than submit to Roman enslavement. The whole seacoast was quickly won over, and they sent a joint

delegation to Crassus asking him to return their hostages if he wished to recover his officers.

9. Caesar was informed of these events by Crassus, and because he was far away he gave orders for warships to be built on the Loire, which flows into the ocean, rowers to be drafted from the Province, and sailors and pilots to be mustered. These measures were quickly taken in hand, and as soon as weather permitted Caesar hurried to join his army. The Veneti and likewise the other states learned of Caesar's coming and at the same time realized the gravity of their offense: they had arrested and thrown into chains ambassadors, a title which has always been sacred and inviolable among all peoples. Their preparations for war accordingly matched the magnitude of their peril, and in particular they began to look to their naval preparations, and with higher hope because they trusted to the advantages of the locale. They knew that the roads were cut by tidal creeks and that our navigation would be hampered by our ignorance of topography and the scarcity of havens. They were sure our army could not long remain in their country because of short supplies. Even if these expectations should all be disappointed they still controlled the sea, whereas the Romans were short of shipping and ignorant of the shoals, harbors, and islands where the fighting would take place: navigation on the vast, open ocean was very different from that in a landlocked sea. Their plans formed, they fortified their towns, stocked them with grain from the countryside, and assembled as many ships as possible at Venetia, where it was certain Caesar would begin the campaign. They secured the alliance of the Osismi, Lexovii, Namnetes, Ambiliati, Morini, Diablintes, Menapii, and

they summoned reinforcements from Britain, which lies over against that region.

10. Such were the difficulties of the war, as explained above, yet urgent considerations moved Caesar to undertake it: the outrageous detention of Roman knights, rebellion after capitulation, defection after yielding hostages, conspiracy involving so many states, but most of all the danger that other peoples might assume the same license if this area were overlooked. Caesar knew that Gauls generally tend to revolution and that their instability makes them very ready to take up arms, knew moreover that men naturally yearn for liberty and loathe slavery; and therefore he decided to divide his army and distribute it over a wide area before other states could join in the conspiracy.

11. Accordingly he dispatched his deputy Titus Labienus with cavalry to the Treveri along the Rhine, with instructions to visit the Remi and other Belgic peoples and hold them to their duty, and to block any attempt the Germans might make (it was said they had been invited to support the Belgae) to force their way across the river. Publius Crassus was ordered to proceed to Aquitania with twelve legionary cohorts and a large body of cavalry, to prevent reinforcements from these peoples being sent into Gaul or any union of such powerful races from being effected. His deputy Quintus Titurius Sabinus, Caesar sent with three legions to the country of the Venelli, Curiosolites, and Lexovii to isolate their strength. He put young Decimus Brutus in command of the navy and the Gallic vessels he had ordered to assemble from the Pictones, Santoni, and other subjugated districts. Decimus was ordered to proceed towards the Veneti as soon as possible, and Caesar him-

self pushed on to the same region with his land forces.

12. Generally the towns of the Veneti were planted at the tips of spits or headlands and afforded approach neither by land, for the tide boiled in from the sea at intervals of twelve hours, nor yet by sea, for when the tide receded the ships were caught in the shallows. Assault on either element was therefore hampered. Occasionally the tide was kept out by massive piles and a dike raised to the level of the town wall; but if the townfolk were so awed by these massive works that they began to have misgivings, they had only to bring up a large number of boats (of which they had enormous quantities) and retire with all their belongings to the next town, where they had similar advantages of position for their defense. These tactics they maintained for a good part of the summer, and the more easily because our shipping was detained by foul weather; sailing was extremely difficult in that rough and open sea with its strong tides and virtual absence of harbors.

13. The design and rigging of their own ships suited these conditions. Their hulls were flatter than ours, and so could more easily ride shallows and ebb tides. Their prows and sterns were high, for protection against high waves and winds. Their timbers were all oak, to withstand the roughest violence. The cross-timbers were a foot thick and riveted with iron bolts as thick as a man's thumb. Iron chains, not ropes, held the anchors. Instead of sails they used finely dressed hides, whether because they had no flax and did not know how to work it, or (as is more probable) because they thought canvas was not stout enough to sustain ocean tempests and violent gales and not suitable for controlling such massive ships. In encounters with their ships ours were superior only in speed and in oar-propulsion; in other respects theirs

were more adaptable and better suited to local wind and weather. They were so stoutly built that our ships could not damage them with their beaks, and so tall that missiles could not easily reach them, nor could they conveniently be caught with grappling irons. Moreover when winds freshened they could ride a storm out easily, and when the tide ebbed rest safely in shoals without fear of rocks or reefs; for our ships all such contingencies were dangerous.

14. After he had stormed a number of towns Caesar realized that all his labor was in vain, for he could not prevent the enemy's escape when he took their towns nor inflict injury upon them; he therefore resolved to await his fleet. As soon as it arrived and was sighted by the enemy, about 220 of their ships fully equipped with every kind of weapon and ready for action came out of harbor and ranged to meet our fleet. Neither Brutus, who commanded it, nor the tribunes and centurions assigned to individual vessels were clear as to what course to follow or what tactics to adopt. They knew they could not hurt the enemy with their beaks, and even when they raised their turrets the tall enemy sterns overtopped them, so that they could not well shoot their missiles from a lower position, and those shot by the Gauls struck with heavier impact. One device our people prepared proved very useful. Very sharp scythes were firmly attached to the ends of long poles to make an instrument like a grappling hook. With these they caught the halyards which fastened the sails to the masts, and then rowed off smartly so that the ropes were severed. Thereupon the yards naturally collapsed, and since the Gallic ships relied wholly on their rigging, the usefulness of their vessels was destroyed immediately their sails were down. The battle then devolved solely

upon courage, in which our men easily proved superior, particularly since the action took place in full view of Caesar and the whole army (they occupied high hills which afforded a full view down to the sea) and any exploit was sure to be noticed.

15. When the yards collapsed, as we have said, two or three of ours surrounded individual enemy ships and the soldiers swarmed aboard in a rush. When several had been stormed in this way the natives realized what was happening, and since they could contrive no countermeasure they hastily fled for safety. They had already headed their ships in the direction of the wind when so dead a calm fell that they were unable to budge. This afforded us a lucky chance to finish the business; our ships isolated and stormed theirs one by one. The battle lasted from forenoon till sunset; at night a very few out of their armada were able to reach land.

16. This battle brought the campaign against the Veneti and the whole seacoast to an end. All their young manhood and all the older men of intelligence or prestige had there assembled, and every one of their ships had concentrated there. These lost, the survivors had no place to go nor any means of defending their towns. And so they surrendered themselves and all their property to Caesar. Caesar resolved to exact severe punishment, to make the natives more scrupulous in observing the rights of ambassadors in the future. Their senators were all put to death, and the others sold into slavery.

17. While the campaign against the Veneti was in progress, Quintus Titurius Sabinus with the troops Caesar had assigned to him reached the territory of the Venelli. Their chieftain Viridovix was also commander-in-chief of all the insurgent states and had collected an

army and other forces from among them. Within the last few days the Aulerci, Eburovices, and Lexovii had put their senates to death for refusing to sanction the war, closed their gates, and joined Viridovix. Desperadoes and brigands foregathered from every part of Gaul, moreover, lured from farming and regular work by the prospect of pillage and love of fighting. Sabinus' camp was well situated in every respect and he kept within it although Viridovix faced him at a distance of only two miles and led his forces out daily to offer battle. Soon not only the enemy grew contemptuous of Sabinus but even some of our soldiers reproached him; he created such an impression of cowardice that the enemy grew bold enough to approach the rampart of the camp. This course Sabinus followed because he judged it improper for a subordinate to engage so numerous an enemy, especially in the absence of the commander-in-chief, unless on advantageous ground or if a favorable opportunity offered.

18. When the natives were convinced that Sabinus was afraid, he chose a clever Gaul from the auxiliaries he had with him who was exactly suitable to his purpose and induced him by liberal rewards and promises to go over to the enemy for an object which he explained. The man came over, posing as a deserter, described the panic of the Romans, explained that Caesar himself was hard pressed by the Veneti, and said that Sabinus would steal out of his camp not later than the following night to go to Caesar's assistance. At this news all clamored for an immediate attack on the camp, not to lose so good a chance for a decisive blow. Many factors contributed to this decision: Sabinus' hesitation during the days preceding, the deserter's corroboration, their own lack of food, for which they had made inadequate provision,

the hope engendered by the Venetian insurrection, and men's propensity to wishful thinking. So actuated, they would not let Viridovix and the other generals leave the council before they had obtained their permission to take arms and press on to the camp. They were as exultant with this permission as with an assured victory, and they collected brushwood and faggots to fill up the Roman trenches, and so marched on the camp.

19. The camp was on high ground which sloped down gradually for about a mile. They rushed up this slope to give the Romans the least possible time to fall in and arm, and so arrived breathless. Sabinus harangued his men and gave them the signal they longed for, and ordered sorties from two gates against an enemy encumbered with bundles. Thanks to the favorable ground, the awkwardness and exhaustion of the enemy, our soldiers' courage and the experience they had gained in previous battles, the enemy was incapable of facing a single charge but turned tail at once. With energy unimpaired our men pursued the hampered enemy and cut a large number of them down. The cavalry rounded up the rest and only a few survived to escape the rout. Thus Sabinus was informed of the naval battle and Caesar of Sabinus' victory at the same time, and all the states at once surrendered to Sabinus. The Gallic temper is impetuous and quick to go to war, but their character is irresolute and not steadfast in the face of disaster.

20. About this same time Publius Crassus arrived in Aquitania, which in extent and population can be reckoned, as has been pointed out above, as a third of Gaul. He knew he would have to campaign in a region where the legate Lucius Valerius Praeconinus had been killed a few years before and his army routed and from which the proconsul Lucius Mallius was forced to flee

with the loss of his equipment, and realized that he would have to use especial care. Accordingly he provided for his commissary, collected auxiliaries and cavalry, in addition called up by name many brave soldiers from Toulouse and Narbonne (states in the Province of Gaul adjacent to Aquitania), and marched his army into the territory of the Sotiates. Upon intelligence of his approach the Sotiates raised a large force, including cavalry in which they were especially strong, and attacked our column on the march. First there was a cavalry engagement, and then when their cavalry was defeated and ours in pursuit, they suddenly uncovered their infantry, which they had posted in an ambush in a valley. These attacked our scattered cavalry and renewed the action.

21. The battle was long and fierce, for their earlier victories gave the Sotiates confidence in their courage and they thought the safety of all Aquitania depended upon them, and the Romans were eager to show what they could do under a youthful leader in the absence of the general and of supporting legions. After suffering many casualties the enemy turned tail, and when he had killed a large number Crassus proceeded directly to assault the stronghold of the Sotiates. When they offered determined resistance he used sheds and towers. The enemy countered now with a sortie and now by driving mines to the rampart and sheds; in this the Aquitani are very expert, for there are many copper mines and quarries in various parts of their country. But when they realized that our diligence rendered their efforts nugatory they sent a deputation to ask Crassus to receive their surrender.

22. Their request was granted and they proceeded to hand their weapons over as ordered. But while the at-

tention of all our men was focused on this transaction,
their commander-in-chief Adiatumnus went into action
in another part of the town with 600 devoted followers
whom they call *soldurii*. The rule of this order is that
they share in the enjoyment of all life's advantages with
the friends to whom they have committed themselves,
and if the friend succumbs to any violence they either
share his fate or commit suicide; there is no record of
one who refused to die when the man to whose friendship he had committed himself was killed. It was with
such followers that Adiatumnus attempted his sortie,
but a shout was raised in that part of the fortification.
The soldiers ran to arms, and after a sharp engagement
Adiatumnus was driven back into the town. But he petitioned Crassus for the old terms of surrender and obtained his desire.

23. After receiving their arms and hostages Crassus
moved into the territory of the Vocates and Tarusates.
The natives were alarmed when they learned that within
a few days of his arrival he had stormed a town
so strongly fortified by nature and art, and began to
send deputies in every direction, to enter into conspiracy, to exchange hostages, and to prepare their forces.
They even sent emissaries to the peoples of Nearer Spain
adjoining Aquitania to request reinforcements and
leaders. Their arrival gave them great resources and
great confidence for their undertaking. The leaders they
chose were those who had served with Quintus Sertorius
throughout his Spanish career and who were credited
with the highest mastery of military science. They set
about choosing sites, entrenching camps, and blockading
supply lines according to Roman practice. Crassus observed that whereas his own small numbers forbade di-
viding his army up, the enemy could roam at will and

blockade the roads and leave adequate guards for their camp, that in consequence the transport of food and supplies was hazardous, and that the numbers of the enemy were increasing daily, and therefore resolved to fight a decisive battle without delay. He referred the question to a council, and upon their unanimous approval appointed the day following for the battle.

24. At dawn he marched all his forces out and formed them in a double line with the auxiliaries placed in the center, and waited to see what tactic the enemy would adopt. Because of their numbers and warlike reputation and the fewness of our men, they were sure it was safe for them to fight, but they judged it safer to blockade the roads and cut us off from supplies and so obtain a victory without casualties. If food shortage should compel the Romans to attempt a withdrawal, they planned to attack them on the march while they were burdened with their packs and depressed in spirit. This was the plan their leaders approved, and accordingly they kept to their camp when the Romans moved forward. Crassus saw through their design. But the enemy's hesitation and the impression of fright this created made our men all the keener for the fight and there was general murmuring against delaying an assault on the camp. Crassus harangued his troops and pushed on to the camp with an enthusiastic army.

25. Some filled up the trenches, others cleared the rampart and redoubts of defenders with volleys of missiles, and the auxiliaries, in whom Crassus had no great confidence as fighting men, passed up stones and weapons and carried turf for a ramp, and so presented the appearance and impression of fighters. The enemy likewise fought with courage and determination, and the missiles they threw from their commanding position

were effective. Meanwhile cavalrymen who had made
a circuit of the camp reported to Crassus that the rear
gate was not so carefully fortified and offered an easier
approach.

26. Crassus urged his cavalry commanders to stimulate their men by large bonuses and promises and explained what he wanted done. Following his instructions
they led out the cohorts which had been left to guard
the camp and were therefore fresh, and guided them to
the above-mentioned weaker position by a circuitous
route to avoid their being sighted from the enemy
camp. They demolished the fortifications and gained a
foothold in the camp before the enemy could clearly see
them or know what was happening. When our main
force heard the shouting from that quarter their energies
were redoubled, as generally happens when victory is in
prospect, and they attacked with greater vigor. Surrounded on all sides and in utter despair, the enemy
flung their colors over their fortifications and fled to seek
safety. Our cavalry chased them over the broad open
plain; of the 50,000 who are known to have gathered
from Aquitania and the Cantabrian country scarcely a
fourth survived. Late at night our cavalry returned to
camp.

27. Upon news of this battle the greatest part of
Aquitania surrendered to Crassus and sent hostages on
their own initiative. Included in the number were Tarbelli, Bigerriones, Ptianii, Vocates, Tarusates, Elusates,
Gates, Ausci, Garumni, Sibuzates, Cocosates. A few remote tribes trusted the lateness of the season (winter
was approaching) and failed to follow their example.

28. Though all Gaul had been subdued, the Morini
and Menapii remained under arms and had not sent
Caesar envoys to treat of peace. At about this same

time, though summer was nearly over, Caesar marched
against these peoples, in the belief that the campaign
could be finished speedily. But these tribes began to use
tactics very different from the other Gauls. They knew
that even the strongest tribes had been overwhelmingly
defeated when they fought in open battle, and so they
took themselves and all their belongings to the endless
forests and marshes they owned. Caesar arrived at the
outskirts of the forest and began to entrench a camp;
no enemy was to be seen. But when our men were scattered at their tasks, they suddenly flew out of all parts of
the forest and attacked them. Our men quickly seized
arms and drove them back into the forest with considerable loss; but in carrying their pursuit too far in impassable terrain they lost a few of their own.

29. The succeeding days Caesar set about cutting
down the forest, and to prevent surprise flanking attacks on his unarmed soldiers, he piled all the timber he
felled in the direction of the enemy, building it into a
barricade on either flank. By working with incredible
speed a large space was cleared within a few days; the
enemy's cattle and the hind part of their baggage was in
our possession, and they were themselves making for
the thicker forests. But the weather then forced the dis-
continuance of our work, and the constant rain made it
impossible to keep the soldiers under canvas any longer.
And so, after ravaging their whole countryside and
burning their villages and farms, Caesar led his army
back and quartered them for the winter among the
Aulerci, Lexovii, and other peoples which had recently
been under arms.

IV 55 B.C.

1. In the winter following, the consular year of Gnaeus Pompey and Marcus Crassus, the Germanic Usipetes and also Tencteri crossed the Rhine in large numbers not far from its mouth. What impelled them to cross was harassment by the Suebi over a period of years; the pressure of war had made farming impossible. The Suebi are the largest and most warlike of all the German tribes. They are said to possess a hundred cantons, from each of which they draft a thousand soldiers annually for campaigns outside their territory. Those who remain at home support themselves and the others, and in the year following they take their turn in the field while the others stay home. This insures continuity in both farming and the theory and practice of arms. Private and individual ownership of land does not exist among them, nor is it lawful to work the same farm longer than a year. They use little grain but live mainly on milk and meat and are much given to hunting. Their mode of life, their diet, their daily exercise, their freedom from restraint (from childhood they are subjected to no duty or discipline and do nothing whatever against their will) fosters their strength and produces a gigantic breed. Moreover they have trained themselves, even in the coldest regions, to wear nothing but skins, which are so scanty as to leave a large part of the body bare, and they bathe in rivers.

2. They admit traders, rather to market their booty

than out of a desire for imports. They do not import even horses, which the Gauls are extremely fond of and buy at high prices, but use native animals, which, though inferior and ugly, are made capable of very hard work by constant exercise. In cavalry engagements they frequently dismount to fight on foot; but their horses are trained to stand in their tracks, for quick refuge in case of need. By their standards nothing is so vile or effeminate as the use of saddles, and however few they may be, they will venture to attack saddled cavalry however numerous. They forbid the import of wine altogether, on the ground that its use makes men effeminate and too soft to work.

3. They regard it the highest communal distinction to have the largest possible area adjoining their frontiers unoccupied; this they take as proof that a large number of states cannot cope with them. In one direction, for example, a tract of some 600 miles is said to be uninhabited. On another side their nearest neighbors are the Ubii, whose state was at one time large and flourishing, by German standards. They are somewhat more civilized than other Germanic peoples because they touch the Rhine, are frequently visited by traders, and, because of their proximity, have grown accustomed to Gallic manners. The Suebi had repeatedly made war on the Ubii, but found them too numerous and powerful to dispossess; they did, however, make them tributary, and greatly reduced their power and prestige.

4. The Usipetes and Tencteri, of whom we have spoken, were in the same case. For several years they withstood Suebian pressure, but eventually they were driven from their country, and after three years of wandering in many parts of Germany, reached the Rhine. The district was inhabited by the Menapii, who had

farms, buildings, and villages on either side the river.
They were so terrified by the approach of this horde that
they abandoned their buildings on the far side of
the river and posted guards on the near side to keep the
Germans from crossing. The latter tried every expedient,
and since they could not force their way for want of
boats nor steal across because of the Menapian patrols,
they pretended to return to their home country. After
marching for three days they turned again, and their
cavalry covered the whole distance in a single night.
Upon hearing from their patrols that the Germans had
withdrawn, the Menapii had returned to their villages
on the far bank. The Germans attacked them, all unsuspecting, slaughtered them, and seized their boats.
Before the Menapii on the near bank knew what was
afoot, the Germans crossed the river, seized their buildings, and lived off their stores the remainder of the winter.

5. When news of this reached Caesar he decided to
take no chances with the Gauls for fear of their instability; they are capricious in choosing a course and prone
to revolution. It is characteristic of them that they force
travelers to stop, even when they are unwilling, and
question them on any news or rumors they may have
heard, and in the towns the crowd surrounds traders
and forces them to say where they have come from and
what they heard there. On the basis of such hearsay they
enter upon grandiose plans which they inevitably regret, for they credit rumor unquestioningly and their
informants lie to please them.

6. Knowing their character Caesar started to rejoin
his army earlier than usual, to anticipate more serious
eventualities. On his arrival he found his suspicions con-

firmed. A number of states had sent representatives to invite the Germans to spread south of the Rhine on the promise that all their demands would be met. Lured by such prospects the Germans had broadened their range and had reached the territory of the Eburones and Condrusi, dependencies of the Treveri. Caesar summoned the Gallic chieftains and, because he thought it prudent to conceal what he knew, lulled and reassured them; he requisitioned cavalry and announced a campaign against the Germans.

7. After he had arranged for his commissary and selected his cavalry, he began marching to the localities where the Germans were reported. When he was within a few days' march of them a deputation approached him and spoke as follows: The Germans were not the aggressors but if provoked would not refuse to fight, for it was a hereditary principle with them to resist any who attacked them without asking mercy. But so much they would say: They had not come to Gaul of choice but had been driven from their home. If the Romans desired their good will they might find them useful friends; they should either assign them lands or allow them to keep what they had won by force of arms. Only to the Suebi, whom the very gods could not match, did they acknowledge themselves inferior; there was no one else on earth whom they could not beat.

8. Caesar made a suitable reply, of which the upshot was this: No friendship could exist between them if the Germans remained in Gaul. It was not just for people who could not defend their own territory to seize others', nor were there vacant lands in Gaul which could be justly assigned, especially to so large a multitude. They might settle, if they wished, in the country of the

Ubii; Ubian envoys were there present to complain of Suebian abuses and to ask his assistance, and he would order the Ubii to receive them.

9. The envoys said they would report Caesar's offer to their people and return in three days after it had been considered; they asked that he refrain from moving his camp forward in the meanwhile. Caesar said this concession was impossible. He had learned that a large detachment of their cavalry had been sent across the Meuse a few days before to plunder and forage in the country of the Ambivariti, and suspected they were playing for time against the return of this cavalry.

10. The Meuse rises in the Vosges mountains in the country of the Lingones, receives a tributary from the Rhine called Waal, whereby it forms the island of the Batavi, and then flows into the Rhine not more than eighty miles from the ocean. The Rhine rises in the country of the Lepontii, who live in the Alps, and runs in a long and swift course through the territories of the Nantuates, Helvetii, Sequani, Mediomatrices, Triboci, and Treveri. As it nears the ocean it divides into several channels which form many very large islands; a number of them are occupied by savage and cruel tribes who are believed to live on fish and birds' eggs. Then the Rhine empties into the ocean by many mouths.

11. When Caesar was not more than twelve miles from the enemy the envoys returned to him as they had agreed to do, and begged him, as he was marching on, not to advance any further. When this petition was denied they asked Caesar to send instructions to the cavalry at the head of his line to refrain from fighting, and also to give them permission to send envoys to the Ubii. If the chiefs and senate of the Ubii would pledge their faith on oath, the Germans would accept the conditions

Caesar had offered. For accomplishing this mission they requested a term of three days. Caesar suspected that the object of these stipulations was the same—to gain time for the return of the absent cavalry, but he declared that that day he would advance no more than four miles, to get water; for the day following he desired that the largest possible number of Germans gather before him so that he might examine their claims. To the commanders of the cavalry, which had gone forward in full force, he sent messengers with instructions not to attack the enemy, and if attacked to remain on the defensive until he came up with the main body.

12. The enemy had no more than 800 cavalry, for those who had crossed the Meuse to forage had not yet returned. Our cavalry numbered 5,000 and anticipated no hostility because the enemy ambassadors who had begged a truce had just left Caesar. But directly they caught sight of our men, the enemy attacked and threw them into confusion. When our men rallied, the Germans leapt to the ground, following their usual tactic, unhorsed many of our men by stabbing their horses in the belly, and drove the rest into such a panic that they never drew rein until they came in sight of our column. In that engagement seventy-four cavalrymen were killed, including Piso, a gallant Aquitanian of noble lineage whose grandfather had been king among his people and had received the title of Friend from the Roman senate. When his brother was cut off by the enemy Piso went to his aid and rescued him, but his own mount was wounded and he was unhorsed. He resisted bravely as long as he could, but he was surrounded and fell covered with wounds. His brother who was now out of the fight saw this from a distance; he spurred his horse on, flung himself on the enemy, and was killed.

13. After such a battle Caesar felt it impossible to receive envoys and entertain proposals of people who had
treacherously and insidiously made an unprovoked attack when they had sued for peace. To wait until the
enemy forces were increased by the return of their cavalry he judged the height of madness, and in view of the
Gauls' instability he realized how great an impression
the Germans had made upon them with a single battle
and resolved not to allow them time to concert their
plans. He had communicated his determination not to
lose a day in forcing battle to his legates and quaestor.
Then a lucky opportunity presented itself. Early the next
morning a large party of Germans, including all their
notables and elders, presented itself at Caesar's camp,
as treacherous and deceitful as ever. Their ostensible
object was to exculpate themselves for the battle they
had fought the day before contrary to the agreement
they had themselves requested, and they also hoped to
inveigle Caesar into extending the truce. Caesar was de-
lighted to have them in his power and ordered them
detained. He himself led his forces out of camp; the cavalry he posted at the rear of the column because he
thought the recent engagement had demoralized it.

14. Caesar speedily covered eight miles with a triple
line and reached the enemy's camp before the Germans
could sense what was afoot. The speed of our onset and
the absence of their own leaders unnerved them suddenly and completely. There was time neither to plan
nor to take arms, and they were too confused to know
whether to advance against the enemy or stand on the
defensive or fly for safety. As their cries and scurrying
betrayed their condition, our men burst into their camp,
goaded by their treachery of the day before. Those
quick enough to seize weapons made a brief stand,

fighting amidst their carts and baggage, but the remaining crowd of women and children (the Germans had left home and crossed the Rhine with their all) began to disperse in flight. Caesar sent cavalry to hunt them down.

15. When the Germans heard the shrieks behind them, and saw their kin cut down, they threw their weapons away, abandoned their standards, and flung out of the camp. At the confluence of the Meuse [Moselle?] and Rhine they despaired of further flight; many were killed and the rest threw themselves into the river, where they perished of panic, exhaustion, and the force of the current. The enemy had numbered 430,000 and our men had been apprehensive of a difficult war, but all returned safe to camp, with only a handful wounded. Caesar gave the Germans detained in his camp permission to leave, but they were afraid of being tortured to death by the Gauls, whose fields they had ravaged, and said they preferred to remain with him. He gave them leave to do so.

16. Upon the conclusion of the German campaign many considerations determined Caesar to cross the Rhine, of which the most compelling was to show the Germans, who were so ready to invade Gaul, that a Roman army could and would cross the Rhine and terrify Germany. Another consideration was the fact that the cavalry force of the Usipetes and the Tencteri which had crossed the Meuse to pillage and forage, as I mentioned above, and had not been present at the battle, had withdrawn across the Rhine into the territory of the Sugambri, after the rout of their countrymen, and had joined forces with them. When Caesar sent messengers to the Sugambri to demand the surrender of the people who had made war upon himself and the Gauls, they

replied that the Rhine was the limit of Roman power:
if Caesar thought the Germans had no right to cross into
Gaul without his permission, how could he claim authority or power beyond the Rhine? Furthermore the Ubii,
who were the only people beyond the Rhine who had
sent envoys to Caesar, entered in alliance, and delivered
hostages, earnestly begged Caesar to support them
against heavy Suebian pressure. If state commitments
prevented his doing so, they asked that he merely bring
an army across the Rhine: this would suffice to give
them strength for the present and hope for the future.
The defeat of Ariovistus and this latest victory had so
enhanced the fame and prestige of Caesar's army even
among the remotest tribes of Germany, they said, that
the advertisement of their friendship with Rome would
afford them security. For transporting the army they
promised a large flotilla of boats.

17. For the reasons mentioned above Caesar was determined to cross the Rhine, but he thought it hardly
safe to cross in boats and deemed it unworthy of his own
or his country's dignity to do so. And so, though the
construction of a bridge presented great difficulties by
reason of the width, rapidity, and depth of the river, he
nevertheless resolved to make the attempt or else not to
cross at all. The type of bridge he adopted was as follows. Wooden poles, a foot and a half thick, sharpened
a little from the end and adapted to the varying depth
of the stream, were coupled in pairs at intervals of two
feet. These were lowered into the river by floats and
driven home with rams, not vertically like ordinary piles,
but tilted at an angle in the direction of the current.
Next a similar set of piles, parallel to the first but sloping
against the powerful thrust of the current, was carried
across the stream forty feet further down. Beams two

feet wide, fitting into the intervals between the piles of each couple, were laid across, the whole framework being kept in position by a pair of under-braces running from either side. Since they were held apart and yet clamped together, the structure was stable and it was so designed that, the greater the force of the current, the more closely were the piles locked together. The trestles thus constructed were interconnected by boards running in the direction of the bridge, and these were overlaid with poles and wattle-work. Finally, to break the impact of the stream, piles were driven diagonally from either shore and at the center formed a sort of buttress which was connected with the main fabric of the bridge. A similar structure was erected a little above the bridge, so that if the natives should launch tree trunks or barges to demolish it, these fenders might lessen their force and so prevent injury to the bridge.

18. Within ten days after the collection of timber began the whole work was finished and the army crossed over. Caesar left a strong guard at either end of the bridge and pushed on into the Sugambrian territory. Meanwhile deputations from several states came to ask for peace and friendship: Caesar made a courteous response and directed them to bring hostages. But the Sugambri had prepared to decamp, at the instigation of the Tencteri and Usipetes, whom they had received, as soon as work on the bridge began, and now they evacuated their territory, carried all their property away, and hid in isolated forests.

19. Caesar remained in their country a few days, burned all their villages and buildings, cut down their crops, and then withdrew to the territory of the Ubii. He promised to help the Ubii if the Suebi should attack them, and received certain intelligence from them.

When the Suebi heard of the construction of the bridge from their patrols they convoked a council, as was their practice, and sent messengers in all directions bidding the people to evacuate their towns, convey their children, wives, and property to the forests, and to muster all hands capable of military service at a rendezvous, virtually at the center of the Suebian holdings. Here they were awaiting the coming of the Romans, determined to fight to the end at that spot. Caesar had achieved all the objectives for which he had resolved to cross the river—to overcome the Germans, punish the Sugambri, and relieve the pressure on the Ubii—and he felt that the eighteen days he had spent across the Rhine had satisfied the demands of honor and utility. Upon intelligence of the Suebian concentration, therefore, he withdrew to Gaul and destroyed the bridge.

20. Very little of summer was left, and winter comes early in Gaul because its trend is northerly; nevertheless Caesar was intent on an expedition to Britain. He knew that the enemy had been reinforced from Britain in almost all the Gallic campaigns, and thought that even if the season were too short for operations it would still be useful merely to visit the island, and see what manner of men were there and learn the terrain, the harbors, the landing-places. The Gauls knew practically nothing about these things; none but traders ever go there and the traders know only the coast and the area across from Gaul. Though Caesar consulted traders from all parts he could ascertain nothing about the size of the island, the native tribes and their strength, their military tactics or civil institutions, nor what harbors might accommodate a fleet of large vessels.

21. To procure this information before making the venture, Caesar dispatched a galley with Gaius Voluse-

nus, whom he judged competent for the mission, with instructions to investigate the situation fully and report back as quickly as possible. Caesar himself marched all his forces to the country of the Morini, which affords the shortest crossing to Britain. Here he ordered all shipping from the neighboring districts and the fleet which he had built the previous summer for the Venetian campaign to concentrate. Meanwhile his plan became known and was communicated to the Britons by traders, and deputations from several of the communities in the island came to promise hostages and to submit to the authority of the Roman people. Caesar heard them, made them liberal promises, urged them to abide by their decision, and sent them home. With them he sent Commius, whom he had made king over the Atrebates when he defeated them, and who enjoyed high prestige in Britain; he had confidence in Commius' resourcefulness and courage, and believed he was loyal to himself. His orders were to visit as many communities as he could, urge them to a policy of loyalty to Rome, and advertise his own impending arrival. Volusenus reconnoitered the terrain as fully as possible for a man who did not venture to disembark and trust himself to the natives, and in five days returned to report his observations to Caesar.

22. During the interval Caesar spent in making his fleet seaworthy, deputations from a large section of the Morini approached him to exculpate their earlier hostility. It was because they were uncivilized and ignorant of our ways that they had made war on the Roman people, they alleged, and would now promise to carry out all his orders. Caesar thought the offer most opportune; he had no wish to leave an enemy at his rear, the season was too far advanced for a campaign, and he thought

Britain more important than petty conquests. He required a large number of hostages, therefore, and on
their delivery received the Morini under his protection.
About eighty transports, enough, in his judgment, to
carry two legions, were assembled and concentrated;
the extra warships he had he assigned to the quaestor,
the legates, and the auxiliary commanders. Eight miles
off there were eighteen additional transports, which adverse winds prevented from joining the concentration;
these he assigned to the cavalry. The remainder of the
army he assigned to the generals Quintus Titurius Sabinus and Lucius Aurunculeius Cotta to be used against
the Menapii and the cantons of the Morini which had
sent no deputations. He ordered the legate Publius Sulpicius Rufus to hold the port with a garrison he considered adequate.

23. When these assignments were completed, the
weather being favorable, he cast off before midnight; the
cavalry he ordered to proceed to the farther harbor,
there embark, and follow him. They were slow in carrying out this assignment; Caesar himself reached Britain
with the leading flotilla about nine in the morning and
there saw the enemy forces posted on the hills under
arms. The terrain was such, with precipitous cliffs overhanging the sea, that missiles could be thrown from the
heights down on the beach. Judging the spot highly un-
suitable for a landing, Caesar lay at anchor until the early
afternoon, waiting for the remainder of his fleet. Meanwhile he convoked the generals and the tribunes, and
told them what he had learned from Volusenus and what
he wanted done. He warned them that tactical requirements, especially in an operation at sea, were fluid and
variable; they must therefore follow orders closely and
act briskly. When the council had been dismissed and

wind and tide were favorable, he gave the signal for weighing anchor and moved on about seven miles, where he grounded his ships on an open and level beach.

24. But the natives realized what the Romans intended. They sent forward their cavalry and charioteers —a kind of warrior they habitually employ—and following up with the rest of the force attempted to prevent our men from disembarking. Landing was difficult for the reasons following. The size of the ships made it impossible for them to run ashore except in deep water; the soldiers did not know the ground, and with their hands burdened and themselves weighed down by their cumbrous arms, they had to jump down from their vessels, keep a foothold in the surf, and fight the enemy all at once; while the enemy had their hands free, knew the ground perfectly, and could stand on dry land or advance a little into the water, throw their missiles boldly, and spur their horses into the sea, to which they were trained. Our men were unnerved by these handicaps and being inexperienced in this kind of warfare, they did not show the dash and energy they generally did in land battles.

25. When Caesar noticed this, he ordered the galleys, with the look of which the natives were not familiar and which were easier to handle, to sheer off a little from the transports, row hard and range along the enemy's flanks, and thence to dislodge them and clear them away with slings, arrows, and artillery. This tactic proved very serviceable. The natives were alarmed at the shape of the ships, the motion of the oars, and the novelty of the artillery; they halted and then retired a little space. Then, while our soldiers were hesitating, chiefly because of the depth of the water, the standard-bearer of the Tenth, with a prayer that his act might redound to the success

of the legion, cried: "Leap down, men, unless you want
to betray your eagle to the enemy; I, at least, shall have
done my duty to my country and my general." As he
said this, in a loud voice, he threw himself overboard and
began to advance against the enemy with the eagle. Then
our men called upon one another not to suffer such a
disgrace, and with one accord leaped down from the
ships. Seeing this their comrades from the nearest ships
followed them and advanced close to the enemy.

26. Both sides fought with spirit. But our troops became greatly confused; they could not keep rank nor
stand firm nor follow their respective standards, but, as
they came from one ship or another, attached themselves
to whatever standard they came upon. The enemy, on
the other hand, knew all the shallows; and when, standing on shore, they observed a few men disembarking
one by one, they spurred their horses on, many surrounding few, and attacked them before they were ready.
Others got on the exposed flank of the entire company
and discharged their missiles at them. When Caesar noticed this, he ordered the warships' boats and scout-boats
manned, and sent them to support any party he saw in
difficulties. As soon as they got upon dry land our men,
with their comrades close behind, charged the enemy
and routed them, but they could not pursue them far
because the cavalry had not been able to keep their
course and make the island. This was the only failure in
Caesar's traditional good luck.

27. As soon as the defeated enemy recovered from
their rout they sent a peace commission to Caesar and
promised to deliver hostages and obey his commands.
With the commissioners there came Commius the Atrebatian, who, as has been related above, had been sent
ahead to Britain by Caesar. They had seized him and

thrown him into chains as soon as he disembarked, while he was delivering Caesar's instructions in the character of an ambassador; now after the battle they sent him back. In their petition for peace they laid the blame for the offense upon the rabble and begged forgiveness on the grounds of ignorance. Caesar protested that they had made war upon him without provocation after they had themselves sent ambassadors to the continent to ask him for peace, but said that he would pardon their ignorance, and asked for hostages. Some they delivered at once; the rest, they said, had to be fetched from considerable distances and would be delivered within a few days. Meanwhile they ordered their people to go back to their fields, and chieftains began to come in from all sides and place themselves and their communes under Caesar's protection.

28. After peace had been concluded, on the fourth day of our arrival in Britain, the eighteen ships carrying cavalry, as mentioned above, set sail from the upper port with a gentle breeze. When they neared Britain and were in sight of our camp, so violent a storm arose that none could hold its course; some were driven back to their starting point, and others were swept down, at great hazard, to the lower, westerly, part of the island. They anchored nevertheless, but shipped so much water that they were forced to stand out to sea despite the darkness and make for the continent.

29. That night there happened to be a full moon, which usually makes ocean tides very high; but our men did not know this. The warships which Caesar had used to ferry the army over and had beached became water-logged, and at the same time the storm buffeted the transports moored at anchor. It was impossible for our men to handle the ships or do anything to save them. Many

were smashed and the rest lost their cordage, anchors, and other rigging and were made useless. The whole army was in consternation; there were no other ships to carry them back, no materials for refitting the damaged ships, and, because it had been understood that they would winter in Gaul, no provision for wintering in Britain.

30. Aware of this situation, the British chieftains, who had gathered at Caesar's camp after the battle, discussed its possibilities amongst themselves. They knew that the Romans had no cavalry or ships or grain, and surmised that their soldiers were few from the smallness of the camp—it was particularly small because Caesar had brought his legions without heavy equipment—and they judged their best course was to renew hostilities, cut our men off from grain and supplies, and draw the campaign out into the winter. They were sure that if they could defeat this force or prevent its return, no one would ever invade Britain in future. And so they made a new compact and began to slip away from the camp and secretly to recall their followers from the countryside.

31. Though Caesar had not yet ascertained their design, the disaster to the ships and the interruption in the delivery of hostages made him suspect what did in fact happen, and he prepared countermeasures for any contingency. Grain was brought in from the fields daily, the timber and bronze of the ships most severely damaged were used to repair the others, and other materials for repairs were ordered brought from the continent. The soldiers applied themselves willingly and energetically, and all but the twelve ships lost were made tolerably seaworthy.

32. While these repairs were in progress one legion,

the Seventh, had been sent, in due course, to fetch grain. So far nothing suspicious had occurred; some of the natives were still in their fields, and some went in and out of our camp. The pickets at the camp gate reported to Caesar that an unusual quantity of dust was visible in the direction the legion had taken. Caesar suspected what had happened—the natives had hatched some scheme. He ordered the cohorts on outpost duty to march with him to the scene, two others to take their place at the outpost, and the rest to arm and follow immediately. When he had proceeded some distance from the camp he saw that the legion was in trouble; they were huddled in a mass and assailed by missiles from all sides and could hardly hold their ground. The grain having been harvested elsewhere, the enemy surmised our men would come to the one sector where any was left and had taken cover in the nearby woods by night. Then when our men had scattered, laid their arms aside, and were busy reaping, they attacked. They killed a few, threw the rest into confusion before they could form up, and surrounded them with their cavalry and chariots.

33. The technique of chariot fighting is as follows. First they ride all over the field hurling missiles, and the terrifying horses and clatter of wheels is usually enough to confound the enemy. When they have worked their way among the squadrons of their own cavalry they leap down from their chariots and fight on foot. Meanwhile the drivers gradually withdraw from the battle and park their vehicles in such a way that if the charioteers are hard pressed by a numerous enemy they will have an easy retreat to their own side. In action, therefore, they exhibit the mobility of cavalry and the steadiness of infantry. Daily practice and training enables them to check

their horses at a gallop down a steep hill, turn them, sprint along the whiffletree, perch on the yoke, and get back into the car in a flash.

34. The novelty of these tactics had unnerved our men, and Caesar's support was most timely. At his arrival the enemy stood still, and our men recovered morale. But at this point Caesar did not think the occasion suitable for bringing on a pitched battle, and so kept to his position and after a short interval led his legions back to camp. During these operations, while all our men were preoccupied, the natives remaining in the fields made off. There followed several days of continuous bad weather which kept our men in camp and prevented the enemy from fighting. Meanwhile the natives had dispatched messengers in all directions to advertise the fewness of our soldiers and to point out what great opportunities for plunder and for liberating themselves permanently would accrue to them if they drove the Romans from their camp. By these means they speedily collected a great host of foot and horse and marched on our camp.

35. Caesar foresaw that what had happened on previous occasions would be repeated: if the enemy were beaten back their speed would carry them out of danger. However, he obtained about thirty horsemen whom Commius, the Atrebatian mentioned above, had brought over, and he formed his legions up in front of the camp. Battle was joined; the enemy could not long withstand the assault of our men and turned tail. Our men pursued as far as their speed and endurance allowed, and killed a good many; then they burned all buildings over a wide area and returned to camp.

36. On the same day envoys sent by the enemy came to Caesar to sue for peace. Caesar doubled the number

of hostages he had previously demanded and ordered them delivered on the continent, for the equinox was near and as his ships were shaken he did not think it wise to risk a winter crossing. He weighed anchor a little after midnight, when the weather was favorable, and all the ships reached the continent safe. But two of the transports were unable to make the same port as the rest and drifted a little further south.

37. The approximately 300 men disembarked from their transports were hurrying towards camp when the Morini, whom Caesar had subdued before he set out for Britain, surrounded them in the hope of plunder and ordered them to lay their arms down if they did not wish to be killed. At first the Morini were but few, but when our men formed a square to defend themselves the din brought about 6,000 more natives to the scene. When Caesar was informed he sent all the cavalry from the camp to rescue his men. Meanwhile our men withstood the enemy onslaught and fought most gallantly for more than four hours; they sustained a few wounds but killed many of the enemy. After our cavalry came into sight the enemy threw their weapons away and turned tail, and great numbers of them were killed.

38. On the next day Caesar sent his legate Titus Labienus with the legions he had brought back from Britain to punish the rebellious Morini. The marshes which had served as their refuge the year before were dried up, leaving them no retreat, and almost all fell into the hands of Labienus. Quintus Titurius and Lucius Cotta found that the Menapii had all hidden in their thickest forests when they led their legions against them; they devastated their fields, cut down their crops, and burned their buildings, and so returned to Caesar. Caesar quartered all the legions among the Belgae for the win-

ter. Only two of the British tribes sent hostages there; the others failed to do so. Upon receipt of Caesar's dispatches the senate decreed a thanksgiving of twenty days for these achievements.

V 54 B.C.

1. When, in the consulship of Lucius Domitius and Appius Claudius, Caesar left his winter quarters to go to Italy, as he was accustomed to do each year, he charged the legates whom he had given command over the legions to build as many ships as they could during the winter and to repair the old ships. He gave instructions regarding proper size and design. To facilitate loading and beaching he made the ships somewhat lower than is normal in the Mediterranean; he had observed that the waves were smaller because of the frequent ebb and flood of the tides. To enable them to carry more freight and numerous pack-animals he made the vessels somewhat broader than is usual in other seas. He ordered all to be fitted for oar-propulsion, for which lowness is a great advantage. Materials for fitting the ships he ordered brought from Spain.

When he had finished the assizes in Hither Gaul he set out for Illyricum because he heard that the borders of the Province were being ravaged by inroads of Pirustae. Upon his arrival he levied soldiers from the communities and ordered them to muster at a given point. When this became known to the Pirustae they sent envoys to explain that the raids were not officially inspired and to declare their readiness to give full satisfaction for the injuries committed. Caesar heard them and bade them deliver hostages by a specified time; if they failed to do so he would make war upon their state. The hostages were delivered, in accordance with his orders, and he appointed arbiters to assess the damage one state had inflicted upon the other and fix the penalty.

2. When these matters had been attended to and the assizes completed he returned to Hither Gaul and from there proceeded to rejoin his army. Upon his arrival he visited the cantonments and found that despite severe shortages of materials the extraordinary diligence of the soldiers had produced 600 ships of the type described above and twenty-eight men-of-war; they were virtually ready to be launched in a few days. He congratulated the soldiers and explained to the supervisors of the work what he wanted done. He ordered all the vessels to concentrate at Boulogne, from whose harbor he knew there was an easy crossing to Britain, which was about thirty miles from the continent. For this purpose he left what seemed a suitable force, and himself proceeded to the territory of the Treveri with four light-armed legions and 800 cavalry; these people had not attended his assemblies or obeyed his orders and were said to have solicited assistance from the Germans across the Rhine.

3. This people is the strongest of all Gaul in cavalry and possesses large forces of infantry. As we have shown above, it lies along the Rhine. There were two rivals for the chieftainship, Indutiomarus and Cingetorix. The latter came over to Caesar, as soon as he heard he was approaching with the legions, assured him that he and his followers would remain loyal and not betray the friendship of the Roman people, and explained what was taking place among the Treveri. But Indutiomarus, on the

other hand, prepared for war. He mustered cavalry and
infantry and concealed those not of military age in the
Ardennes forests, which cover an enormous stretch from
the Rhine through the center of the Treveri to the frontier of the Remi. But when he found that some of the
chieftains, out of attachment to Cingetorix and because
they were frightened by the approach of our army, had
gone to Caesar to plead for themselves since they could
do nothing for their state, Indutiomarus was afraid he
might be completely deserted and sent envoys to Caesar,
with the following plea: He had been unwilling to leave
his followers and approach Caesar because he wished to
be in position to keep the state loyal, for with the departure of the nobility the common people might be so
foolish as to backslide. Now the state was under his control, and if Caesar would have it so he would come to
his camp and place his own and his people's fate in Caesar's custody.

4. Caesar knew well enough what Indutiomarus' motives were and what had induced him to change his designs, but he was loath to spend the summer among the
Treveri when everything was ready for a British campaign, and so he ordered Indutiomarus to present himself with 200 hostages. They were duly brought, including the chieftain's son and all his relatives whom Caesar
had specifically named, and Caesar reassured him and
encouraged him to remain loyal. But this did not prevent
Caesar from summoning the chiefs of the Treveri one by
one and reconciling them to Cingetorix; this was not
only a recognition of Cingetorix' services, but he realized that it was very important to enhance the prestige
of a man who had shown such extraordinary devotion to
Caesar's cause. Indutiomarus was vexed at the diminu-
tion of his authority among his own people; he had been

hostile towards us before, but his resentment now burned much hotter.

5. This business settled, Caesar and his legions marched to Boulogne, where he learned that the sixty vessels which had been built among the Meldae had been driven from their course by a storm and forced to return to their port of origin; the rest were completely fitted out and ready to sail. Cavalry from all Gaul, to the number of 4,000, and the nobility of all the states had assembled at the same place. Of the latter he decided to leave those of proven loyalty in Gaul and to take the remainder with him as hostages, for fear of insurrection in Gaul during his absence.

6. Among these chieftains was the Aeduan Dumnorix, of whom mention has been made above. Him particularly Caesar resolved to keep at his side because he knew he was a revolutionary, ambitious for rule, high tempered, and possessed great prestige among the Gauls. Moreover Dumnorix had asserted in an assembly of the Aedui that Caesar had conferred kingship over them upon him. The Aedui resented this claim but dared not send Caesar a deputation to reject the appointment or beg him to reconsider. This Caesar learned from his private connections. At first Dumnorix petitioned that he be left in Gaul on various grounds: he was unused to sailing and afraid of the sea, there were religious scruples which forbade his leaving. But afterwards, when he met with resolute refusal and realized there was no hope of obtaining his wish, he began to buttonhole the Gallic chieftains individually and to urge them to remain on the continent, suggesting that Caesar had some purpose in stripping Gaul of its nobility: he was afraid to put them to death in the sight of Gaul but would massacre them when he had carried them across to Britain. He

pledged his word and demanded their oath that they
would act in concert according to what they perceived
to be the interest of Gaul. Word of this was communicated to Caesar by several persons.

7. Upon this intelligence he resolved, because of his
high esteem for the Aeduan state, to restrain and deter
Dumnorix by what means he could. But when he saw
that his madness proceeded further he conceived it his
duty to prevent Dumnorix from injuring himself and
Rome. For the approximately twenty-five days that he
lingered at Boulogne (the northwest wind which is constant in that area at every season prevented his sailing)
he made every effort to keep Dumnorix loyal, but at the
same time kept informed of all his plans. Finally, when
the weather was favorable, he ordered infantry and cavalry to embark. While all hands were preoccupied, Dumnorix and the Aeduan cavalry started on their homeward
journey without Caesar's knowledge. When he was informed of the fact Caesar suspended his departure, and
laying all other business aside, dispatched a large part of
his cavalry to pursue Dumnorix with orders to bring him
back; if he should refuse obedience and resist he was to
be killed. A man who disregarded an order when the general was present could not be expected to behave ration-
ally when he was absent. When he was bidden to return
he began to resist, to defend himself, and to appeal to
the loyalty of his followers, shouting that he was a free
man and belonged to a free country. But pursuant to
orders, the man was surrounded and killed, and the
Aeduan horse all returned to Caesar.

8. This business dispatched, Caesar left Labienus on
the mainland with three legions and 2,000 cavalry to
guard the harbor, secure the grain supply, maintain surveillance over events in Gaul, and take such action as

the occasion and situation warranted, and himself, with
five legions and the same number of cavalry as he had
left on the mainland, weighed anchor about sunset with
a gentle southwest wind. About midnight the wind fell;
he was carried from his course and at dawn saw Britain
behind him on his left. Then he followed the changing
tide and plied his oars to make the part of the island
which he had found convenient for disembarking the
summer before. Here the prowess of the soldiers must
be applauded; their unflagging rowing enabled the heavy
transports to keep pace with the men-of-war. Landfall
was made with the entire fleet about noon, but not an
enemy was in sight. Caesar subsequently learned from
prisoners that a large group had indeed assembled at
that point but had been frightened away by the large
number of our ships—with those newly built and the
private vessels which individuals had made for their own
use, more than 800 were to be seen at once—and had
quitted the shore to hide in the highlands.

9. Caesar disembarked his army and chose a site suitable for a camp. When he learned from prisoners where
the enemy forces were situated, he left ten cohorts and
300 cavalry by the shore to guard the vessels, and shortly
after midnight marched towards the enemy. He was
not uneasy about his ships for he had left them moored
with Quintus Atrius in charge. During the night he advanced about twelve miles, where he came in view of
the enemy forces. With their cavalry and chariots they
advanced to the river, and from a higher position began
to interdict our passage and to give battle. When they
were repulsed by our cavalry they took cover in the
forest at a place admirably protected by nature and art,
which they had previously prepared, apparently for use
in their civil wars. Every access was blocked by heaps of

tree trunks. They themselves carried on guerrilla fighting from the forest, and kept our men from entering their stronghold. The men of the Seventh Legion, however, formed a testudo and built a ramp to their fortifications and so took the place and drove them from the forest at the cost of minor casualties. But Caesar forbade them to carry the pursuit too far, both because the terrain was unfamiliar and because a good part of the day was spent and he wished to use the remainder for fortifying his camp.

10. On the following morning he sent infantry and cavalry, in three detachments, to pursue the fugitives. They had advanced some distance and had sighted the rear of the enemy when horsemen sent by Quintus Atrius came to inform Caesar that on the previous night a great storm had battered almost all the ships and cast them on shore. Neither could anchors and cables hold nor could sailors and pilots resist the storm's violence to prevent the ships from running foul of one another. The losses were therefore severe.

11. Upon this intelligence Caesar recalled his legions and cavalry and ordered them to halt while he himself returned to the ships. He found that the dispatches brought him were accurate: some forty vessels had foundered, and the refitting of the remainder appeared to require great effort. Accordingly he drafted carpenters from the legions and ordered others fetched from the mainland. He wrote Labienus to build as many ships as he could with the legions at his disposal. And though the task involved much toil and effort he decided it was best for all the ships to be beached and enclosed in a continuous line of entrenchment with the camp. This required ten days and nights of incessant labor on the part of the soldiers. When the ships were beached and the

camp perfectly fortified Caesar left the same force as
before to guard the ships and himself marched back to
the point whence he had returned. Here he found much
larger forces of Britons assembled. The supreme command had been entrusted by common consent to Cassivellaunus; his territory was separated from the maritime
states by the river called Thames and extended inland
for about eighty miles. Previously he had waged incessant war with the other states, but our advent moved the
Britons to give him command over the whole war.

12. The interior of Britain is inhabited by people who
assert, on the basis of tradition, that they are indigenous,
but the seacoast by people who crossed over from Belgium for war and pillage and then settled in the country
and began to farm it; almost all are called by the names
of the states of their origin. The country is thickly pop-
ulated, there are many buildings very like the Gallic
style, and there are numerous cattle. For money they use
either brass or iron rods of specified weight. Tin is produced in the midlands and iron along the coast, but in
small quantities; their bronze is imported. There is wood
of various kinds, as in Gaul, except firs and beech. The
eating of hare, hen, or goose is forbidden, but they breed
them for pleasure. The climate is more temperate than
Gaul, and the frost less severe.

13. The shape of the island is triangular, with one side
facing Gaul. Of this side one corner is at Kent, towards
the east, where ships from Gaul usually land; the lower
corner looks south. This side extends for about 500 miles.
The second side faces Spain and the west. On this side
is Ireland, which is thought to be half as large as Britain, and the same distance from it as Britain is from
Gaul. In the channel between the two is the island called
Man, and there are thought to be several lesser islands

also. Of these some authors say that for thirty continuous days in winter they have night. Our inquiries revealed nothing of the kind, but we did see by our water-clocks that the nights were shorter than on the continent. The length of this side, by their calculation, is 700 miles. The third side is to the north and has no land facing it, but one corner points towards Germany. The length of this side is reckoned to be 800 miles, so that the circuit of the whole island amounts to 2,000 miles.

14. Of all the Britons the most civilized are those in Kent, all of which is along the coast. Their habits do not differ much from the Gauls'. The inland people do not sow grain but live on milk and meat and wear skins. All Britons stain themselves with woad, which makes them blue and more terrifying to confront in battle. Their hair they wear long, but they shave all the rest of their bodies except the head and upper lip. Ten or a dozen, particularly brothers or fathers and sons, hold wives in common, but the issue is attributed to the one to whom the wife was first married as a maid.

15. The enemy horse and chariots engaged our cavalry briskly on the march, but our men everywhere had the upper hand and drove them into the forests and hills. But when they had killed a number they pursued too eagerly and lost some of their own. But after an interval they suddenly dashed from the forest to fall upon our unsuspecting men, who were busy entrenching their camp, and delivered a sharp attack upon the pickets posted in front of the camp. Caesar supported them with two cohorts, each the chief of its legion. These took position with only a small space between them, but while our men were confounded by their novel mode of fighting, they boldly broke through their midst and then retired without loss. In that battle the tribune Quintus La-

berius Durus was killed. When additional cohorts were sent up the enemy was repulsed.

16. This engagement, fought in front of the camp in full view of everyone, made it plain that our men were not a fit match for such adversaries. They could not pursue an advantage because of their heavy armor nor venture far from their standards; nor could our cavalry engage except at great peril, for the Britons would purposely retreat, and when they had drawn our cavalry a little distance from the legionaries, leap down from their chariots and exploit the advantage of fighting on foot. In a cavalry engagement this tactic involved equal danger whether we pursued or retreated. Another disadvantage was that they never fought in a mass but widely scattered, and they had their posts dispersed at intervals so that they could relieve one another, and fresh soldiers could take the place of the weary.

17. On the next day the enemy took position at a distance in the hills; they showed themselves only in small groups, and attacked our cavalry with less energy than the day before. At noon, when Caesar had sent three legions and all the cavalry under command of Gaius Trebonius to forage, they suddenly swooped down on the foragers from all directions, even up to the legions and standards. Our men counterattacked vigorously, beat them back, and pressed their pursuit, seeing the legions close behind to support them. They drove the enemy headlong and killed a large number, giving them no chance to rally and make a stand or leap down from their chariots. In this rout their auxiliaries, who had gathered from all parts, deserted them, and thereafter they were never able to muster their full force against us.

18. Apprised now of their plan, Caesar marched his army to the territory of Cassivellaunus towards the

Thames, a river which can be forded on foot at only one
point, and that with difficulty. Upon his arrival there
he observed a large enemy force drawn up on the far
bank. The bank was protected by sharp stakes fixed in
the ground, and there were similar stakes in the river
bed, covered by the water. This Caesar had learned from
prisoners and deserters. He sent his cavalry forward and
ordered the legions to follow at their heels. Though only
their heads were above water, they moved with such
speed and dash that the enemy could not sustain the assault of legions and cavalry, abandoned the bank, and
took to flight.

19. Cassivellaunus, as we have shown above, gave up
hope of open battle and dismissed the larger number of
his forces, but retained about 4,000 chariots. Retiring a
little from the road and taking cover in impassable and
overgrown places, he kept watch over our march. From
the districts he knew we would traverse he drove cattle
and natives from the fields into the forests, and when our
cavalry ventured too far afield to forage and lay waste
he sent his chariots out of the forest, through tracks and
trails. Our cavalry fought them at a great disadvantage,
and fear of such encounters restricted their movements.
Caesar's only recourse was to forbid their ranging away
from the legionary column and to restrict damage to
the enemy by devastation and burning to what the legionaries had energy for after their exhausting marches.

20. Meanwhile the Trinobantes, virtually the strongest people in that area, made overtures to Caesar. Mandubracius, whose father had been their king, had been
killed by Cassivellaunus, and Mandubracius himself
had escaped death only by fleeing to Caesar on the continent and putting himself under his protection. Through
a deputation to Caesar the Trinobantes promised to sur-

render to him and do his bidding; they petitioned him
to protect Mandubracius from Cassivellaunus and send
him back to govern and rule them. Caesar asked for
forty hostages and grain for his army, and sent Mandubracius back. They obeyed his orders promptly, and
sent the hostages and grain as specified.

21. Observing that the Trinobantes were now protected against Cassivellaunus and secured from injury
by the soldiers, the Cenimagni, Segontiaci, Ancalites,
Bibroci, and Cassi sent delegations to surrender to Caesar. From them he learned that Cassivellaunus' stronghold, fortified by forests and marshes and containing
large numbers of men and cattle, was not far distant.
The Britons call a stronghold a place in the forest fortified with a rampart and trench where they customarily
foregather to avoid enemy incursions. To this place Caesar proceeded with his legions, and found it excellently
protected by nature and art. Nevertheless he promptly
attacked from two directions, and after a short resistance
the enemy proved unable to withstand and fled the
stronghold in another direction. A great quantity of cattle was taken and many of the fugitives were caught
and killed.

22. While these operations were in progress in the interior, Cassivellaunus sent messengers to Kent, which
was by the coast, as we have shown above, and was governed by four kings, Cingetorix, Carvilius, Taximagulus,
and Segovax. He ordered them to make a sudden attack
with their combined forces upon our naval camp. When
they reached the camp our men made a sortie, killed
large numbers, captured a noble chief named Lugotorix,
and retired without loss. Upon news of this battle Cassivellaunus was moved by his numerous setbacks, the devastation of his country, and in particular by the defec-

tion of his allies, to send Caesar emissaries to offer surrender through the mediation of Commius the Atrebate.
Caesar had decided to winter on the continent to forestall sudden commotions in Gaul; moreover little was
left of the summer, and he knew the operation might be
prolonged. He therefore ordered hostages and fixed an
annual tribute for Britain to pay to the Roman people;
he also gave strict orders that Cassivellaunus should do
no hurt to Mandubracius or the Trinobantes.

23. With these hostages in hand Caesar led his army
back to the sea, where he found his fleet refitted, and
launched it. Because his captives were so numerous and
some of his ships had foundered in the storm, he decided
to transport the army in two voyages. Not a single ship
carrying soldiers, as it happened, though the fleet was
so large and the crossings so numerous, was lost, neither
then nor the year before. But of those sent back empty
from the continent, both those that had carried one load
across and the sixty which Labienus built subsequently,
very few reached their destination; almost all the rest
were driven back. When after a considerable wait, Caesar found they had not come and feared the imminence
of the equinox might make navigation impossible, he
crowded the men on board perforce and set sail at ten
o'clock in serene weather. He made land at dawn, with
all his ships safe.

24. He beached his ships and held an assembly of
the Gauls at Amiens and then, because drought had
caused a scarcity of grain that year, he was compelled
to alter his practice of previous years and distribute the
legions in several areas for the winter. One he assigned
to the Morini, under the legate Gaius Fabius; another to
the Nervii, under Quintus Cicero; a third to the Esubii
under Lucius Roscius; a fourth to the Remi, at the fron-

tiers of the Treveri, under Titus Labienus. Three legions
he quartered among the Belgae, under the quaestor Marcus Crassus and the legates Lucius Munatius Plancus
and Gaius Trebonius. One legion, recently recruited
across the Po, and five cohorts he sent to the Eburones,
who live mainly between the Meuse and the Rhine and
were ruled by Ambiorix and Catuvolcus; command over
these soldiers he assigned to Quintus Titurius Sabinus
and Lucius Aurunculeius Cotta. By such a distribution
of the legions he thought the shortage of grain could
most easily be met. Yet all these cantonments were within
a circuit of a hundred miles, except Roscius', which was
in a very quiet and subdued district. Caesar himself resolved to remain in Gaul until he knew the legions had
secured and fortified their several cantonments.

25. Among the Carnutes there was a man of noble
lineage named Tasgetius, whose forebears had been kings
over their people. In recognition of his courage and loyalty and his outstanding cooperation in all Caesar's campaigns, Caesar restored him to the throne of his fathers.
That year, which was the third of his rule, his enemies,
with the avowed complicity of many of the citizens, assassinated him, and the matter was reported to Caesar.
The numbers of those involved made Caesar apprehensive that they might instigate rebellion, and he ordered
Lucius Plancus with his legion to proceed rapidly from
Belgium to the country of the Carnutes, there to arrest
and dispatch to him the persons he found implicated in
the assassination of Tasgetius. In the meanwhile he was
informed by the officers in charge that they had reached
their winter cantonments and had fortified them.

26. Within fifteen days of their settlement, riots and
rebellion were suddenly raised by Ambiorix and Catuvolcus. They had reported to Sabinus and Cotta at the

frontiers of their domain and had delivered grain to their cantonments, when messengers from Indutiomarus the Treveran instigated them to revolt. They suddenly overwhelmed a wood-gathering detachment and marched to attack the camp in great force. Our men promptly took arms and mounted the rampart, and the Spanish cavalry charged out of one of the gates and gained the advantage in a cavalry engagement. The enemy gave their attempt up and retired from the assault. Then, as their custom was, they shouted for one of our people to come out for a conference; they had something of common interest to say, they declared, which they hoped would assuage the conflict.

27. To confer with them Gaius Arpineius, a Roman knight and a close friend of Quintus Titurius, was sent out, and with him a Spaniard named Quintus Junius, who had gone on several missions to Ambiorix for Caesar. Ambiorix spoke to them as follows: "I am greatly indebted to Caesar for the kindnesses he has shown me. Thanks to him I am freed from the tribute I used to pay my neighbors the Aduatici and have recovered my son and nephew whom the Aduatici had received as hostages and were holding in chains as bondmen. My part in the assault in the camp was without my own consent or wish, but at the compulsion of my people; the nature of my authority is such that my power over my people is no greater than theirs over me. The state opened hostilities because it was unable to withstand the sudden uprising of the Gauls. Of this my own humility is a proof: I am not so naïve as to think that my resources could vanquish the Roman people. Gaul had agreed to a common plan, and this is the day appointed to attack all Caesar's cantonments, so that no legion can come to the assistance of another. It is not easy for Gauls

to refuse cooperation with other Gauls when the object is the recovery of their common freedom. Now I have discharged my duty to my country I can offer recompense for Caesar's kindnesses. In the name of our friendship, Titurius, I beg and admonish you to see to your own and your soldiers' safety. A huge band of Germans hired by the Gauls have crossed the Rhine and will be here in two days. You must decide, if you wish to leave your cantonment before the neighboring peoples become aware of your route, whether you will take your soldiers to Cicero, who is about fifty miles away, or to Labienus, who is somewhat further. I promise to assure you safe conduct through my territory and will give my oath. This course will benefit my people, who will be relieved of the cantonment, and be a proper return to Caesar for his services." After this speech Ambiorix departed.

28. Arpineius and Junius reported what they had been told to the generals, who were disturbed by the unforeseen development and thought the suggestion, though it came from an enemy, should not be disregarded. What actuated them mainly was the extreme unlikelihood that so lowly and ineffectual a people as the Eburones would venture war against the Roman people on their own initiative. They referred the question to a council, where the debate was vigorous. Lucius Aurunculeius and many of the tribunes and senior centurions were of opinion that no risks should be taken and that their winter quarters should not be abandoned without orders from Caesar. They pointed out that their fortifications could withstand any number of Germans: had they not bravely withstood the first enemy assault and inflicted serious losses upon him? There was no lack of provisions, and in the meanwhile reinforcements from nearby canton-

ments and from Caesar would reach them. They capped
their argument with the declaration that nothing could
be more frivolous or more cowardly than to adopt measures of the highest moment on the advice of an enemy.

29. In opposition Titurius vociferated that it would be
too late to act when the enemy had been joined by the
Germans and was concentrated in strength or when disaster had befallen the neighboring cantonments. The
time for consultation was short. Caesar must have gone
to Italy, for otherwise the Carnutes would not have resolved to murder Tasgetius, nor would the Eburones, if
Caesar were near, have so despised us as to assail our
camp. Facts, he said, and not the enemy's advice, swayed
him. There was the Rhine, and the Germans were ag-
grieved at the death of Ariovistus and our recent victories; all Gaul was aflame at the humiliation of subjection to Roman authority and the extinction of their proud
military reputation. And finally, who could imagine that
Ambiorix would take so extreme a step without certain
assurances? His proposal, he declared, was safe in either
event: if his apprehensions were baseless, they could
reach the nearest legion with no danger; but if all Gaul
had conspired with the Germans their only salvation
was speed. What was the upshot of the proposal of Cotta
and the other dissenters? Even if there was no present
danger they must anticipate a long siege and starvation.

30. In the ensuing debate Cotta and the senior centurions resisted strenuously; whereupon Sabinus said, in
a voice loud enough for many of the soldiers to hear,
"Have your way, if you like. I am no more afraid of
death than any of you. But these men must understand
that it is from you they should demand an accounting
for any disaster that may befall. If you would only allow
it they could be united with the other cantonments by

day after tomorrow and face the chances of war with their comrades, and not perish by sword or starvation alone and isolated from the rest."

31. As the council was breaking up officers button-holed the opponents and pleaded with them not to let their stubborn disagreement endanger the general wel-fare. Staying or leaving would involve no difficulty if only they approved a single course, but there would be no hope of safety if they quarreled. The argument con-tinued till midnight, when Cotta, much moved, yielded and Sabinus won. Orders were issued to march at dawn, and the rest of the night the soldiers were all awake, each man calculating what he could carry with him and how much of his winter gear he would have to leave behind. Everything conceivable was done to convince the sol-diers that their march at dawn would be dangerous, and the danger was increased by their fatigue and sleepless-ness. And so they left the camp at dawn in a very long column and with great quantities of baggage, in the as-surance that Ambiorix' advice came from a devoted friend, not an enemy.

32. The noises and stirring during the night revealed the imminent departure to the enemy, who set an am-bush in two bodies in a suitable spot deep in the forest, about two miles away, where they awaited the Romans. When a large part of our column had descended in a broad valley, they suddenly showed themselves on either side of the valley, attacked the rear and blocked the as-cent of the van, and began to engage with a great ad-vantage of terrain.

33. Then at last did Titurius, who had been blind to what must happen, run up and down in great trepidation and marshal the cohorts, but with hesitation and in a manner which made his helplessness obvious; this usu-

ally happens when people have to make their plans while
action is in progress. But Cotta, who had foreseen the
possibility of an attack on the march and accordingly
advised against it, did everything possible for the common safety; he encouraged and heartened the soldiers
like a general, he fought like a man in the ranks. The
length of the column made personal supervision difficult;
because the officers could not foresee the requirements
of disparate sectors, they ordered the men to abandon
their baggage and form into a square. Such a tactic is
proper in such a situation, but the results were bad, for
it disheartened our soldiers and enhanced the enemy
morale, for the move seemed a confession of panic and
despair. Inevitably also it happened that as the soldiers
were separated from their standards individuals hurried
to find and snatch their most precious belongings from
the baggage, and consequently there was shouting and
wailing everywhere.

34. But the natives kept their heads. Their leaders had
passed the order down their lines that no one must leave
his post. All that the Romans left would be their booty,
kept safe for them; all they need think about was victory. Though their general and the goddess luck had
forsaken them our men staked their hope of survival on
courage and fought with great gallantry. In whatever
quarter a cohort charged, there a large number of the
enemy fell. On observing this Ambiorix passed the order
to discharge weapons from a distance and not approach
too close to our men but give ground wherever the Romans charged. Their light armor and the agility acquired
by long practice would keep them from harm, and when
the Romans retired to their standards they could resume
the offensive.

35. These directions the Gauls observed most care-

fully. When a cohort charged forward from the square
the enemy fled nimbly. But in the meanwhile part of
the square was left unprotected and missiles could be
hurled in on the open flank. Again, when our men began
to retire to the point they had left, they were surrounded
by the body that had retired and those adjacent to them.
On the other hand, if they chose to hold their ground
there was no opportunity for gallantry, and it was impossible for so dense a mass to avoid missiles showered
by so large a host. Harassed by so many disadvantages,
nevertheless, and despite their severe losses, they kept
up their resistance, and during the greater part of a day,
from dawn till two in the afternoon, their conduct was
worthy of their reputation. Titus Valentius, a brave and
highly respected soldier who had been a senior centurion
the year before, had both his thighs pierced by a pike.
His peer Quintus Lucanius was killed fighting bravely
to help his son who was surrounded. Lucius Cotta the
legate received a sling wound in the mouth as he was
encouraging the cohorts and centuries.

36. Disturbed by these developments Quintus Titurius
sent his interpreter to Ambiorix, whom he saw encouraging his men at a distance, to ask for quarter for himself
and his men. To this appeal Ambiorix answered that if
Titurius wished to confer with him he might do so. He
hoped he could prevail on his host to grant the Roman
soldiers quarter; Titurius himself he would certainly not
harm, and for this pledged his honor. Titurius reported
Ambiorix' answer to Cotta (who was wounded) and
suggested that they leave the battle to parley with
Ambiorix, in the hope that they could procure their own
and their soldiers' safety. Cotta said he would not go to
an armed enemy, and persisted in his refusal.

37. Sabinus then ordered the tribunes and senior cen-

turions who were present near him to follow him. When
they drew near Ambiorix he was ordered to throw down
his weapons; he obeyed the order and bade his men
do likewise. Meanwhile, as they were discussing terms
and Ambiorix had purposely embarked on a long dis-
course, they were gradually surrounded more closely and
then killed. Then the Gauls shouted for victory, as is their
custom, and raised their wail for a charge against our
lines, which they threw into confusion. There Lucius
Cotta died fighting, with the larger part of the soldiers,
and the remnant took shelter in the camp they had left.
When Lucius Petrosidius, an eagle-bearer, was overwhelmed by the enemy host he threw the eagle inside
the rampart and himself died fighting bravely in front
of the camp. With difficulty the men sustained the enemy
assault till nightfall, and at night, in despair of survival,
they killed themselves to a man. A handful that had escaped out of the battle made their way through the path-
less forest to Titus Labienus' cantonment and gave him
an account of what had happened.

38. Elated by his victory Ambiorix with his cavalry
started immediately for the Aduatici, who adjoined his
realm. He marched day and night without halting, and
ordered the infantry to follow. When he had roused the
Aduatici by his account of the victory, he reached the
Nervii on the day following and urged them not to lose
the opportunity of winning their liberty forever and
avenging the injuries they had received at the hands of
the Romans. He pointed out that two generals and a
large part of the army had been destroyed; it would be
an easy matter to overwhelm and massacre the legion
quartered with Cicero, and he promised his assistance
in the enterprise. The Nervii were readily persuaded.

39. Accordingly messengers were sent forthwith to the

Ceutrones, Grudii, Levaci, Pleumoxii, Geidumni, all of whom were their dependencies, bidding them muster the strongest bands possible and swoop suddenly upon the cantonment of Cicero, who had not yet heard of the death of Titurius. Here too it happened, as was inevitable, that a number of soldiers who had gone into the forest to fetch wood for the fortifications, were intercepted by the sudden descent of the cavalry. When these men were cut off the Eburones, Nervii, Aduatici, and all their allies and dependents began to attack the legion in great force. Our men quickly took arms and mounted the rampart. The assault was hard to withstand because the enemy had put all their hope in speed, in the conviction that victory that day would make them victors forever.

40. Cicero immediately sent dispatches to Caesar, offering large rewards if they were carried through; but all the roads were blocked and the couriers intercepted. During the night 120 towers were built, with incredible speed, out of the lumber which had been brought to fortify the camp, and finishing touches were put on the works where they seemed to need them. On the next day the enemy attacked the camp in much greater force and filled up the trench, but our men resisted as they had the day before. It was the same on the days following. No hour of the night was free from work, no opportunity was given the sick or wounded to rest. All that was needed for the next day's attack was got ready during the night: numerous pointed stakes were hardened in fire, quantities of heavy siege javelins prepared, towers were boarded up, screens and crenellations were woven of wicker. Cicero himself, though his health was frail, never spared himself to rest even at night; finally the soldiers of their accord, crowded about him and insisted that he must spare himself.

41. Then the Nervian chieftains and nobles who had had some introduction to Cicero or connection with him asked for a conference, which was granted. Their arguments were the same as Ambiorix had used with Titurius: all Gaul was in arms, the Germans had crossed the Rhine, Caesar's and the other cantonments were under attack. They spoke also of the death of Sabinus, and pointed to Ambiorix in corroboration. Cicero was mistaken, they said, if he expected support from men who were themselves desperate. Still, their attitude towards Cicero and the Roman people was such that they would deny them nothing except establishing winter quarters in their country; they did not wish the practice to become regular. They would allow the Romans to depart from their cantonment and proceed without fear wherever they wished. To this Cicero gave a simple answer: It was not the habit of the Roman people to accept terms from an armed enemy; if they would lay their arms down he would intercede for them and they might send representatives to Caesar; such was Caesar's justice that he could hope they would obtain their request.

42. This hope frustrated, the Nervii circumvallated the cantonment with a rampart ten feet high and a trench fifteen feet wide. This technique they had learned from contact with us during the years preceding, and had received instruction from captives taken from our army. But since they had no proper tools they were compelled to cut turf with their swords and carry earth in their hands and capes. Their vast numbers, incidentally, can be estimated from the fact that they completed fifteen miles of circumvallation in less than three hours. On the days following they began to erect towers to the height of the rampart and to prepare siege-hooks and scythes, as their prisoners taught them.

43. On the seventh day of the siege they took advantage of a sudden stiff breeze to fling heated darts and sling-shots of heated clay at our huts, which were thatched after the Gallic fashion. The thatch quickly caught fire, which the strong wind spread over the whole area of the camp. As if victory were already gained and secured the enemy raised a great shout and began to bring up their towers and sheds and scale the rampart on ladders. But so great was our soldiers' courage and presence of mind that though they were surrounded by scorching flames and overwhelmed with showers of missiles, and although they knew that their baggage and all their possessions were burning up, not only did no one abandon his post on the rampart to go elsewhere, but they would even scarcely look back, but continued to fight gallantly, one and all. That was far our worst day, but even so it resulted in many enemy casualties, dead and wounded, because they crowded so close under our rampart that the hindmost prevented those in front from retiring. When the fire had abated somewhat and the enemy had brought up a tower to touch the rampart, the centurions of the third cohort withdrew from their position, taking their men with them, and began to call and beckon to the enemy to come in if they liked; but not a one ventured to advance. Then they were chased away by stones thrown from every direction and the tower was burned down.

44. In that legion were two very brave centurions who were near promotion, Titus Pullo and Lucius Vorenus. They were in constant rivalry as to which would win advancement first, and each year they quarreled about the promotion. When the fighting at the rampart was at its briskest Pullo called out: "Why hesitate, Vorenus? What better opportunity do you expect to dis-

play your courage? This day will settle our dispute." So
saying he advanced outside the fortification and charged
where the enemy seemed thickest. Nor would Vorenus
remain behind the rampart, but followed his rival to
maintain his reputation. When he had got within a short
distance of the enemy he hurled his pike and pierced
one who started to run forward. The enemy covered him
with their shields as he lay wounded and unconscious,
and all threw their weapons at Pullo and kept him from
advancing. One pierced his shield and stuck in his belt;
this put his scabbard askew, and as he was hampered
by efforts to draw his sword with his right hand the
enemy surrounded him. His rival Vorenus ran up and
came to his assistance. The crowd at once turned from
Pullo, whom they thought wounded by the spear-point,
to Vorenus. Vorenus plied his sword in hand-to-hand
fight, killed one man, and was gradually pushing the others back when in his eagerness he stumbled in a depres-
sion and fell. As he was now surrounded Pullo came to
his assistance, and the two of them killed many of the
enemy and got back safe to their fortifications, with
much applause. Fortune's intervention in the rivalry of
these two was such that one contender's help saved the
life of the other and it was impossible to decide which
of the two proved braver than the other.

45. Day by day the defense became more difficult and
hazardous, chiefly because so many were killed or
wounded that few were left to fight, and Cicero sent dispatches to Caesar with increasing frequency. Some of
the couriers were caught and tortured to death in sight
of our soldiers. There was a solitary Nervian in camp,
Vertico by name, a man of good birth who at the beginning of the siege had taken refuge with Cicero and had
done him loyal service. By the promise of liberty and

large rewards Vertico persuaded a slave of his to carry a letter to Caesar. The man attached the message to his pike, and being himself a Gaul moved among the Gauls without arousing suspicion and so made his way to Caesar. Thus was information of the danger to Cicero and his legion brought.

46. It was about five in the afternoon when Caesar received the message. At once he sent a messenger into the country of the Bellovaci, to Marcus Crassus the quaestor, who was encamped at a distance of twenty-five miles; Crassus was to march at midnight and join him at once. Crassus started upon receipt of the order. Caesar sent another courier to the legate Gaius Fabius to bid him march his legion into the country of the Atrebates, through which he knew he would himself have to march. Labienus he ordered to bring his legion to the country of the Nervii, if he could do so consistently with the public interest. As the rest of the army was somewhat too far away he did not think it wise to wait for it. From the nearest winter cantonments he collected about 400 horsemen.

47. About nine in the morning Crassus' outriders informed Caesar that Crassus was approaching, and he advanced twenty miles that day. He assigned a legion to Crassus and put him in charge of Amiens, because the army's baggage, the hostages of the various states, the public records, the grain supply for the whole winter had been there concentrated and deposited. Fabius and his legion joined Caesar on the march, according to orders, with but a brief delay en route. Labienus had learned of the death of Sabinus and the destruction of his cohorts and knew the Treveri were marching against him in full force. His departure might look like flight, and he might not be able to withstand an attack, es-

pecially when the enemy were elated by their recent
victory. His dispatches to Caesar therefore explained
the danger in leading his legion out of its cantonment,
in view of what had happened at Liège and in consideration of the fact that the entire forces of the Treveri, foot
and horse, had taken a position only three miles from his
camp.

48. Caesar approved his decision, and although he had
only two legions instead of the three he expected, he
saw that success was just possible with speed. He advanced into the Nervian territory by forced marches,
and from prisoners he learned what was going on in Cicero's camp and what great danger he was in. By a large
bounty he induced one of his Gallic horsemen to carry
a letter to Cicero; this he wrote in Greek characters so
that his plans should not become known to the enemy
if it were intercepted; and he instructed the man, if he
could not get into the camp, to tie the letter to the thong
of a spear and throw it inside the entrenchment. He
wrote that he had started with the legions and would
soon arrive, and he exhorted Cicero to keep up his proven
courage. The Gaul was apprehensive and threw the spear
as had been directed, but it chanced to catch in a tower
and was not noticed by our troops for two days. On the
third day a soldier sighted it, took it down, and brought
it to Cicero. Cicero read it over, and then read it out to
a parade of the troops, to their great joy. Soon the smoke
of beacons was seen in the distance, and all doubt about
the coming of the legions was dispelled.

49. When their patrols reported Caesar's approach to
the Gauls they quitted the siege and marched to meet
him with their entire force, which amounted to some
60,000 men. Through the same Vertico who was mentioned above, Cicero found a Gaul who would carry a

dispatch to Caesar and urged him to travel with care and diligence. He wrote that the enemy had turned away to meet Caesar in full force. The letter reached Caesar about midnight, and he communicated its contents to his men and gave them courage to fight. At dawn he broke camp and had gone some four miles when he sighted the enemy host across a valley with a creek. It was a hazardous thing for a force so greatly outnumbered to engage on unfavorable ground, and since he had relieved the pressure on Cicero he could postpone action without misgivings. He therefore halted and pitched camp in the best position possible; and though he needed but little space, having only 7,000 men and no baggage, he further reduced its size by narrowing the passageways, with the object of making it seem contemptible to the enemy. Meanwhile he sent scouts in all directions to discover the most convenient means of crossing the valley.

50. That day minor cavalry skirmishes were fought near the creek, but both armies kept to their camps, the Gauls because they were expecting larger forces which had not yet arrived, and Caesar in the hope of enticing the enemy into a position of his choosing. His desire was to fight on his side of the valley, in front of his camp, and if this could not be managed to cross the valley and creek with a minimum of danger by the paths his patrols had scouted. At dawn the enemy cavalry rode up to our camp and engaged our cavalry, who, at Caesar's direction, purposely gave ground and retired to the camp. At the same time he ordered the ramparts on all sides of the camp to be raised to a greater height and the gates to be blocked—all this to be done with demonstrations of confused haste to suggest great fear.

51. The feint induced the enemy to cross the valley

and take an unfavorable position. They approached the
rampart, from which our troops had been withdrawn,
and hurled missiles inside the fortifications from all directions, and sent criers around the ramparts to proclaim
that any Gaul or Roman who wished might safely come
over to them before nine o'clock; after that hour they
would not be received. So contemptuous were they that
some tried to pull our rampart apart with bare hands
and others to fill up the trench—the single layer of turf
with which we had blocked the gates for appearance's
sake fooled them into thinking the gates could not be
broken down. But then Caesar charged out of all the
gates and launched a cavalry attack which speedily
routed the enemy. Not one stood to fight, but many were
killed and the rest disarmed.

52. Caesar judged further pursuit imprudent because
of intervening forests and marshes, nor was the enemy in
position to do any mischief, and so with all his forces intact he reached Cicero that same day. He admired
the towers, sheds, and fortifications the enemy had built,
and on parading the legion, discovered that not one man
in ten was unwounded. This was a measure of the peril
they had undergone and of the gallantry of their defense. He paid public tribute to Cicero and the legion
and cited by name the centurions and tribunes to whose
valor Cicero testified. The details of the debacle of Sabinus and Cotta he ascertained from prisoners, and on
the next day described the action to an assembly of the
soldiers and consoled and encouraged them. The losses
incurred through the rash fault of a legate, he explained,
must not dishearten them, for by grace of the immortal
gods and their own valor the affront was avenged; the
enemy's elation had been short-lived, and their grief
should last no longer.

53. In the meanwhile news of Caesar's victory had been brought to Labienus by the Remi with incredible speed. Though Cicero's cantonment was some sixty miles distant and Caesar had not reached it till nearly three in the afternoon, the Remi were shouting at the gates of Labienus' camp before midnight to notify him of the victory and felicitate him. Indutiomarus had resolved to attack Labienus' camp on the following day, but when the news reached the Treveri he decamped during the night and took all his forces back to their country. Caesar sent Fabius and his legion back to their winter cantonment and himself resolved to winter with three legions in three cantonments near Amiens. The commotions that disturbed Gaul decided him to remain with the army for the winter. When Sabinus' disastrous debacle was advertised, virtually all the Gallic states began to plan for war. Couriers and embassies were dispatched in all directions, they kept one another informed of their plans and where they intended to initiate hostilities, and they held nocturnal conclaves in desert spots. Hardly a day passed during the winter but that Caesar was troubled by some intelligence concerning subversive movements on the part of the Gauls. For instance, Lucius Roscius whom he had given command over the Thirteenth Legion notified him that a large force of Gauls from the states called Armorican had mustered to attack him and were within eight miles of his cantonment, but that they had withdrawn at news of this victory, and so speedily that their retreat looked like a rout.

54. Caesar summoned the chieftains of the several states, and by overawing some with his full knowledge of what they were about and encouraging others he kept a great part of Gaul to their obligations. But the

Senones, a very strong people and highly reputed among
the Gauls, had sought by official action to execute
Cavarinus, whom Caesar had designated to be their king.
Cavarinus' brother Moritasgus was the reigning king
when Caesar arrived in Gaul, and his ancestors before him had been kings. When he got wind of their intentions Cavarinus fled, and the Senones pursued him
to the frontier and unthroned and banished him. They
then sent representatives to explain their action to Caesar, who directed their entire senate to wait upon him.
They refused to comply. So impressed were the barbarians with their bold aggressiveness and so great was the
transformation of their morale that virtually every state
except the Aedui and the Remi fell under suspicion.
These two Caesar had always shown special honor, the
Remi because of their long and uninterrupted loyalty to
Rome, and the Aedui for their recent services in the
Gallic campaign. Their restiveness was not surprising;
among other considerations was chagrin that their once
paramount reputation for warlike prowess had been so
humbled that they now had to obey the orders of the
Roman people.

55. All through the winter the Treveri and Indutiomarus were busy sending embassies across the Rhine,
intriguing with the various tribes, promising money, advertising that a large portion of our army had been killed
and only a small fraction survived. But no German tribe
could be persuaded to cross the Rhine; they had tried it
twice, in Ariovistus' war and the migration of the
Tencteri, and would not tempt Fortune a third time.
Disappointed in this hope Indutiomarus nevertheless
began to levy and train troops, procure horses from
neighboring states, and allure exiles and outlaws from all
Gaul by large bonuses. So great was the prestige he built

up among the Gauls that ambassadors flowed in to solicit his good will and friendship, officially and individually.

56. When he saw that he was being thus solicited, that the Senones and Carnutes were pricked by consciousness of their guilt on the one hand, and the Nervii and Aduatici were mobilizing for war against Rome on the other, and when he was certain he would not lack for volunteers if he would initiate a campaign beyond his frontiers, he convoked a council of war. The Gallic usage is to commence a war by ordering all adults to present themselves under arms, and he that is last to come is done to death with many tortures in the sight of the multitude. At this council Indutiomarus declared his son-in-law Cingetorix, who was chief of the rival faction and had followed Caesar with unswerving loyalty, as we have shown above, a traitor and confiscated his goods. This done, he stated to the council that he had received appeals from the Senones, Carnutes, and many other Gallic states, and intended to march through and devastate the country of the Remi; but first he would attack Labienus' camp. Then he issued instructions.

57. The camp in which Labienus kept sheltered was well situated and strongly fortified, and he had no fears for himself and his legion; his only concern, indeed, was not to lose an opportunity for a successful operation. When he was informed, by Cingetorix and his relatives, of the speech Indutiomarus had made to the council, therefore, he sent commissioners to the neighboring states to raise cavalry, who were to report to him on a fixed day. In the meanwhile Indutiomarus' cavalry roamed about near our camp almost daily, sometimes to study the site of the camp and sometimes to talk with and frighten our men. Many missiles were hurled inside

the rampart, but Labienus kept his men within their
fortifications and used every possible means to confirm
the enemy's impression that he was afraid.

58. Day by day and with growing contempt Indutiomarus came nearer our camp. The cavalry from the
neighboring states which Labienus had procured were
introduced one night, and the guards were so carefully
controlled within the camp that the Treveri could not
possibly get wind of the reinforcement. Indutiomarus
followed his custom of riding up to the camp, and
wasted a great part of the day there. His horsemen discharged their missiles and challenged our men in insulting language to fight. Our men made no reply, and towards evening the Treveri decided to leave, in a scattered and disorderly fashion. Labienus launched a
sudden attack with all his cavalry from two gates. His
strict orders were that when the enemy was surprised
and routed (he foresaw this would happen, and it did)
the whole attack should be centered on Indutiomarus.
They must not strike a blow until Indutiomarus was
killed, for he did not wish any distraction to afford Indutiomarus a respite for escape. He offered large
rewards for killing Indutiomarus. To support the cavalry he sent cohorts out. Fortune seconded man's designs; attacked by the whole body, Indutiomarus was
caught and killed in the ford of the river and his head
brought back to camp. Then the cavalry returned to the
pursuit and killed as many as they could. Upon intelligence of this defeat, all the forces of the Eburones and
Nervii which had mustered dispersed, and thereafter
Caesar had a quieter Gaul.

VI 53 B.C.

1. Several factors led Caesar to expect a more serious disturbance in Gaul, and he commissioned his generals Marcus Silanus, Gaius Antistius Reginus, and Titus Sextius to draft new troops. He also requested Gnaeus Pompey to call up the troops from Cisalpine Gaul which he had sworn in during his consulate and order them to join Caesar. Pompey was now proconsul but was staying near the capital, while retaining his military authority, for political reasons. For the future as well as the present Caesar thought it expedient to convince Gaul of Rome's enormous resources by showing that it could not only quickly make any war losses good but even enlarge its army. Pompey acceded to the request out of patriotism and friendship, and Caesar's officers completed their levy promptly; before winter was done three legions—twice the number of cohorts lost with Quintus Titurius—were organized and mobilized. The size and speed of this increment showed what Roman organization and resources could do.

2. After Indutiomarus was killed, as we have shown, the Treveri conferred the command upon his kin, who persisted in attempts to rouse the neighboring Germans by promises of money. When they failed to persuade their next neighbors they tried remoter tribes, and when they found some compliant they exchanged oaths and gave hostages as security for their subsidies. They procured Ambiorix' adhesion to their league by a covenant.

Intelligence of these arrangements determined Caesar to
plan his campaign promptly. Everywhere he looked war
preparations were afoot: the Nervii, Aduatici, and
Menapii were united under arms with all the Germans
this side the Rhine; the Senones had ignored his summons and were in league with the Carnutes and neighboring peoples; the Treveri were sending a series of
deputations to rouse the Germans.

3. Before winter was over, therefore, Caesar assembled the four nearest legions for an unexpected descent on the Nervii and captured a large quantity of
cattle and humans before they could either concentrate
or escape. He bestowed the booty on his soldiers, devastated the countryside, and forced the Nervii to surrender and deliver hostages. This business speedily
dispatched, he led the legions back to their cantonments.
Early in the spring he convened the customary Gallic
assembly, which all except the Senones, Carnutes, and
Treveri attended. Their absence he regarded as a prel-
ude to armed rebellion, and to show his sense of its
paramount importance he adjourned the meeting to
Paris. The Parisii adjoined the Senones and in the past
the two had formed a single state, but they appeared
not to be implicated in the subversion. On the same day
that he announced the adjournment from his headquarters, he started with his legions and reached the
country of the Senones by forced marches.

4. Upon news of Caesar's approach Acco, the leader
of the plot, ordered the populace to gather in their
strongholds, and they tried to do so; but before they
could manage news came that the Romans had arrived,
and they abandoned their design perforce. They sent
deputies to beg Caesar's forbearance, with the Aedui,

the traditional protectors of their state, to be their advocates. Caesar readily granted the Aedui the pardon
they asked and accepted their excuses; the summer season should be devoted to the impending war, he
thought, not to judicial inquiry. He required a hundred
hostages, and handed them over to the Aedui for safe-
keeping. The Carnutes also sent a deputation and hostages to Caesar, employing as advocates the Remi,
whose dependents they were; Caesar's response was the
same. Caesar then adjourned the council and ordered
the states to supply cavalry.

5. With this sector of Gaul subdued, Caesar devoted
all heart and soul to the campaign against the Treveri
and Ambiorix. Cavarinus with the cavalry of the
Senones he ordered to accompany him, to prevent any
disturbance in the state in consequence of his hot temper
or the enmity he had earned. These matters settled, he
tried to divine Ambiorix' intentions, for he was convinced Ambiorix would not fight a pitched battle. Adjoining the territory of the Eburones were the Menapii,
protected by unbroken marshes and forests; alone of
the Gauls they had never sent Caesar a deputation to
treat of peace. He knew that Ambiorix had a connection
with these people, and understood that they had made
friends with the Germans through the Treveri. He
thought it advisable to deprive Ambiorix of these supports before attacking him, for despair might push him
to take cover among the Menapii or join the Germans
across the Rhine. Pursuant to this plan he sent the baggage of the whole army to Labienus in the Treveran
country and ordered two legions to join him; Caesar
himself with five legions lightly equipped marched towards the Menapii. The Menapii had mustered no force

because they relied on the protection of their terrain;
they betook themselves, and carried their belongings,
into the forests and marshes.

6. Caesar divided his forces with his legate Gaius
Fabius and quaestor Marcus Crassus, and the three
columns advanced on rapidly constructed causeways,
burning buildings and villages and seizing quantities
of cattle and men. This forced the Menapii to send a
delegation to sue for peace. Caesar accepted hostages
and warned them that he would treat them as enemies
if they admitted Ambiorix or his agents within their
borders. This attended to, he left Commius the Atrebatian with cavalry to keep surveillance over the Menapii
and himself proceeded against the Treveri.

7. While Caesar was engaged with this business the
Treveri had mustered large forces of foot and horse and
were making ready to attack Labienus, who had been
quartered in their territory for the winter with a single
legion. They were only two days' distance from him
when they learned that the two legions dispatched by
Caesar had arrived, so they pitched camp fifteen miles
off and decided to wait for German reinforcements.
Labienus was aware of their intention, and in the hope
that their rashness might give him an opening for
a battle, Labienus advanced with twenty-five cohorts
and a large body of cavalry, leaving five cohorts to
guard the baggage, and entrenched a camp one mile
from the enemy. Between him and the enemy was a
river with steep banks and difficult to cross. He had no
intention of crossing it, and did not think the enemy
would. Their expectations of reinforcements were increasing daily, and Labienus remarked openly in a
council that since the Germans were said to be approaching he would not jeopardize himself and his

army but would strike camp the following dawn. This
was quickly reported to the enemy, for of the numerous
Gallic cavalry it was natural that some should favor the
Gallic side. At night Labienus summoned the tribunes
and senior centurions, propounded his plan to them,
and to create an impression of panic, ordered the strik-
ing of the camp to be noisier and more confused than
is customary in Roman armies. This made the departure
look like a rout; and since the camps were so close, their
scouts informed the enemy before morning.

8. The Gauls urged one another not to let the booty
they craved slip out of their hands; with the Romans in
panic it was waste of time to wait for German reinforcements, and it ill beseemed their dignity for their
large force to shrink from attacking a puny band, especially when it was in flight and hampered. The rear of
our column had scarcely got beyond the entrenchment
when the Gauls unhesitatingly crossed the river to fight
on unfavorable ground. This is what Labienus had surmised, and to entice the whole body across the river
he calmly continued his pretense of marching away.
Then when he had sent his baggage forward a little and
parked it on a hill, he said: "Soldiers, this is the chance
you wanted. You have the enemy cornered in a bad
position. Show your general the same prowess you have
so often shown our commander-in-chief; imagine that
he is here and looking on." At the same instant he ordered the column to wheel into battle line and posted
the cavalry, except for a few squadrons detached
to guard the baggage, on the flanks. Our men quickly
raised the battle cry and discharged their javelins at the
enemy. When they saw the men they thought were fleeing advance to attack them, they could not even meet
the first charge but fled in rout to the nearest woods.

Labienus hunted them down with the cavalry, killed a
great many, took many prisoners, and a few days later
received the tribe's surrender. When the Germans coming to help them heard of the rout of the Treveri they
went back home. Indutiomarus' kin, who had instigated
the insurrection, followed them out of the country. The
civil and military headship was given to Cingetorix,
whose loyalty, as we have shown, had remained steadfast.

9. Caesar was determined to cross the Rhine, after he
passed from the country of the Menapii to that of the
Treveri, for two reasons: first, the Germans had sent the
Treveri reinforcements against him, and second, to deprive Ambiorix of an asylum. In keeping with this decision he started to build a bridge a little above the point
where he had crossed before. Since the principle of construction was now established and familiar, the work
was finished in a few days, thanks to the willing energy
of the men. Caesar left a strong garrison at the bridge-
head in the country of the Treveri to forestall any sudden uprising, and took the rest of his forces including
the cavalry across. The Ubii had previously surrendered
hostages and accepted terms; now they sent representatives to clear themselves and explain that they had kept
faith and had supplied no reinforcements to the Treveri.
They begged and implored him to spare them and not
punish the innocent for the guilty out of indiscriminate
hatred of Germans. If he wished additional hostages
they promised to supply them. Upon investigation Caesar found that the reinforcements had been sent by the
Suebi; accordingly he accepted the exculpation of the
Ubii and inquired into routes leading to the Suebi.

10. Some days later he was informed by the Ubii that
the Suebi were concentrating their forces and notifying

their dependencies to supply contingents of foot and horse. Upon this intelligence Caesar secured his commissariat and chose a suitable place for a camp. He instructed the Ubii to convey their cattle and belongings from the countryside to their strongholds, in the hope that shortages might induce inexperienced natives to fight at a disadvantage; he also directed them to send relays of scouts into the Suebian country to ascertain what they were about. These orders were carried out, and in a few days Caesar received a report to the effect that the Suebi with all their own and their allies' forces had retired to the remotest parts of their country as soon as they received definite intelligence of the Roman army. Their refuge was an immense forest called Bacenis, which stretched far into the interior and formed a natural barrier to protect the Cherusci and Suebi from hostile inroads against each other. It was at the edge of this forest that the Suebi had determined to await the coming of the Romans.

11. This seems a suitable point in the narrative to describe the mores of Gaul and Germany and the points of difference between them. In Gaul factions are the rule, not only in all states and cantons and districts but almost in individual households. Those they judge to possess the highest authority are the leaders, and to their decision they submit all important questions of policy. The object of this ancient institution seems to have been to assure the common people of support against the powerful; each leader protects his followers against oppression and fraud, for if he did not he would lose all his authority. The same principle applies to Gaul in its entirety, for the tribes too are grouped in two factions.

12. At Caesar's arrival in Gaul the leaders of one faction were the Aedui, and of the other the Sequani.

Traditionally the Aedui possessed the highest prestige and many dependencies, and to compensate for their inferior position the Sequani made an alliance, by great sacrifices and promises, with the Germans and Ariovistus. By several successful battles and the extirpation of the Aeduan nobility their power had advanced to the point where they annexed a large part of the Aeduan dependencies. They had secured the children of the principal families as hostages and had exacted an oath that no measures unfriendly to the Sequani would be countenanced. They seized and held the territory adjoining theirs, and had attained paramount power over all Gaul. It was this pressure which had constrained Diviciacus to beg the senate's help in Rome, but he had returned without accomplishing his mission.

Caesar's arrival changed the situation. Their hostages were returned to the Aedui, their dependencies restored, and new ones acquired through Caesar's influence; the tribes allied to them found their status improved materially and politically. The influence and prestige of the Aedui were enhanced in other respects also, and the Sequani lost their primacy. Their place was taken by the Remi, and since it became known that they stood as high in Caesar's favor as the Aedui, tribes whom ancient animosities prevented from joining the Aedui now accepted the hegemony of the Remi. The Remi were careful to protect their interests, and so secured the new authority they had suddenly acquired. The situation then was that the Aedui were regarded as preëminent, with the Remi standing next in importance.

13. Throughout Gaul only two classes are of any account or enjoy any distinction; the masses are treated almost as slaves, exercise no initiative, and are never taken into counsel. The greater part, when crushed by

debt or heavy taxation or oppressed by powerful individuals, bind themselves in slavery to the nobles, who exercise over them all the rights masters have over slaves. One of the two classes consists of the Druids, the other of the Knights. The former officiate at divine worship, regulate sacrifices public and private, and expound questions of ritual. Numbers of young men resort to them for study and hold them in high respect. They are judges in nearly all disputes, whether public or private, and in cases of crimes or murders or disputes about inheritances or boundaries, they settle the matter and fix awards and penalties. Any who do not abide by their decision, whether an individual or a tribe, they excommunicate, and this is their severest penalty. People under the interdict are regarded as impious monsters: everybody avoids them and shuns their approach and conversation for fear of incurring pollution; they cannot appear as plaintiffs or share in any distinction. The Druids are all under one head, who possesses the highest authority among them. At his death either the most eminent of his fellows succeeds, or if there are several on an equality, the headship is decided by a vote of the Druids, or sometimes actually by force of arms. At a certain season the Druids meet at a sacred spot in the country of the Carnutes, the reputed center of all Gaul. Here litigants assemble from all parts, and abide by their decisions and sentences. It is believed that their doctrine was discovered in Britain and thence imported into Gaul; and today most people who wish to study the subject thoroughly go there to learn it.

14. As a rule the Druids keep aloof from war, and do not pay taxes with the rest. They are exempt from military service and all obligations. Attracted by these great privileges many young men voluntarily foregather to

receive their doctrine and many are sent by parents and relatives. It is said that they learn a great many verses by heart, and accordingly many remain as students for twenty years. It is against the principles of the Druids to commit their doctrines to writing, though for other business, public or private, they use Greek characters. I suppose their motive is twofold: they do not wish their doctrine to become common property or their disciples to trust writing rather than memory. It is true that reliance upon documents tends to relax diligence in memorization. The doctrine they most strive to inculcate is that souls do not die, but pass from one body to another. This they regard as the greatest incentive to courage, for fear of death is then cast aside. They also hold long discussions about the heavenly bodies and their movement, the size of the universe and of the earth, the order of nature, the power and capacities of the immortal gods, and this lore they pass on to their disciples.

15. The other distinguished class is the Knights. When their services are required for war—and before Caesar's intervention this happened annually, whether they were themselves the aggressors or had to repel the aggressions of others—all participate, and the number of a man's retainers is the measure of his resources and rank. This is the only form of influence and power they recognize.

16. The whole Gallic race is addicted to religious ritual; consequently, those suffering from serious maladies or subject to the perils of battle sacrifice human victims or vow to do so. The officiants they employ are Druids. It is their belief that human life must be rendered for human life if the divinity of the immortal gods is to be appeased. There are regular public sacrifices of

the same character. Some weave huge figures of wicker, and fill their limbs with live humans, who are then burned to death when the figures are set afire. They suppose that the gods prefer this execution to be applied to thieves, robbers, or other malefactors taken in the act; but in default of such they resort to the execution of the innocent.

17. The god they particularly worship is Mercury, of whom there are a great many images. They regard him as the inventor of all crafts, the pathfinder and guide, and the most powerful patron of gain and trafficking. Next they rank Apollo, Mars, Juno, and Minerva, of whom their conceptions are virtually the same as other peoples': Apollo averts disease, Minerva initiates arts and crafts, Jove holds dominion over the heaven-dwellers, and Mars regulates war. To Mars they generally vow whatever spoils they may take when they decide on battle. After victory they sacrifice all livestock captured, and the other property they concentrate in one place. Such dedicatory heaps are to be seen in con-secrated spots in many of their states, and it is extremely rare that an individual should disregard scruple and either conceal an item of booty or appropriate a dedica-tion. For such an offense the penalty is death under tor-ture.

18. The Gauls claim that they are all descended from Dis Pater, on the authority of Druid tradition. That is why they designate measurements of time not by days but by nights; in observing birthdays and the first of the month or the year they make the day follow the night. Among other social usages a principal difference from other people is that they do not permit their sons to approach them in public until they are sufficiently

grown for military service, and they consider it reprehensible for a young boy to appear in public in the presence of his father.

19. Husbands set aside from their own property an
amount equivalent to the dowry they receive from their
wives and the two are lumped together. A joint account
is kept of the total, and the income saved, and the sur-
vivor receives both shares with accumulated profits.
Husbands hold power of life and death over their wives
as over their children. When a noble head of a house
dies his relatives foregather, and if the death seems suspicious, they examine the wives under torture, like
slaves, and if guilt is established they execute with fire
and all manner of torture. Gallic funerals, considering
their standard of living, are showy and expensive. They
throw into the flames everything they think the deceased was fond of, even animals; only a little before
our time slaves and dependents to whom the deceased
were known to have been attached were cremated with
them at the conclusion of the regular obsequies.

20. It is ordained by law, among the states whose
government is reckoned efficient, that anyone who receives political information by news or hearsay from
neighboring peoples must report it directly to the magistrate without communicating it to anyone else, for experience has shown that headstrong and inexperienced
persons may be so alarmed by false rumors as to be pre-
cipitated into unauthorized and criminal measures. The
magistrates use their discretion to suppress intelligence
or publish it. Political discussion is not allowed in a regular assembly.

21. German institutions are very different. They have
no Druids to preside over ritual, and no inclination to
sacrifice. As gods they recognize only those they see are

directly useful—Sun, Fire-god, Moon; the others they
have not even heard of. Their whole life consists of
hunting and war; they are inured to toil and deprivation
from infancy. Those that retain their virginity longest
are most highly esteemed, for they believe that conti-
nence contributes to height and strength and energy. To
have had intercourse with a woman before the age of
twenty is scandalous. But prudery does not enter in, for
they bathe in the rivers promiscuously and their furs
and short reindeer cloaks leave much of the body bare.

22. The Germans are not agricultural; their diet is
mainly milk, cheese, and meat. No one owns a specific
plot with definite boundaries; annually the magistrates
and chieftains assign fields of appropriate size and loca-
tion to tribes or clans who form a body, and in the following year they are compelled to move. Various reasons are alleged for this practice: long attachment might
make them give up warlike proclivities for agriculture;
they might become ambitious to expand their holdings
and the more powerful dispossess the lowlier; they might
build too solidly to avoid cold and heat; they might suc-
cumb to greed, which is the source of factions and dis-
sension; they want to keep the common people content
and orderly by showing them that their property was on
a level with that of the most powerful.

23. For a state the highest distinction is to be surrounded by the widest possible belt which they have
desolated and left uninhabited. It is a mark of their
prowess, they think, that their neighbors have been dis-
possessed and driven away and that none dares settle
near them; they also believe that it contributes to their
security to eliminate the danger of sudden invasion. For
the management of a war, aggressive or defensive, they
choose supreme commanders who are vested with

power of life and death. In time of peace there is no central authority; the chiefs of districts and cantons administer justice among their own people and settle quarrels. Brigandage involves no disgrace when it is carried on outside a given state's territory; it is rather applauded as a means of training the young and correcting laziness. When a chieftain states in council that he will lead an expedition and asks for volunteers to declare themselves, so many as approve the man and his project rise and promise their support, and the crowd applauds them. Any who do not keep their promise to participate are accounted deserters and traitors and forfeit all trust for the future. To misuse a guest is sacrilege. Any who visit them, for whatever reason, they protect from injury and regard as privileged; all houses are open to them, and they share in meals.

24. There was a time when the Gauls were more warlike than the Germans; they made war against the Germans and planted colonies across the Rhine because their own territory was too small for their dense population. Thus the Volcae Tectosages seized and settled the most fertile part of Germany, round the Hercynian forest—I note that Eratosthenes and other Greeks had heard of this place, under the name Orcynia. They occupy their settlement to this day, and enjoy a high reputation for probity and prowess. Because they have continued in the same poverty, privation, and hardship, the diet and dress of the Germans have remained unchanged. But the Gauls are plentifully supplied with articles of utility and luxury because of their proximity to our provinces and their acquaintance with imports from abroad. Gradually they have become habituated to inferiority; after repeated defeats in battle they do not even pretend to equality with the Germans.

25. The extent of the above-mentioned Hercynian forest is a nine days' journey for a light traveler; there is no other way to define it, for they have no system for measuring distances. Starting from the frontiers of the Helvetii, Nemetes, and Rauraci it follows the line of the Danube to the frontiers of the Daci and Anartes. Then it turns to the left through regions remote from the river and its broad sweep touches on many peoples. There is no one in this part of Germany who can affirm that he has reached the end of the forest, though he may have traveled for sixty days, or who has heard where it begins. It is known to produce many species of wild animals never seen elsewhere. Because of their marked differences from other animals the following may deserve to be recorded.

26. There is a stag-shaped ox from whose forehead, between the ears, there rises a single horn, taller and straighter than the horns we know; the tip divides into tines, like hands and branches. Male and female are alike, in shape and in size of horns.

27. Then there are the animals called elk. Their shape and piebald hides are like a goat's but they are somewhat larger. Their horns are blunt, and their legs have no knots or joints. They do not lie down to sleep, and if they happen to be knocked down cannot raise themselves to a standing position. For beds they use trees, against which they lean for support and thus get a little sleep. Hunters who track them to their haunts loosen the roots of the trees or cut through them to leave them seem to stand firm, and when the elk lean against them, as is their habit, their weight brings the weakened trunk down and they collapse with it.

28. A third species is called aurochs. They are only a little smaller than elephants, and have the appearance

and color and shape of bulls. They are very strong and very swift, and attack any man or beast they see. The natives are much concerned to trap these animals in pits and kill them. This kind of hunting trains the young men and hardens them. Those who have killed the most bring the horns to a public place as evidence and are applauded for their achievement. These animals cannot be domesticated or tamed even if they are taken very young. The size, conformation, and appearance of their horns are very different from those of our oxen. They are much sought after by the natives, who fit the rims with silver and use them for goblets at their grandest feasts.

29. When Caesar ascertained, through the Ubian scouts, that the Suebi had retired into their forests he decided not to advance further. As we have shown above, the Germans are not agricultural, and Caesar feared a shortage of grain. But in order to keep the natives apprehensive of his returning, and also to delay any reinforcements they might send, he broke down 200 feet of the bridge where it touched the banks of the Ubii, after he had taken his army across, and at the western end erected a four-story tower, fortified the position heavily, and posted a garrison of twelve cohorts to guard the bridge. He placed young Gaius Volcatius Tullus in charge of the position and the garrison, and as soon as the grain began to ripen set off for his campaign against Ambiorix through the Ardennes forest. This is the largest in all Gaul and extends from the banks of the Rhine and the frontiers of the Treveri to the country of the Nervii, a stretch of more than 500 miles. He sent Lucius Minucius Basilus ahead with all the cavalry on the chance that speed and a lucky conjuncture might enable him to strike a blow. Caesar instructed him to

forbid fires in camp, to give no intimation of his approach, and said that he would follow directly.

30. Basilus obeyed instructions and accomplished his journey sooner than anyone could expect. He caught many men off their guard in the open country, and upon information received from them pushed on to a place where Ambiorix was said to have halted with a retinue of horse. Great is the power of fortune, in war as in all else. It was a stroke of fortune that Basilus came upon Ambiorix unwary and unready and appeared in person before any report or rumor of his approach came through; but it was equally a stroke of fortune that Ambiorix himself escaped death, though all his military equipment was lost and his carriage and horses seized. A contributory cause was the circumstance that the building, like most Gallic houses, was surrounded by a forest: to escape the heat they find sites near woods and rivers. In that small space Ambiorix' friends and retainers were able to hold off the attack of the Roman cavalry, and while they were fighting one of his people put him on a horse and the woods covered his flight. Fortune was very instrumental both in exposing him to danger and in delivering him from it.

31. Why Ambiorix failed to concentrate his forces is a question. It may have been deliberate, because he did not think the time right for a decisive battle, or he may have been forestalled by the unexpected arrival of our cavalry, assuming that the rest of the army was at their heels. In any case, he broadcast instructions over the countryside bidding every man shift for himself. Some took refuge in the Ardennes forest, some in the vast marshes; those nearest the ocean hid in the islands formed by the tides. Many left their own country and entrusted themselves and their possessions to utter

strangers. Catuvolcus, who was king of half the
Eburones and had shared Ambiorix' project, was now
an old man incapable of the exertions of war or flight;
he called imprecations down upon Ambiorix for having
instigated the scheme and took his life with a yew, a
tree very common in Gaul and Germany.

32. The Segni and Condrusi, German tribes and
counted as such, situated between the Eburones and
Treveri, sent envoys to beg Caesar not to count them
as enemies or assume that all the Germans this side the
Rhine were in league. They protested that they had
never dreamed of war nor given Ambiorix any support.
Examination of prisoners established the fact, and Caesar assured them that he would not invade their territory if they would hand over any Eburones that had
taken refuge with them. Then Caesar distributed his
forces in three divisions and deposited the baggage of
all the legions at Aduatica. This is the name of a fort
practically in the center of the territory of the Eburones,
where Titurius and Aurunculeius had established their
winter quarters. Among other considerations which
favored the site was the fact that the fortifications built
the year before were intact, and this saved the soldiers
labor. To guard the baggage Caesar left the Fourteenth
Legion, one of three newly recruited and brought from
Italy. He entrusted command over the legion and camp
to Quintus Tullius Cicero, and assigned him 200 cavalry.

33. When Caesar had divided the army he ordered
Titus Labienus with three legions to move towards the
ocean into the districts bordering on the Menapii, and
sent Gaius Trebonius with the same number to ravage
the district adjacent to the Aduatici. With the remaining
three legions Caesar resolved himself to proceed to the
Scheldt, which flows into the Meuse, and to the remote

parts of the Ardennes where he had heard Ambiorix had
gone with a few cavalry. At his departure Caesar
asserted that he would return in a week, on the day rations were due to be issued to the legion on garrison
duty. He urged Labienus and Trebonius to return on
the same day also, if the military situation made it fea-
sible, so that they could pool their impressions of the
enemy strategy and form a fresh plan of campaign.

34. There was no organized body of natives, as we
have mentioned above, no stronghold, no garrison under
arms. The population had dispersed in all directions,
and individuals had settled wherever some remote
valley or forest glen or impenetrable morass offered any
hope of protection or survival. These retreats were well
known in their own neighborhood, and extreme care
was necessary to insure the safety, not of our army as a
whole (massed troops were in no danger from an enemy
dispersed in panic), but of individual soldiers, though
this too concerned the welfare of the whole army. For
one thing, the lure of plunder enticed many far afield;
for another, the dark and unmarked forest tracks were
impracticable for groups in formation. If Caesar chose
to finish the business and extirpate the whole scoundrelly crew he would have had to break up his units and
send out numerous small detachments; if he chose to
keep his formations together, as required by the established practice of the Roman army, the natives would
have the advantage of terrain, and they were bold
enough to ambush scattered parties and cut them off.
In this difficult situation every possible care was taken,
on the principle that it was better to sacrifice an opportunity to injure the enemy if the injury would involve loss on our part, though the soldiers were all on
fire to punish the enemy. Caesar sent messengers to in-

vite the neighboring states, with the prospect of plunder, to ravage the Eburones. His object was to risk Gallic lives, rather than the legionary soldiers, in the forests, and at the same time pour in so large a host that the whole breed and name of the Eburones should be annihilated in requital. Large numbers quickly assembled from all sides.

35. While this operation was in progress in all parts of the Eburonian territory, the seventh day, which Caesar had appointed for his return to the legion guarding the baggage, was approaching. Here one can observe the potency of fortune in war and what momentous chances it sets on foot. The enemy were dispersed in panic, as we have pointed out, and there was no organized body to cause the least apprehension. News reached the Germans across the Rhine that the Eburones were being pillaged and that everyone had been invited to share the plunder. The Sugambri, who are nearest the Rhine, and who, as we pointed out above, had sheltered the fugitive Tencteri and Usipetes, mustered 2,000 cavalry. Thirty miles below the point where the bridge was built and where Caesar had left a garrison they crossed the Rhine on barges and rafts. They entered the nearest part of the Eburonian territory, caught many scattered fugitives, and seized a quantity of cattle, which barbarians particularly prize. The lure of plunder led them farther; the Sugambri are natural fighters and freebooters, and no marsh or forest can stop them. They asked their prisoners where Caesar was, and found that he was on a long journey and that his army was gone. One of the prisoners added: "Why go after this wretched and puny stuff when you can be rich men in an instant? In three hours you can reach Aduatica, where the Roman army had deposited all its wealth. The garrison is not big

enough even to man the wall, and not a soul ventures outside the entrenchment." At this prospect the Germans cached the plunder they had already taken and pushed on to Aduatica, with their informant serving as their guide.

36. In obedience to Caesar's instructions Cicero had been very careful to keep the soldiers inside the camp all during the week, not even allowing a sutler to pass beyond the entrenchment, but on the seventh day he began to doubt that Caesar would keep his appointment, for he had heard that he had gone a longer distance and there was no word of his return. At the same time he was touched by complaints of men who said his strictness in not allowing egress from camp was like being besieged. Nor did he anticipate any mishap in a radius of three miles with nine legions and a large force of cavalry to oppose an enemy that was scattered and all but wiped out. And so he sent five cohorts to harvest nearby fields, between which and the camp there was only one hill. A number of legionaries on the sick list had been left behind in camp, and some 300 of them, who had recovered in the course of the week, were sent in a separate command. Permission to leave was also given to a large number of sutlers and a quantity of pack-animals which had been stabled in the camp.

37. It was just at this critical moment that the Germans rode up. Without checking their gallop they straightway tried to crash into the camp by the rear gate. That part was screened by a wood, so that they were not seen until they were quite near, so near that the traders whose booths were under the rampart had no chance to retreat. Our men were startled by the unexpected action, and the cohort on guard barely withstood the first rush. The enemy swarmed round the

other sides, looking for an opening. The circuit was protected by terrain and fortification, but our men found it
hard to defend the gates. The whole camp was in consternation; men asked one another what the trouble
was, and no one knew where the men should fall in
or the companies move. One man declared the camp was
captured, another insisted that the victorious barbarians
had come from destroying the army with its general.
Most conjured up superstitious fancies suggested by the
locale, and saw vivid pictures of the disaster of Cotta
and Titurius, who had fallen, they imagined, in that
same fort. The general panic confirmed the impression
the barbarians had received from their prisoners' story,
to the effect that there was no garrison inside. They
tried hard to break through and urged one another not
to let such an opportunity slip from their hands.

38. One of the sick men left behind with the garrison
was Publius Sextius Baculus; he had served under Caesar as senior centurion, and has been mentioned in connection with earlier battles. He had been five days without food, and now uneasy about his own and the others'
safety he walked out of his tent unarmed, and saw that
the enemy threat was most critical. He grabbed weapons
from bystanders and posted himself at the gate, where
he was followed by the centurions of the cohort
on guard duty. Together they stood the brunt of fighting for a short time. Sextius was seriously wounded and
fell unconscious; he was barely saved by being dragged
from hand to hand. But the respite was sufficient for the
rest to pull themselves together, man the defenses, and
make a show of resistance.

39. Meanwhile the harvesting party had finished and
overheard the shouting; the cavalry rode forward and
realized the great danger. Here there was no fortification

to shelter the frightened men; they were new recruits with no battle experience, and stood gaping at their tribunes and centurions waiting for some direction. None was so stalwart as not to be alarmed by the emergency. The barbarians sighted the standards from a distance and desisted from their attack. First they believed that the legions which their prisoners told them had gone farther afield had returned; when they realized they were only a negligible handful they charged from all sides.

40. The sutlers dashed to the nearest hill, from which they were promptly dislodged. Then they scurried into the regular formations, which increased the soldiers' terror. Some proposed a quick dash to the camp, since it was so near, in wedge formation; even if part were cut off and killed the rest could be saved. Others proposed to take a position on the hill, where they would meet the same risk together. The veterans, of whom we said that they had gone out under a separate command, disapproved. Instead they heartened one another and then dashed through the enemy under the leadership of Gaius Trebonius, the Roman knight who was their commander, and reached camp without a single casualty. The sutlers and cavalry who followed their rush were saved by the gallantry of the soldiers. But those who had taken their stand on the hill had still learned nothing about fighting. They could neither stick to the plan they had adopted and defend themselves in a superior position, nor could they imitate the speed and energy which they saw had saved the others, but when they tried to get back to camp they only got themselves into a bad position. The centurions, many of whom had been promoted for gallantry from lower grades in other legions to higher grades in this, fought

bravely, not to lose the credit they had earned, and
died. Their heroism made an opening in the enemy line
which enabled part of the soldiers to get back to camp
safe beyond all hope; part were surrounded by the barbarians and killed.

41. The Germans lost hope of storming the camp
when they saw that the fortifications were now manned,
and so retired across the Rhine with the plunder they
had cached in the forest. Even after they were gone the
panic persisted, so that when Gaius Volusenus, who had
been sent ahead with the cavalry, arrived that night, he
could not make the men believe that Caesar and the
army were close behind, all intact. Terror had laid such
hold of their minds that in their distraction they
declared that the cavalry had escaped when all the rest
of the force had been annihilated, and argued that the
Germans would never have attacked the camp if the
army were intact. Caesar's arrival dispelled their fears.

42. Aware of the vicissitudes of war, Caesar's only
complaint upon his return was that the cohorts had been
sent away from their garrison post, for even a slight
chance of mishap should not be risked. Fortune had
shown its power, in his judgment, in the unexpected
onset of the enemy, and even greater power in their re-
pulse from the very rampart and gate of the camp. The
strangest element in the whole episode was that the
Germans, who had crossed the Rhine for the purpose of
ravaging Ambiorix' territory, had by their diversion to
the Roman camp rendered Ambiorix a most welcome
service.

43. Again Caesar proceeded to ravage the enemy
with large numbers of horse which he had collected
from the neighboring states and sent off in every direction. Every hamlet or building anyone could sight was

burned; all the cattle were rounded up; such of the grain as had not been flattened out by the autumn rains was devoured by the swarms of men and beasts, so that even if a man succeeded in hiding for the present he would seem bound to starve to death when the army withdrew. With so large a force of cavalry combing the ground it often happened that prisoners would look round for Ambiorix, whom they had just seen in his flight, and insist that he had hardly got out of sight. The prospect of realizing their hope and justifying their enormous efforts by earning Caesar's great gratitude inspired them to superhuman exertions; but always complete success proved just out of reach. Ambiorix would fling out of his lairs and thickets, hide out at night, and make for other parts. His only escort were four horsemen, all that he dared trust with his life.

44. After ravaging the country in this way Caesar brought his army, with the loss of two cohorts, back to Reims, where he convoked a Gallic council and proceeded to investigate the conspiracy of the Senones and Carnutes. A heavier sentence was pronounced on the ringleader Acco, who was flogged to death in the ancient Roman way. Some who were afraid of being tried fled, and these Caesar interdicted from fire and water. Then he quartered two legions near the frontier of the Treveri for the winter, two among the Lingones, and the remaining six at Agedincum in the country of the Senones, and when he had arranged for the army's grain supply he set out for Italy to hold the assizes.

VII 52 B.C.

1. As Gaul was now quiet Caesar set out for Italy, as he had resolved to do, to hold the assizes. There he heard that Clodius had been murdered and was informed that the senate had decreed a mass levy of the youth of Italy. He proceeded to conscript troops throughout the Province. The news quickly reached Transalpine Gaul, where the natives embellished it with rumors to which the circumstances gave verisimilitude, to the effect that internal disturbances were detaining Caesar in the capital and making it impossible for him to join the army. These people were already chafing at subjection to Rome, and with this incentive they began, openly and boldly, to make plans for war. Their leading men met together in secluded woodland spots, where they deplored the execution of Acco and pointed out that they were all liable to the same fate. They lamented the common lot of Gaul, and offered rewards and ample promises to induce men to take the initiative and risk their lives to redeem Gallic freedom. They declared that their first effort must be to cut Caesar off from his army before their clandestine plans were divulged. This would be easy, for the legions would not venture out of their cantonments in the absence of the general, nor could the general reach his legions without an escort. Their last word was that it was better to die fighting than to forfeit their ancient military glory and the liberty their ancestors had bequeathed to them.

2. As a result of this agitation the Carnutes declared they would face any danger for the common welfare and promised to strike the first blow. Since the interchange of hostages at that juncture might advertise their enterprise, the Carnutes asked the pledge of a solemn oath. With standards trooped (this is a very solemn rite according to Gallic usage) all present swore that they would not forsake the Carnutes after they struck the first blow. The Carnutes were applauded, a day was fixed for the offensive, and the assembly dispersed.

3. When the day came the Carnutes, under a pair of desperadoes named Cotuatus and Conconnetodumnus, swooped down upon Cenabum at a given signal, massacred the Roman citizens settled there for business reasons, and plundered their goods. The victims included Gaius Fufius Cita, a reputable Roman knight to whom Caesar had assigned charge of the commissary. The news quickly spread to all the states of Gaul. Whenever anything notable happens the Gauls spread the news by shouting across the countryside and then others take the call up and pass it on to their neighbors. This is what they did then; the dawn raid at Cenabum was known in the country of the Arverni, a distance of some 160 miles, early that night.

4. The Arvernian Vercingetorix, son of Celtillus, a young man of high position whose father had held the highest power in Gaul and had been sentenced to death for aspiring to kingship, called his dependents together and fired their enthusiasm for liberation. When his design became known there was a rush to arms. His uncle Gobannitio and other chieftains were against tempting fortune and tried to stop him. He was expelled from the town of Gergovia, but persisted and conscripted needy and desperate men in the countryside. With this band

in hand he won every countryman he met to his views, urging them to take arms for their common liberty. When he had raised a large force he ejected his opponents who had driven him out of the state. His followers proclaimed him king, and he sent embassies to all quarters adjuring the tribes to keep faith. He soon won the support of the Senones, Parisii, Pictones, Cadurci, Turoni, Aulerci, Lemovices, Andi, and all other maritime tribes, and they unanimously conferred the supreme command upon him. Armed with this power he requisitioned hostages from these states and ordered fixed quotas of soldiers sent him at once. He directed each state to manufacture a specified quantity of arms by a specified date, and paid special attention to the cavalry. He coupled his great diligence with stern discipline and coerced waverers by severe punishment. Those guilty of major offenses he executed by fire and every species of torture; lesser culprits he sent home with ears cut off or one eye gouged out, to serve as a warning to deter others by the harshness of the penalty.

5. With such ruthlessness Vercingetorix speedily raised an army. Part of his forces he sent under an extremely daring Cadurcan named Lucterius into the country of the Ruteni, while he himself marched against the Bituriges. Upon his approach the latter sent representatives to their overlords the Aedui to request help in resisting the enemy invasion. Upon advice of the legates whom Caesar had left with the Roman army the Aedui dispatched a force of cavalry and infantry to support the Bituriges. At the river Loire, which is the boundary between the Aedui and the Bituriges, these reinforcements halted for a few days and then returned without venturing to cross the river. They explained their return to the Roman legates by declaring that they

feared treachery on the part of the Bituriges, who had planned, they discovered, to surround them on one side if they should cross the river, while the Arverni would surround them on the other. We cannot be sure whether the reason they alleged to the legates was their true motive or whether it was a ruse, and therefore make no positive assertion on the subject. As soon as they withdrew, the Bituriges did join the Arverni.

6. Caesar had learned that the situation in the capital had been improved by Pompey's vigorous measures, and when news of Vercingetorix' insurrection reached him in Italy he started for Transalpine Gaul. Arrived there, he was faced with the difficult problem of joining his army. If he summoned the legions to the Province he knew they might have to fight a battle on the march without him; whereas if he made his way to them he realized it would be unwise to trust himself even to the tribes which were apparently at peace.

7. Meanwhile Lucterius the Cadurcan, who had been sent to the Ruteni, had won that state over to the Arverni. Then he proceeded to the Nitiobriges and Gabali, and when he had received hostages from both and raised a large force, he moved to overrun the Province in the district of Narbonne. When news of this reached Caesar he thought all other plans should be shelved in favor of a march to Narbonne. There he reassured the faint-hearted and posted garrisons among the Ruteni in the Province, the Volcae Arecomici, the Tolosates, and the environs of Narbonne closest to the enemy. Part of the Provincial forces and the supplements he had brought from Italy he ordered to concentrate in the country of the Helvii where it adjoins that of the Arverni.

8. By these measures Lucterius was checked and

forced to retire, for he thought it hazardous to by-pass
our garrisons. Caesar set out for the Helvii. Winter was
at its height, and the deep snow covering the Cevennes,
which separates the Arverni from the Helvii, hindered
movement. But by dint of sweat the soldiers made their
way, by shoveling through snow six feet deep, and
reached the frontiers of the Arverni. These were taken
by surprise, for they thought the Cevennes protected
them like a wall, and at that time of year the tracks were
impassable even for individual travelers. Caesar ordered
his cavalry to range over the widest possible area and
bring the maximum of terror upon the enemy. Rumors
and messengers quickly carried the news to Vercingetorix. In consternation all the Arverni beseeched and implored him to look out for their welfare and not suffer
them to be ravaged by the enemy, for he could see that
they were now bearing the brunt of the war. Vercingetorix yielded to their prayers and removed his camp from
the Bituriges to the Arverni.

9. Caesar had calculated what Vercingetorix would
do, and after a two days' halt left the army in charge of
young Brutus and went off ostensibly to raise additional
infantry and cavalry. He directed Brutus to scour the
widest possible area with his cavalry and said he would
endeavor to return within three days. These arrangements made, Caesar headed for Vienne at his best speed,
to the surprise of his own men. At Vienne he picked up
fresh cavalry, which he had sent ahead many days before, and pushed on without halting night or day
through the country of the Arverni, to forestall any designs against his safety they might have, to the country
of the Lingones, where two legions were wintering.
Upon his arrival there he sent for the remaining legions
and concentrated them before word of his presence

could reach the Arverni. Vercingetorix, when he heard of
this move, led his army back to the Bituriges and
marched thence to begin operations against Gorgobina,
a stronghold of the Boii whom Caesar had settled there,
under the suzerainty of the Aedui, when the Boii had
been defeated in the battle with the Helvetii.

10. Vercingetorix' operation confronted Caesar with
an embarrassing decision. If he retained his legions in
one spot for the remainder of the winter, the reduction
of the Aeduan tributaries might cause the defection of
all Gaul, for it would become apparent that Caesar
could not be relied upon to protect his friends; if he left
his winter cantonments prematurely his commissary
would be subject to hazardous exposure. Nevertheless
the risk of any hardship appeared preferable to submitting to an affront which would alienate the good will of
all his partisans. He urged the Aedui to take care of the
food convoys and sent couriers to tell the Boii that he
was coming and to urge them to remain steadfast and
meet the enemy attack with stout hearts. Then he
marched towards the Boii, leaving two legions and the
whole army's baggage at Agedincum.

11. The next day Caesar arrived at Vellaunodunum,
a stronghold of the Senones. In order to leave no enemy
to endanger the food supply at his rear, he resolved to
attack the town, and within two days drew contravalla-
tions around it. On the third day representatives came
out of the town to capitulate, and Caesar ordered them
to stack arms, bring out their draft animals, and deliver
600 hostages. Not to delay his march, Caesar left Gaius
Trebonius to supervise the surrender and himself pushed
on to Cenabum, in the country of the Carnutes. The
Carnutes thought the siege of Vellaunodunum, of
which they had just heard, would be long protracted

and were assembling a garrison to be sent to Cenabum for its protection. Caesar reached the town within two days and pitched camp in front of it. The day being too far advanced, he postponed the assault to the next day and directed the soldiers to make the necessary preparations. He ordered two legions to bivouac under arms because there was a bridge from the town across the Loire and he was afraid the garrison might escape during the night. A little before midnight the townsfolk silently moved out and began to cross the river. This was reported by Caesar's patrols, and he sent the two legions on duty to burn the gates and take possession of the city. All but a handful of the enemy were captured, because the narrow bridge and roads prevented the crowd from escaping. Caesar sacked and burned the town and gave the booty to the soldiers; then he marched his army across the Loire and into the territory of the Bituriges.

12. Vercingetorix abandoned the siege of Gorgobina when he heard of Caesar's approach and marched to meet him. Caesar had commenced operations against Noviodunum, a stronghold of the Bituriges on his route. A deputation from the town had come to beg Caesar for pardon and mercy, and in order to bring his successful operation to speedy completion he ordered them to stack arms, bring out their horses, and deliver hostages. Part of these had already been handed over and the rest of the business was in progress, with centurions and a detachment of infantry sent into the town to collect weapons and livestock, when enemy cavalry, the advance guard of Vercingetorix' column, appeared in the distance. As soon as the townsfolk sighted them and saw there was hope of relief, they raised a shout and proceeded to take up arms, shut the gates and man the wall.

The behavior of the Gauls gave the centurions to understand that some new mischief was afoot, and so they seized the gates with drawn swords and got their men safely off.

13. Caesar ordered his cavalry from the camp and engaged the enemy, and when his men were in difficulties sent to their support some 400 German horse whom he had made a practice of keeping by him from the beginning. The Gauls could not withstand their dash but turned tail and rejoined their column after suffering many casualties. In consternation at this defeat the townspeople seized and brought to Caesar the persons they considered responsible for arousing the mob and surrendered. This business disposed of, Caesar marched to Bourges, the largest and strongest town of the Bituriges and situated in their most fertile district. He was confident that the recovery of Bourges would reduce the state of the Bituriges to his sway.

14. After the successive disasters at Vellaunodunum, Cenabum, and Noviodunum, Vercingetorix called a council of his followers at which he explained that their strategy must be radically changed. Their prime objective must be to interdict the Romans from forage and supplies, and this was easy because they were strong in cavalry and the season of the year was in their favor. Because there was no grass to cut, the enemy must necessarily scatter to find fodder in barns in small parties, which could be picked off by the cavalry day by day. Moreover private interests must be sacrificed to the common cause. To either side of the road as far as foragers could reach, steadings and barns must be burned down. They would themselves be adequately supplied, for they would draw on the resources of the peoples in the theater of operations. The Romans must either starve

or go far afield from their camp at great risk; and
it made no difference whether they killed them or took
their baggage, for without it they could not make war.
Furthermore, every town not rendered impregnable by
fortifications and terrain must be burned, to eliminate
a refuge for their own shirkers and ready stocks for the
Romans to pillage and carry off. If these measures
seemed hard and cruel they must remember how much
harder was the alternative—their wives and children
dragged off into slavery and themselves massacred, the
inevitable fate of the vanquished.

15. Vercingetorix' proposal was approved unanimously, and in a single day the Bituriges set more than
twenty of their cities on fire. The other states did likewise, and everywhere fires blazed out. Though the destruction was a painful blow they consoled themselves
with the thought that victory was virtually assured and
were confident that they would quickly recover their
losses. The question whether Bourges should be burned
or defended was debated in a general council. The Bituriges knelt at the feet of all the Gauls begging them
not to compel them to burn with their own hands well-
nigh the fairest city of all Gaul which was the bulwark
and glory of their state. Its terrain, they declared, made
it easy for them to defend, for it was almost wholly surrounded by river and marsh and its only approach was
very narrow. Their petition was granted; Vercingetorix
at first argued against it but subsequently yielded to
their prayers and to the general feeling on their behalf.
Suitable officers were assigned to defend the town.

16. Vercingetorix followed Caesar by easy stages and
chose for his camp a spot protected by marshes and
forests sixteen miles from Bourges. Regular patrols at intervals throughout the day kept him informed of what

went on in the town, and he issued orders accordingly. He was on the watch for our foraging and grain-gathering parties, and when they necessarily scattered far afield he attacked them and inflicted serious losses, though all possible countermeasures, such as leaving at irregular hours and by different routes, were taken.

17. Caesar's camp stood on the side of the town where a gap in the river and marsh left a narrow approach, as has been remarked, and since the terrain made circumvallation impractical he proceeded to prepare a ramp, form sheds, and erect two towers. He put continuous pressure upon the Boii and Aedui for grain, but the Aedui were unenthusiastic and gave little help, and the Boii were a small and weak state which quickly consumed the little it could produce. The poverty of the Boii, the indifference of the Aedui, and the firing of the farm buildings imposed such scarcity upon the army that for several days they were without grain and staved starvation off only by driving cattle in from remote villages. Yet not a word did they utter unworthy of the majesty of Rome and their past victories. More remarkable, when Caesar addressed the individual legions at their tasks and declared he would abandon the siege if they found their privation too hard, they all begged him not to do so. They had served under his command for many years, they said, without incurring disgrace or leaving any task unfinished, and they would consider it ignominious to abandon a siege they had begun. It was better, they added, to endure any hardship than to fall to avenge the Roman citizens whom the Gauls had treacherously massacred at Cenabum. Such declarations were also made to the centurions and tribunes, who were requested to transmit them to Caesar.

18. The towers were drawing near the wall when

Caesar ascertained from prisoners that Vercingetorix had exhausted his fodder and moved his camp nearer Bourges. He had himself taken the cavalry and the light-armed infantry which regularly fought with the cavalry to set an ambush where he expected our men to come foraging the next day. Upon this intelligence Caesar silently set out at midnight and reached the enemy camp at dawn. The enemy were promptly notified of Caesar's approach by their patrols, hid their carts and all their baggage in thick forest, and deployed their forces on an open elevation. When this was reported to Caesar he ordered his men to stack their packs promptly and ready their weapons.

19. The hill sloped gently upward and was almost completely surrounded by a difficult and viscous marsh not more than fifty feet wide. The Gauls had broken the causeways and kept to their hill with complete confidence in their position. They were formed up by tribes and held every ford and thicket that gave on the marsh, in their commanding position ready and determined to overwhelm the Romans, who would be stuck if they tried to crash through the marsh. Looking at their nearness, a man would think they were ready to fight on virtually equal terms, but if he perceived the disparity of the positions he would realize that their show was empty bravado. Our soldiers were indignant at the enemy daring to face them across so narrow a space and clamored for the battle signal, but Caesar explained what a dear price in lives of brave men the victory must cost. When he saw them eager to face any peril for his honor, he said, he would be guilty of the grossest unfairness if he did not value their lives above his honor. When he had thus pacified the soldiers he led them back

to camp the same day and proceeded to complete the
necessary preparations for the siege.

20. When Vercingetorix returned to his army he was
charged with treachery on the grounds that he had
moved the camp nearer the Romans, that he had gone
off with all the cavalry, that he had left so large a force
without a commander, and that the Romans had so
promptly taken advantage of his absence to make their
advance. These things, it was alleged, could not have
happened fortuitously or without design: Vercingetorix
clearly preferred to rule Gaul by the gift of Caesar
rather than by the favor of his own people. In reply to
these charges Vercingetorix said that he had moved
camp at their own solicitation because of scarcity of
forage; that the decisive factor for shifting the camp
nearer the Romans was the advantage of an easily defensible position; that cavalry could not be used on the
marshy terrain but were useful in the sector to which he
had gone. He had purposely designated no supreme
commander on his departure so that there should be no
one whom mass pressure could force to give battle—
that, he could see, was what they all wanted, because
they were soft spirited and could not endure prolonged
hardship. If it was by chance the Romans had come
they ought to thank Fortune, if by invitation of some
traitor they ought to thank the traitor, for enabling them
to realize, from their commanding position, how few
the Romans were and to despise the abject spirit of men
who dared not fight but ignominiously slunk back to
camp. As for kingship, he had no desire to obtain from
Caesar by treachery what he could hold by victory—a
victory of which he and all the Gauls could be sure.
Nay, they could have the title back if they thought the

honor they conferred upon him was greater than the
security he gave them. "To make sure," he cried, "that
what I say is so, hear these Roman soldiers speak!" He
produced some slaves whom he had caught foraging a
few days before and had tortured and starved. They
had been thoroughly coached on the testimony they
were to give, and said, when they were questioned,
that they were legionary soldiers, that hunger and want
had moved them to steal out of camp and look for grain
or cattle in the field; that the whole army was equally
hungry and too weak to stand up to their work; and
that the general had therefore decided to withdraw if
they made no progress in their siege operations in three
days. "This is what I have done for you," Vercingetorix
exclaimed, "and you accuse me of treason! Thanks to me
and at no cost of your blood you see this great and
victorious army starved out, and I have taken care that
no state will harbor it within its borders in its ignominious retreat."

21. The whole crowd cheered and clashed their weapons—the regular Gallic method of indicating approval
of a speech. They shouted that Vercingetorix was a peer-
less leader, that his loyalty was beyond question, that
the war could not be more shrewdly managed. They decided to throw into the town 10,000 men chosen from
their whole force, for they did not think it prudent to
trust the whole issue to the Bituriges alone, realizing
that ultimate success virtually depended on their holding the town.

22. The extraordinary courage of our soldiers the
Gauls countered with many kinds of contrivances, for
they are an ingenious people, quick to imitate and ap-
ply ideas suggested to them. They diverted our grappling hooks, for example, with nooses, and then pulled

them taut and hauled the hooks inside their walls with windlasses. They undermined our ramps, and very expertly, because they have large iron mines and are familiar with every kind of mining operation. They built platformed towers on every part of their wall and covered them with hides. They made frequent sorties day and night, to set fire to our ramp or attack our soldiers at their work. As the daily building up of our ramp gave our towers greater height, they matched it by adding tiers to their own towers. They opened our mines and hampered their progress with pointed beams hardened by fire and boiling pitch and massive boulders, and so prevented them from reaching their walls.

23. The general design of Gallic walls is as follows. Beams are laid on the ground at two-foot intervals along the entire length of the wall and at right angles to it. These are anchored on the inside and thickly coated with rubble, and the two-foot gaps in the outer face are closed with large stones. When this layer is packed down in position another is added on top, with the beams at the same interval as the first but not touching them. The gaps are again faced with single stones and the fabric thus made tight. Then the same procedure is followed, until the wall reaches its proper height. The alternation of timber and stone kept in straight lines makes a handsome variegated appearance but is also most useful for purposes of defense; the stone resists fire and the timber battering rams, for beams which run to forty feet and are anchored down inside can neither be breached nor pulled apart.

24. These many defensive measures impeded our operations, and frost and continuous rain hampered our men; nevertheless their unremitting labor overcame all

obstacles and within twenty-five days they built a ramp
330 feet broad and 80 feet high. The ramp was almost
in contact with the enemy wall and Caesar was as usual
bivouacking near the scene and urging the soldiers not
to leave working for a moment when, a little before midnight, it was noticed that the ramp was smoking; the
enemy had undermined it and set it on fire. At the same
time a shout was raised all along the wall and a sortie
was made from two gates, at either side of our towers.
Men far up on the wall threw torches and tinder down
on the ramp and poured down pitch and other inflam-
mables; it was hard to figure where to turn first or where
to rally reinforcements. Still, because two legions always
bivouacked under arms by Caesar's order and there were
many men on the work shift, it was quickly arranged
that some should go to oppose the sortie, others should
draw the towers back and make a gap in the ramp, and
all the personnel from the camp should hurry to put the
fire out.

25. The rest of the night was spent with fighting continuing at all points. The enemy was constantly spurred
on by fresh hope of victory. They saw that the screens of
the towers were burned out and noticed that it was not
easy for our men to bring help without cover; relays
of fresh troops took the place of the weary, and they
were convinced that the whole salvation of Gaul depended on that instant of time. Before our eyes there occurred a memorable incident which I feel must not be
passed over. Before the town gate a certain Gaul was
pitching lumps of grease and tow, which were passed
up to him, into the fire near one of our towers. He was
shot in the right side by a quickfiring catapult and fell,
whereupon the man next to him stepped over his body

and carried on with his job. When the second man was similarly shot down a third took his place, and a fourth succeeded the third; that post was not abandoned by the defenders before the ramp fire was put out, the enemy repulsed at every point, and the fighting ended.

26. Since none of their numerous expedients had succeeded the Gauls resolved next day to evacuate the city, as Vercingetorix urged and directed them to do. They hoped that an attempt during the silent hours of night might succeed at no great cost, for Vercingetorix' camp was not far away and the unbroken interval of marshland would retard Roman pursuit. At night, as they were preparing to leave, the housewives ran out into the open and flung themselves at the feet of their menfolk with tearful prayers not to surrender them and their shared children to the tender mercies of the enemy when their sex and tender years prevented them from fleeing. In a crisis fear has no room for pity, and when the women saw that their pleas were ignored they began to scream and show the Romans there would be an exodus. This made the Gauls afraid that the Roman cavalry would seize and block the roads, and in their fright they abandoned their intended flight.

27. Next day Caesar's structures were completed as planned and a tower moved forward. A heavy shower came on, which Caesar regarded an opportune occasion for implementing his plan. The guards on the wall were posted rather carelessly, and Caesar ordered his men to go about their work listlessly, explaining what he wanted done. The legions stripped for action under cover of the sheds, where Caesar exhorted them to pluck at long last the victory which was the fruit of their arduous labors. He announced prizes for those who would

be first to scale the wall, and then gave the signal for
action. Promptly the soldiers dashed out from every
quarter and quickly filled the wall.

28. Panic-stricken by this unexpected development
the enemy were thrown down from wall and towers.
They formed in wedges in the market place and other
open ground, resolved to fight it out in formation if they
were attacked. When they saw that no one came down
to their level but that the whole wall swarmed with
men they grew afraid that every chance of escape would
be cut off, threw their weapons down, and made for the
farthest section of the town in a headlong rush. There,
as they jammed the narrow exits, some were cut down
by our infantry, and some that had got out of the gates
by our cavalry. No one paid any attention to booty; they
were so infuriated by the massacre at Cenabum and by
the toil of the siege that they spared neither the aged
nor women nor children. Actually out of the total number of some 40,000 scarcely 800, who had flung out of
town at the first sound of shouting, got safely to Vercingetorix. He intercepted them late at night and in silence, for fear that the pity they would arouse among
the rank and file if they entered camp in a body might
turn to mutiny. He therefore posted his friends and tribal
chieftains some distance down the road, with instructions
to separate the fugitives and take them to their countrymen in the sections of the camp which had originally
been assigned to each tribe.

29. Next day Vercingetorix convoked a meeting at
which he comforted his men and urged them not to be
disheartened or disturbed by the reverse. It was not by
courage or in open battle that the Romans had won but
by a trick and by expertness in siege operations in which
the Gauls had no experience. To expect unvarying suc-

cess in war, he said, was a mistake. He had himself never approved of defending Bourges, as they could testify; it was due to the short-sightedness of the Bituriges and the excessive complaisance of the rest that this reverse had been sustained. But he would speedily repair it with greater successes. The Gallic states that had held aloof he would manage to win over and so establish a single policy for all Gaul, and a united Gaul would be irresistible to the whole world. This objective, he declared, was already within his grasp. Meanwhile he could fairly ask them, for the sake of the common good, to set about fortifying their camp, the better to repel sudden attack.

30. This speech pleased the Gauls, and particularly so because Vercingetorix himself was not downcast by the disaster and did not hide himself or avoid the sight of the crowd. He was credited with foresight and imagination because before there was any pressure he voted first for burning Bourges and then for evacuating it. And so whereas failure impairs the authority of commanders, Vercingetorix' prestige, on the contrary, was daily enhanced by the defeat. At the same time his assurances about winning other states over raised their hopes. For the first time the Gauls set to work to fortify a camp; their spirit was so stiffened that unaccustomed to labor as they were, they felt they must submit to all that was asked of them.

31. Living up to his promise, Vercingetorix worked hard to win the other states over and offered inducements of presents and promises. For his agents he chose plausible men gifted with subtle speech or easy camaraderie. He saw to it that the refugees from fallen Bourges should be armed and clothed. At the same time, to recruit his diminished strength he requisitioned fixed contingents from the states, specifying the dates on

which they were to be presented in camp. He ordered that all archers (Gaul has a very large number) be sought out and sent to him. In this way the losses at Bourges were speedily made good. Meanwhile King Teutomatus of the Nitiobriges, whose father Ollovico had received the title of Friend from our senate, brought Vercingetorix a large quantity of cavalry, some his own and some he had hired in Aquitania.

32. Caesar halted at Bourges for several days, and the huge stocks of grain and other provisions he found there restored the army after its toil and privation. Winter was almost over, and the new season invited operations. Caesar had resolved to march against the enemy with the hope either of enticing him out of his marshes and forests or of blockading him into submission, when Aeduan notables came to beg his assistance in a serious crisis affecting their state. Their time-honored usage had been to create a single magistrate to exercise royal sway for a year; now their system was imperiled because two magistrates were holding office simultaneously, each claiming that he had been constitutionally elected. One was Convictolitavis, a popular and successful young man, and the other Cotus, a man of distinguished lineage and himself powerful and well-connected, whose brother Valetiacus had held the same office the year before. The whole state was in arms; senate and people were both divided and each of the rivals had his own following. If the dispute were nursed along civil war was inevitable, and only Caesar's energy and influence could prevent such an outcome.

33. To abandon the war and the enemy Caesar thought wasteful, but he was aware that rivalries of this sort give rise to disastrous disturbances and thought it his duty to block such an eventuality. The Aeduan state

was closely bound to Rome, and he had himself fostered it and shown it every mark of distinction; if it should come to violence the less confident party would appeal to Vercingetorix for help. Aeduan law forbade the holder of the supreme magistracy to leave the country, and in order to avoid the appearance of slighting their ordinances Caesar decided to go to their country himself, and summoned their whole senate and the parties to the quarrel to Décize. Almost the whole state assembled, and it was explained to Caesar that Cotus' election had been proclaimed by his brother in a rump assembly held at an unauthorized time and place, whereas the law provided that two members of the same household could not hold the office or even sit in the senate while both were alive. Caesar accordingly compelled Cotus to resign and directed that Convictolitavis, who had been regularly elected by the priests when the office was vacant, should hold the chief magistracy.

34. When he had so decided the issue Caesar urged the Aedui to forget their bickering, put all their differences behind them, and concentrate on the war, in anticipation of the rewards which would be their due when Gaul was conquered. He asked them to send him promptly all their cavalry and 10,000 infantry, for assignment to garrison posts to protect grain convoys. He then divided the army into two parts, giving Labienus four legions to lead against the Senones and Parisii, and leading six himself along the Allier towards Gergovia in the country of the Arverni. Part of the cavalry he assigned to Labienus and part he retained for himself. When Vercingetorix heard of this he destroyed all bridges over the Allier and began to march along the other bank.

35. The two armies marched in sight of one another

and encamped virtually opposite each other, with patrols posted to prevent the Romans from building a
bridge and taking their army across. This was very trou-
blesome to Caesar. Usually the Allier cannot be forded
before autumn, and the river might balk him most of
the summer. To prevent such a delay Caesar pitched
camp in a wooded spot near one of the bridges Vercingetorix had ordered destroyed, and the next day remained hidden there with two legions while the rest of
his forces with all the baggage was sent forward as
usual; to conceal the difference in the number of units he
divided certain of the cohorts. Their orders were to advance as far as they could; when he surmised, from the
time of day, that they had made camp he began to rebuild the bridge on its original piles, the lower portion
of which had remained intact. The work was done with
dispatch and the legions carried across, and when a suitable place had been chosen for a camp Caesar recalled
the rest of his force. When Vercingetorix heard of this
he moved forward by forced marches, to avoid having
to fight against his will.

36. From that point Caesar reached Gergovia in five
days, and after a cavalry skirmish reconnoitered the city.
Its situation on a very high hill difficult of access on
every side made assault hopeless, and Caesar decided
not to begin siege operations before securing his commissariat. Vercingetorix encamped near the town and
grouped the tribal contingents around him at some distance from one another. Every eminence in the commanding range was occupied, and the sight was formidable. The tribal chieftains whom he had chosen to form
his council he ordered to meet with him daily at dawn,
to share intelligence and formulate plans. Scarcely a
day passed without an engagement of cavalry, inter-

spersed with archers, to prove the mettle and capacities
of individual fighters. Opposite the town, at the very
foot of the mountain, there was a hill, sheer on every
side and exceedingly strong. If our men could hold this
hill they could probably cut the enemy off from his
main water supply and restrict his foraging. An enemy
detachment, though not a very strong one, held this
hill, but Caesar moved out of his camp in the silence of
night, dislodged the detachment before reinforcements
from the town could arrive, took possession of the hill,
and posted two legions upon it. He connected the larger
camp with the smaller by a pair of trenches twelve feet
wide, so that soldiers could pass, even one at a time,
without fear of sudden attack.

37. While these operations were in progress at Gergovia the Aeduan Convictolitavis—the man to whom
Caesar adjudged the magistracy, as set forth above—
was bribed by the Arverni. He opened negotiations
with a group of young men headed by Litaviccus and
his brothers, who belonged to a distinguished family. He
shared his bribe with them and bade them remember
that they were free men and born to rule. The only ob-
stacle to inevitable Gallic victory, he said, was the
Aeduan state, whose example restrained the others also;
if it were brought over the Romans would have no foothold in Gaul. He did indeed have some obligation to
Caesar, but only for a decision which he fully deserved;
their common liberty was a greater obligation. There
was no more reason for the Aedui to appeal to Caesar
to arbitrate their internal laws and usages than it would
be for Romans to appeal to the Aedui. The young men
were quickly persuaded by their chief's eloquence and
his bribes, and promised to take the lead in the program. They then canvassed means for carrying it out,

for they were not sure that the state could easily be persuaded to embark on war. The decision was that Litaviccus should take command of the 10,000 who were to be sent to Caesar for the war and be responsible for their conduct, while his brothers went on ahead to Caesar. They also decided on other procedures.

38. When Litaviccus had brought the army within thirty miles of Gergovia he suddenly paraded his troops and tearfully addressed them: "Where are we going, soldiers? All our cavalry, all our nobility, have perished. Two of our leading personages, Eporedorix and Viridomarus, have been charged with treachery by the Romans and executed without trial. This you will learn from men who escaped the massacre; grief at the slaughter of my brothers and all my kin makes it hard for me to tell the tale." Men whom Litaviccus had coached were brought forward and echoed what he had said. They explained that many of the Aeduan cavalry had been done to death on the allegation that they had been in communication with the Arverni: the informants had hidden in the crowd of soldiers and had escaped as the slaughter was going on. The Aedui shouted and begged Litaviccus to take thought for them. "As if this were a time for taking thought," he answered, "as if we were not bound to go to Gergovia and join up with the Arverni! Can we doubt that after their unspeakable outrage the Romans are already hurrying to kill us? Come, if there is any manhood in us, let us kill these brigands!" He pointed to some Roman citizens who were there because they trusted his protection; the large stock of grain and supplies they carried he plundered, and the men he killed with cruel torture. Then he sent messengers throughout the Aeduan country and aroused passions by the same lie about the massacre of the cavalry

and the chieftains; he urged them to follow his example in avenging their wrongs.

39. Eporedorix was a young Aeduan aristocrat with great influence in his country, and his contemporary Viridomarus was equally popular but of lower birth; Diviciacus had introduced him to Caesar, who raised him from a humble status to high position. The young men had come with the cavalry at Caesar's personal summons. There was rivalry between them for preëminence, and in the late altercation concerning the magistracy one had fought for Convictolitavis with all his might and the other for Cotus. When Eporedorix learned of Litaviccus' plot he reported it to Caesar one midnight and begged him not to allow his state to fall away from friendship with Rome by the mischievous scheming of adolescents, as must happen, he pointed out, if so many thousands joined Caesar's enemies, for their relations could not disregard their safety nor the state remain indifferent to it.

40. Caesar was greatly disturbed by this intelligence for he had always been specially considerate of the Aeduan state. With no hesitation then, he marched out of camp with four legions in light order and all the cavalry. At such a crisis there was no time to retrench the camp, for speed was of the essence, and he left the legate Gaius Fabius in charge with two legions. He ordered Litaviccus' brothers arrested, but found they had decamped to the enemy a little before. He urged the soldiers not to mind a hard march, necessary under the circumstances, and their great willingness enabled him to advance twenty-five miles, where he sighted the Aeduan column. He sent the cavalry to delay and then halt their march, but gave strict orders not to kill anyone. Eporedorix and Viridomarus, whom their people sup-

posed dead, he ordered to mingle with the cavalry and
call to their countrymen. When they were recognized
Litaviccus' cheat was detected, and the Aedui stretched
their hands out in token of surrender, threw their arms
away, and began to beg for their lives. Litaviccus and
his retainers escaped to Gergovia; by Gallic custom it
is wicked to desert a liege lord even when his case is desperate.

41. Caesar sent couriers to the Aeduan state to report
that he had of his grace spared men whom he might have
killed by the rules of war. Then, when he had given the
army the three hours of night to rest, he moved towards
Gergovia. About halfway, horsemen sent by Fabius reported a dangerous situation in the camp. The camp had
been assaulted in full force, they said, with fresh attackers relieving the wearied in frequent relays and wearing
our men down by allowing them no respite, for because
of the extent of our camp the same personnel had to man
the rampart continuously. Many had been wounded by
showers of arrows and other missiles of all kinds. Our
artillery had proved very useful in defense. Upon the
enemy retiring Fabius was blocking up all but two of
the gates, fitting screens to the rampart, and preparing
for a repetition of the attack on the next day. Upon this
intelligence Caesar reached camp before dawn, thanks
to the willing energy of his soldiers.

42. The Aedui received Litaviccus' first dispatches
while this action at Gergovia was in progress, and took
no time to verify them. Actuated partly by avarice and
partly by the reckless passion native to the breed, they
regarded a slight rumor as established fact. They looted
the property of Roman citizens, perpetrated murders,
dragged victims off to slavery. Convictolitavis added his
push to the teetering situation and goaded the populace

to frenzy: if they behaved outrageously enough they
would be ashamed to return to sanity. They induced
Marcus Aristius, a military tribune traveling to join his
legion, to leave the town of Cabillonum by giving him a
safe conduct, and compelled the Romans who had settled in the town for business to leave also. The moment
they started the natives attacked them and stripped them
of their baggage. When they resisted the natives kept
their attack up for a day and a night, and when many
had been killed on both sides the natives raised a bigger
mob of armed men.

43. But when word came that all their soldiers were
in Caesar's power they hurried out to assure Aristius
that the government was not responsible for the incident.
They ordered an inquiry on the property that had been
looted, confiscated the goods of Litaviccus and his brothers, and sent representatives to make excuses to Caesar.
Their motive was to obtain the release of their men; but
they were now tainted with crime, captivated by the easy
profit of plunder (many had shared in the looting), and
apprehensive of retribution, and began clandestine preparations for war and sent deputations to other tribes to
promote their intrigue. All of this Caesar understood, but
he spoke to their representatives in the mildest terms
possible, assuring them that he would not judge their
state harshly because of the silly light-headedness of the
mob nor diminish his good will towards the Aedui. But
he did in fact anticipate a general uprising in Gaul, and
to avoid encirclement by all their tribes began canvass-
ing methods of withdrawing from Gergovia and concentrating his army once more. His concern was that his
withdrawal should not look like flight brought on by
fear of insurrection.

44. As he was studying the problem an opportunity

for a successful stroke seemed to offer. On a tour of in-
spection in the lesser camp he noticed that a hill in the
possession of the enemy was bare of defenders, though on
previous days it had been so crowded as to be invisible.
In astonishment Caesar asked the deserters (large numbers had been streaming in daily) why this was, and all
agreed that the crest of the ridge was almost level, but
wooded and narrow where it gave on to the other part
of the town; this Caesar himself had also ascertained
through his scouts. The enemy was extremely anxious
about this approach, for they were convinced that if they
lost it to the Romans, who already held the other hill,
they would be blocked in and cut off from egress and
from foraging. To fortify this position Vercingetorix had
called all hands out.

45. Upon this intelligence Caesar dispatched several
squadrons of horse at midnight with instructions to ride
over the whole area making more noise than usual. At
dawn he ordered a large number of pack-horses and
mules brought out of camp; the pack-saddles were to be
taken off and the muleteers, wearing helmets to make
them look like cavalrymen, were to mount and ride them
over the hills. Some regular cavalry accompanied them
to heighten the effect by moving over a broader area.
All were to make for the same objective by a wide circuit. These movements could be seen from the town, for
Gergovia commanded a view of the camp; but the distance made it impossible to be sure of their meaning.
Caesar sent one legion towards the same hill, but halted
it on low ground after it had advanced a little and concealed it in a covert of woods. Gallic apprehensions were
heightened, and their whole force was brought over to
strengthen the position. When Caesar saw that the enemy camp was deserted he moved his soldiers over from

the larger to the lesser camp, in small groups and with insignia covered and standards concealed so as not to attract attention from the town. He showed the commanders of the individual legions what he wanted done and impressed it upon them that the men must be kept back and not allowed to advance too far in the heat of the fight or expectation of booty. He pointed out that the uneven ground placed them at a disadvantage which speed alone could compensate; surprise, not fighting, was the essence. After the instructions he gave the signal, and at the same time sent the Aedui up by another ascent on the right.

46. From where the plain began to rise to the town wall was 1,200 paces in a straight line without zig-zags, but the distance to be covered was greatly increased by the bends put in to ease the grade. About halfway up the hill, and following its contours, the Gauls had drawn a horizontal six-foot wall of large stones, to retard an attack on our part. The area below the wall was left empty, but the upper part, up to the town wall, was crowded with camps. At the signal our soldiers quickly reached the barrier, crossed it, and seized three camps. This was done so speedily that King Teutomatus of the Nitiobriges was caught taking a nap in his tent and barely got away from the plundering soldiers stripped to the waist and on a wounded horse.

47. Having attained his objective Caesar ordered the retreat sounded and immediately halted the Tenth Legion, which he commanded. Because of the considerable valley intervening the trumpet call did not reach the other legions; nevertheless the tribunes and legates tried to hold the men back, as Caesar had ordered. But the men were so excited by the expectation of a speedy victory, by the flight of the enemy, and by the memory of

their earlier victories that they thought nothing was too
difficult for their valor to accomplish and did not give
over their pursuit until they neared the wall and gates
of the stronghold. The shouting which then arose in all
quarters of the city frightened those farther away into
thinking that the enemy was inside the gates and they
rushed headlong out of the city. Housewives were throwing clothing and money down from the wall and with
bared bosoms and outstretched arms imploring the Romans not to deny quarter to women and children as
they had done at Bourges. Some were handed down
from the wall and gave themselves up to the soldiers.
Lucius Fabius, a centurion of the Eighth Legion, had remarked to his men earlier in the day, as was later veri-
fied, that with the prizes won at Bourges as an incentive
he would let no man mount the wall ahead of him; he
found three men of his squad to boost him up the wall,
and then hauled them up after him one by one.

48. In the meanwhile the Gauls who had assembled
at the other end of the town to fortify it, as we have
shown above, heard the shouting and then were goaded,
by a rapid succession of dispatches declaring that the
Romans were in possession of the stronghold, into sending their cavalry ahead and streaming to the scene of
action in a great throng. Each took his stand under the
wall as soon as he arrived and added to the fighting
strength. When a great force had gathered, the housewives who had been stretching their hands out to the
Romans a moment before began to adjure their own
menfolk from the wall, showing their disheveled hair in
the Gallic fashion and bringing their children out for the
men to see. The Romans were at a disadvantage in numbers and position; moreover they were winded with the

uphill dash and prolonged action and found it hard to withstand fresh and vigorous fighters.

49. When Caesar observed that his men were fighting in a difficult position against increasing enemy forces he grew anxious for their safety and sent word to the legate Titus Sextius, whom he had left in charge of the lesser camp, to lead his cohorts out of camp at once and post them at the foot of the hill at the enemy's sight; his assignment was to deter the enemy from free pursuit if he saw our men driven down from their position. Caesar himself advanced a short distance from his position and then halted his legion to await the issue.

50. Bitter hand-to-hand fighting had continued for some time, with the enemy trusting to position and numbers and our men to courage, when the Aedui were suddenly sighted on our open flank. This was the body Caesar had sent up by a different ascent on the right to create a diversion. The likeness of their armor to the Gauls' terrified our men, who, though they saw that the men's right shoulders were bared (this was the usual and accepted symbol) thought it was an enemy ruse designed to deceive them. At this same moment the centurion Lucius Fabius and his companions who had mounted the wall were surrounded, killed, and flung down. Marcus Petronius, a centurion of the same legion, was overwhelmed by numbers as he was trying to cut down the gate. "I can't save myself and you too," he said, "but at least I can look out for you: it was my appetite for glory that got you in this predicament. When I give you the chance look out for yourselves." He charged into the midst of the enemy, killed two, and pushed the others a little way from the gate. His men tried to save him but he said: "It's no use, my blood and my strength

are failing. Get out while you can and go back to the legion." He fought on and fell, but he had saved his men.

51. Pressure from every direction dislodged our men, with the loss of forty-six centurions. The relentless pursuit of the Gauls was checked by the Tenth Legion, which had taken a supporting position on somewhat smoother ground. The Tenth was in turn covered by cohorts of the Thirteenth, which had left the lesser camp under the legate Titus Sextius and occupied higher ground. As soon as the legions touched level ground they halted and turned their standards to face the enemy. At the base of the hill Vercingetorix withdrew his men into his entrenchments. We had lost nearly 700 men that day.

52. The next day Caesar paraded his troops and reprimanded them for their headstrong heedlessness in deciding for themselves how far to advance and what to do, for not halting when the retreat was sounded, and for ignoring their officers' efforts to restrain them. He explained the potentialities of an unfavorable pitch and mentioned his own attitude at Bourges, where he had caught the enemy without its general or its cavalry but had nevertheless forgone an assured victory to avoid even a small loss the unfavorable ground might cause. Greatly as he admired heroism undaunted by fortifications, a high mountain, a city wall, equally great was his condemnation of presumption and insubordination which made them fancy that they had a truer premonition of victory and the final outcome than had the general. In a soldier obedience and self-control are as essential as courage and heroism.

53. Caesar closed this harangue by encouraging his men not to be downhearted and not to attribute to enemy prowess a reverse due to unfavorable terrain. Caesar's decision to abandon Gergovia was unaltered, but

he led his soldiers out of camp and deployed them in battle formation in a suitable spot. Vercingetorix was still
unwilling to come down to a fair field, and after a light
but successful cavalry engagement Caesar brought his
army back to camp. On the day following the same thing
happened, whereupon Caesar judged that he had done
enough to deflate Gallic vainglory and restore his soldiers' confidence and moved camp to the Aeduan country. Not even then did the enemy pursue. On the third
day Caesar reached the Allier, where he repaired the
bridge and led his army across.

54. There he was accosted by Viridomarus and Eporedorix, who informed him that Litaviccus had gone
with all the cavalry to agitate among the Aedui, and that
it was essential for them to anticipate him and secure
Aeduan allegiance. Caesar was by now convinced of
Aeduan treachery on many grounds and thought the
departure of Viridomarus and Eporedorix would only
hasten the tribe's revolt; nevertheless he decided not to
detain them, to avoid the imputation of injustice or of
fear. At their departure Caesar briefly rehearsed his services to the Aedui. When he had received them under his
protection they were humble indeed—driven into their
towns, stripped of all their fields, robbed of all their resources, subjected to tribute, abjectly forced to deliver
hostages. He had brought them to prosperity and power,
so that they were not only restored to their former state
but plainly surpassed all the prestige and influence they
had ever enjoyed. After imparting this lesson he dismissed them.

55. The Aeduan town of Noviodunum is situated at
a convenient point on the banks of the Loire. Here
Caesar had deposited all the Gallic hostages, the grain,
the public funds, and a large part of his own and the

army's baggage, and here was the depot for the numerous mounts he had purchased for this campaign in Italy
and Spain. On reaching this town Eporedorix and Viridomarus learned what had transpired in their state. The
Aedui had received Litaviccus at Bibracte, their most
influential city, where he had been joined by their supreme magistrate Convictolitavis and a great part of the
senate; and ambassadors had been sent to Vercingetorix
to negotiate peace and alliance. Eporedorix and Viridomarus thought the opportunity too good to miss. They
killed the guards and the businessmen at Noviodunum
and divided the money and horses. The hostages of the
various states they transferred to the officials at Bibracte.
The town, which they did not believe they could hold,
they burned down, to prevent the Romans' using it.
What grain they could load on boats they carried away;
the rest they spoiled with water and fire. They began
themselves to raise forces in the neighboring districts, to
post garrisons and detachments along the banks of the
Loire, and to display their cavalry everywhere in order
to terrify the Romans and if possible cut them off from
provisions or compel them to retire to the Province under stress of famine. This expectation was strengthened
by the circumstance that melting snows had so swollen
the Loire that it seemed quite unfordable.

56. On learning this Caesar decided that speed was essential; if building bridges was going to be hazardous,
it was better to fight before larger enemy forces were
concentrated. The alternative of reversing his plan and
making for the Province he regarded as wholly unac-
ceptable, however justified by reasonable apprehensions.
Not only would such a course involve disgrace and humiliation, not only would the barrier of the Cevennes
and the state of the roads make it difficult, but Caesar

was extremely anxious for Labienus and the legions he had sent with him in a separate body. And so by long marches day and night he reached the Loire before anyone could expect him. The cavalry found a ford serviceable for the emergency: their arms and shoulders cleared the water enough for them to carry their weapons. A line of horse broke the force of the current, and the enemy were panicked by their unexpected approach. This enabled Caesar to bring his army across; he replenished his army with the grain and plentiful livestock he found in the fields, and proceeded on his march to the Senones.

57. While Caesar was thus occupied Labienus left the recruits newly arrived from Italy at Agedincum to guard the baggage, and himself set out for Paris with four legions. The town is situated on an island in the Seine. When the enemy learned of his approach large forces from the neighboring tribes assembled. Supreme command was given to Camulogenus the Aulercan, who was called to that distinction, though he was superannuated, because of his high military competence. When he observed that an unbroken marsh flowed into the Seine and made movement difficult in the whole region, he took his position at the marsh and resolved to prevent our men from crossing it.

58. Labienus at first tried to bring up sheds, fill the marsh with hurdles and earth, and so build a road across it; but when he realized the project was too difficult he silently left camp, after midnight, and retraced his march to Metiosedum, a Senonian town situated, as we have earlier remarked Paris was, on an island in the Seine. He seized some fifty boats, and quickly lashed them together and threw his soldiers across. The townfolk (and many had been called away in service) were stunned by the surprise, and Labienus took possession

of the town without effort. He rebuilt the bridge which the enemy had cut down during the days preceding, took his army across, and began to march downstream to Paris. This move was reported to the enemy by fugitives from Metiosedum, whereupon they ordered Paris burned and its bridges destroyed; then they moved from the marsh to the banks of the Seine and halted at the level of Paris opposite Labienus' camp.

59. By now Caesar's withdrawal from Gergovia was being advertised and there were rumors of the Aeduan rebellion and a successful uprising in Gaul. In conversation the Gauls asserted that Caesar was blocked off from his route and the Loire and was hurrying back to the Province under stress of famine. The Bellovaci, who had been disloyal even before the Aeduan revolt was known, now began to muster armed bands and openly prepare for war. With the situation so far altered, Labienus realized his plans must be completely revised. Now he was concerned not with seeking an advantage over the enemy and forcing him to engage but rather to bring his army safe back to Agedincum. On one side of him the Bellovaci, who had the highest reputation for prowess in Gaul, were exerting pressure, and the other was held by Camulogenus with a well-equipped army ready to fight; and a very large river cut his legions off from the baggage and its garrison. Suddenly confronted with such enormous hazards Labienus saw that the solution must lie in his own efficiency.

60. Towards evening he convoked a council and urged his officers to execute orders promptly and energetically. To each of the vessels which he had brought down from Metiosedum he assigned a knight, with orders to move downstream silently at the end of the first watch and wait for him there. Five cohorts which he

considered least reliable in action he left to garrison the
camp, and the other five cohorts of the same legion he
ordered to march upstream, with all the baggage, and
to make a great clatter. He also procured some small
boats which he ordered to row upstream also with great
splashing of oars. After a short interval he himself silently marched out with three legions to the rendezvous
with the vessels.

61. Upon his arrival the enemy patrols posted all
along the river were surprised and overpowered by our
men in a fierce storm which suddenly arose, and under
the guidance of the knights assigned to the task the army
with its cavalry were quickly ferried over. Almost simultaneously, just before dawn, the enemy received word
that there was extraordinary commotion in the Roman
camp, that a large column was advancing upstream,
that the splash of oars was heard parallel to the column,
and that troops were being ferried across the river a little downstream. From this intelligence they imagined
that the legions were crossing at three points and that
the revolt of the Aedui had frightened them into general
retreat; accordingly they divided their own forces into
three parts also. A garrison was left opposite the camp,
a detachment was sent to Metiosedum to advance to a
level with the flotilla, and the rest of their forces
marched against Labienus.

62. By daybreak all our men had been ferried over
and the enemy line was in sight. Labienus urged the men
to bear their proven gallantry and past brilliant successes
in mind and to imagine that Caesar himself who had so
often led them to victory was present in person. He then
gave the signal for battle. At the first shock the right
wing, where the Seventh Legion was posted, threw the
enemy back and put them to flight. On the left the

Twelfth Legion spitted the forward ranks of the enemy
with spears, but the rest resisted stoutly and not one
showed any inclination to flight. The enemy general
Camulogenus fought alongside his men and cheered
them on. The issue was still in doubt when the tribunes
of the Seventh were apprised of the situation on the left
wing, whereupon they appeared at the enemy's rear and
charged. Not even then did a man of the enemy
give ground; all were surrounded and killed, and Camulogenus shared their fate.

The detachment left opposite Labienus' camp moved
to support their comrades when they heard that battle
had been joined and occupied a hill, but they could not
withstand the rush of our victorious soldiers. They were
caught up in the rout, and those not protected by the
woods or mountains were killed by the cavalry. This
business dispatched, Labienus returned to Agedincum,
where the baggage of the whole army had been left, and
from there marched in full force to join Caesar.

63. When the defection of the Aedui was advertised
the war took on larger proportions. Embassies were dispatched in all directions and brought every resource of
influence, prestige, and money to bear to win the tribes
over. They got hold of the hostages whom Caesar had
lodged with them and intimidated waverers by execut-
ing them. The Aedui invited Vercingetorix to come and
cooperate in planning the campaign, and when he consented they entered a claim for the supreme command.
When agreement could not be reached a pan-Gallic
council was convoked at Bibracte, which was largely attended by representatives from many tribes. The question was submitted to a vote, and Vercingetorix was
unanimously elected general. The Remi, Lingones, and
Treveri were not represented, the former two because

they adhered to the friendship of Rome, and the Treveri because they were remote and were under German pressure. That is why they remained neutral throughout the war and assisted neither side. The Aedui were chagrined at being refused leadership; they lamented their changed estate and missed Caesar's patronage, but having once committed themselves to war they dared not adopt a separatist program. The young hopefuls Eporedorix and Viridomarus chafed but obeyed Vercingetorix.

64. Vercingetorix requisitioned hostages from the new tribes, and specified a date for their delivery. He ordered all the cavalry, amounting to 15,000, to concentrate at once. He would be content with the infantry he already had, he said, for he would not tempt Fortune in a pitched battle but keep the enemy from grain and forage, which his abundance of cavalry made an easy task. The Gauls must spoil their own grain and burn their own barns and without misgivings, for the loss of their property would secure them permanent sovereignty and freedom. These measures taken, he ordered the Aedui and Segusiavi, who adjoin the Province, to provide 10,000 infantry, added 800 horse, and put the force under command of Eporedorix' brother, with orders to make war on the Allobroges. On the other side he sent the Gabali and the Arvernian cantons nearest the objective against the Helvii, and also the Ruteni and Cadurci to devastate the territory of the Volcae Arecomici. On the other hand, his secret agents and emissaries sought to win the Allobroges over, in the hope that their resentment at the earlier war had not yet subsided. He promised money to the Allobrogian chiefs and dominion over the whole Province to their state.

65. To meet these various emergencies the legate Lucius Caesar raised twenty-two cohorts in the Province

itself and posted detachments at the points threatened.
On their own initiative the Helvii gave battle to their
invading neighbors but were repulsed, with the loss of
their chief Gaius Valerius Domnotaurus, son of Caburus,
and a number of others, and forced into their walled
strongholds. The Allobroges posted a series of units along
the Rhone and protected their frontier carefully and ef-
ficiently. Caesar realized that the enemy's superiority in
cavalry blocked all roads and made reinforcement from
the Province and Italy impossible: accordingly he communicated with the German tribes across the Rhine
whom he had subdued in previous years and procured
from them cavalry and light-armed infantry trained to
fight along with cavalry. The Germans' horses were
found unserviceable, when they arrived, and Caesar assigned them mounts taken from tribunes, other mounted
officers, and reënlisted veterans.

66. During this interval the Arvernian contingent and
the cavalry requisitioned from all Gaul were concentrating for the enemy. To be in position to protect the Province Caesar was marching through the outlying territory
of the Lingones towards the Sequani, when Vercingetorix
halted his greatly enlarged army in three camps about
ten miles from the Romans. He called his cavalry commanders to a council, where he declared that the hour
of victory had come: the Romans were retreating to their
Province and abandoning Gaul. For securing liberty for
the present this was enough, he said, but it offered no
guarantee for peace and tranquillity for the future, for
the Romans would return when they had enlarged their
forces and would never put an end to the war. Their
strategy must be to attack the baggage train; if the infantry came to its support the delay would make it im-

possible for them to march, but if, as he felt sure was more likely, the infantry abandoned the baggage to save their skins they would lose their essential equipment and their prestige. As for the Roman cavalry, the present company had every reason to be sure that not a man of them would dare stir outside the column, and to add to their confidence he would display all his forces in front of their camps to demoralize the enemy. The Gallic cavalry commanders clamored for a solemn pledge that no man who failed to ride through the enemy column twice should be received into a house or have access to his children or parents or wife.

67. The proposal was approved, and all were duly sworn. The next day the enemy cavalry was divided into three sections, two of which made demonstrations on our two flanks while the third began to block the van of our column. Informed of this move Caesar also divided his cavalry into three sections and ordered them to attack. There was simultaneous fighting on all fronts. The column halted, with the baggage enclosed within the legions. If our men seemed to be in difficulty at any point or getting the worst of it Caesar ordered the infantry to advance and wheel into line; this retarded the enemy pursuit and gave our men assurance of support. At length the Germans on the right gained the top of a ridge from which they dislodged the enemy and drove them with heavy losses to the river where Vercingetorix and his infantry were stationed. Thereupon the rest of the Gallic horse were afraid of being surrounded and took to flight. There was slaughter everywhere. Three high-ranking Gauls were taken prisoner and brought to Caesar: Cotus, a cavalry commander, Convictolitavis' rival in the recent election; Cavarillus, commander of

infantry after the defection of Litaviccus; and the Eporedorix who had commanded the Aedui in their war
against the Sequani before Caesar's coming.

68. After the rout of all his cavalry Vercingetorix withdrew the forces he had posted in front of his camps and
proceeded towards Alesia, a stronghold of the Mandubii,
ordering his baggage to leave camp at once and follow.
Caesar withdrew his baggage to a nearby hill and left
two legions to guard it; he pursued the enemy as long as
daylight allowed and killed some 3,000 of their rear
guard. The next day he pitched camp near Alesia. The
enemy were cowed by the defeat of their cavalry, in
which they had put their chief reliance; Caesar reconnoitered the terrain and began circumvallation, heartening
the soldiers to the task.

69. Alesia was situated on the top of a hill so high that
it seemed impregnable except by blockade. The base of
the hill was washed by rivers on two sides, and in front
there was a plain stretching some three miles. On the
other sides there was a circuit of hills at a moderate distance from the stronghold and of equal altitude with it.
Below the wall, where the hill looked towards the east,
the ground was covered with Gallic troops, who had fortified themselves with a trench and a six-foot rubble wall.
The lines of investment which the Romans began had a
perimeter of eleven miles. There were camps at strategic points and twenty-three redoubts to prevent surprise
attacks; these were garrisoned by day and manned by
strong bivouacs at night.

70. When the work was in progress a cavalry engagement took place in the plain which, as has been mentioned, extended for three miles in the gap in the hills.
Both sides fought vigorously. When our men were in
difficulties Caesar sent the Germans in and deployed

the legions in front of the camp to prevent sudden attack by the enemy infantry. The support of the legions raised our morale; the enemy were put to flight, got into each other's way because of their numbers, and were piled up at the gates, which had been left too narrow. The Germans pressed in hot pursuit up to their fortifications, where there was a great slaughter; some abandoned their horses and tried to cross the trench and clamber over the rubble wall. Caesar ordered the legions posted in front of the rampart to make a short advance. The Gauls inside their fortifications were no less terrified; they thought they would be charged at once, and called to arms. Some burst into the town in their panic, and Vercingetorix ordered the gates closed, so that his camp should not be deserted. After much slaughter the Germans retired with the numerous horses they had taken.

71. Vercingetorix now resolved to evacuate all his cavalry by night before the Romans could complete their entrenchments. His parting instructions were for each to go to his own tribe and draft every man of military age. He reminded them of their obligations to him and adjured them to take thought for his safety and not deliver to enemy torture the champion of their common liberty who had served them so well. If they proved remiss, he declared, 80,000 picked men would perish with him. He calculated that his grain would suffice for short rations for thirty days, and might last somewhat longer with frugal management. With these instructions he sent the men out silently in the second watch through a gap in our works. He ordered all grain to be brought to his headquarters, on pain of death for disobedience. The quantities of cattle which the Mandubii had rounded up he distributed man by man. He ordered the grain to be doled out sparingly and a little at a time. He with-

drew into the town all the forces he had stationed in front of it. Such were his plans for conducting the campaign until the Gallic reinforcements should arrive.

72. Caesar was informed of these measures by deserters and prisoners, and set about building fortifications of the following kinds. He dug a twenty-foot trench with perpendicular walls, as wide on the bottom as the distance between the rims. The rest of the construction was placed 800 paces back of the trench, for since the extent of the enclosure made it difficult to man with a continuous ring of troops he wished to eliminate the possibility of a flying night attack upon our works by the massed enemy or of missiles reaching our men while they were at work during the day. Behind the 800-pace stretch he dug two trenches fifteen feet wide and of the same height, and filled the inner one, where it crossed the plain or depressions, with water drawn from the river. Behind the trenches he built a rampart and palisade twelve feet high, to which he attached a breastwork and battlements with large antlers projecting from the juncture of the breastwork and rampart to retard an enemy ascent. Around the entire circuit he erected towers at intervals of eighty feet.

73. While these huge projects were under way timber and grain also had to be brought in, and since our men had to go some distance from the camp our numbers were reduced, and occasionally the Gauls made attempts on our works by mass sorties from the town through several gates. To meet this threat Caesar thought it wise to add to the fortifications to render them defensible by a smaller number of soldiers. Tree trunks or stout branches were cut down, stripped, and sharpened at the end, and continuous trenches five feet deep were dug. The stumps were let down into these, firmly

anchored so that they could not be torn loose, with the boughs projecting above. These were woven together and interlaced in rows of five, and anyone that stepped in would impale himself on very sharp stakes. These the men called "gravestones." In front of these, pits three feet deep were dug, gradually tapering to the bottom and arranged diagonally in the pattern of a quincunx. Into these, smooth logs of the thickness of a thigh, with the tops tapering and hardened in fire, were let down so that no more than four inches projected above ground. To fix the stumps fast and make them steady the earth was tamped down for a foot from the bottom; the rest of the pit was covered over with twigs and brush to hide the trap. There were eight rows of this kind, at intervals of three feet. The men called them "lilies" from their resemblance to that flower. In front of these, foot-long blocks, into which iron hooks had been sunk, were wholly buried in the ground, thickly scattered over the whole field. These the men called "spurs."

74. After these devices were finished Caesar constructed corresponding works of the same type, following the most level ground the terrain afforded, to face the other way, against attack from the outside. This was to prevent the garrison of the fortified area from being encircled by however large an enemy force. And to forestall the need for dangerous expeditions out of camp, Caesar ordered all his men to provide themselves with a month's supply of fodder and grain.

75. During these operations at Alesia a council of Gallic chieftains overruled Vercingetorix' proposal to draft all men of military age and voted for a specified contingent from each tribe. In too large a host they feared that discipline could not be maintained, nor contingents kept distinct, nor provisioning be systematic. The quotas as-

signed were: Aedui, with their dependents Segusiavi, Ambivareti, Aulerci, Brannovices, Blanovii—35,000; Arverni, together with Eleuteti, Cadurci, Gabali, and Velavii, who are vassals of the Arverni—the same number; Sequani, Senones, Bituriges, Santoni, Ruteni, Carnutes—12,000 each; Bellovaci—10,000; Lemovices—the same; Pictones, Turoni, Parisii, Helvetii—8,000 each; Suessiones, Ambiani, Mediomatrici, Petrocorii, Nervii, Morini, Nitiobriges—5,000 each; Aulerci Cenomani—the same; Atrebates—4,000; Veliocassi, Lexovii, Aulerci Eburovices—3,000 each; Rauraci, Boii—2,000 each; all the states touching the ocean, commonly called Armorican, including Curiosolites, Redones, Ambibarii, Caletes, Osismi, Veneti, Lemovices, Venelli—together 30,000. Of these the Bellovaci did not make up their quota on the grounds that they would fight the Romans on their own account and at their own discretion and would not submit to anyone's orders. At the request of Commius, however, they sent 2,000 men along, out of consideration of their ties with him.

76. This Commius, as has been mentioned above, had rendered Caesar loyal and valuable service in Britain some years before, in recognition of which Caesar had granted his state immunity from taxation, restored its rights and laws, and had given him rule over the Morini. But so single-minded was all Gaul to assert its liberty and recover its ancient renown in war that they could be swayed by no favors or past friendships but one and all devoted all their energies and resources to the war in hand. When they had collected 8,000 cavalry and about 250,000 infantry they reviewed and organized their forces in the country of the Aedui and designated their officers. Supreme command was given to Commius the Atrebatian, Viridomarus and Eporedorix

the Aeduans, and Vercassivellaunus the Arvernian, a cousin of Vercingetorix. With these were associated representatives of the states to advise in the direction of operations. Eager and full of confidence they started for Alesia, everyone assured that the mere sight of such a host was irresistible, especially in a battle on two fronts; an attack would be launched from the city while these huge forces of horse and foot would appear on the other side.

77. But the besieged in Alesia did not know what was going on in the Aeduan country. The day on which they expected their people to relieve them had gone by, and their grain was exhausted. They convoked a council to consider their fate, at which some voted for surrender and some for a sortie while they still had strength. Because of its extraordinary and inhuman cruelty the speech of Critognatus, a man of noble birth and high influence, must be recorded. "Of the motion of those who style abject slavery capitulation," said he, "I will say nothing; I do not think they should count as citizens or be admitted to this council. I address myself to those who advocate attack; their proposal, you all agree, shows a vestige of our traditional gallantry. But it is faint-heartedness, not courage, to chafe at a short term of privation. It is easier to find men who will court death than men who will be patient under suffering. Yet I would support their proposal—so highly do I respect its advocates—if the loss involved were only of our own lives. But our decision must consider Gaul as a whole, which we have summoned to help us. If 80,000 of their kith and kin are killed in one place, what will be the morale of men who have to fight almost over their very corpses? Do not deprive of your help men who have risked everything for your sake; do not suffer folly

or rashness or want of fortitude to lay all Gaul low and
subject it to eternal bondage. Do you doubt their loyalty
and constancy because they have not come at the hour
appointed? But do you imagine that the Romans are
working at those farther trenches every day for relaxation? If you cannot have confirmation from the Gauls
because every approach is blocked, you can be sure that
they are coming on the evidence of the Romans; that is
what is frightening them into working day and night.
What is my suggestion then? To do what our forefathers
did in their much lesser war against the Cimbri and
Teutones. When they were driven into their strongholds
and reduced to need like ours they sustained life by the
bodies of those whose time of life made them useless for
war. Even if we had no precedent I would consider it a
noble thing to create one for the sake of liberty and hand
it down to posterity. There is no similarity between that
war and this. The Cimbri ravaged Gaul and inflicted
grievous hurt upon it, but they eventually left our borders and pushed on to other lands; our rights and laws
and fields and liberty they left us. But what do the Romans desire, what is their ambition? Out of sheer envy
to settle in the fields and territories of men whose renown and warlike power they have come to know and
to lay the yoke of perpetual slavery upon them. Their
wars are waged out of no other policy. If you are not
aware of what goes on in distant regions look at Gaul
adjoining you. It has been reduced to a province, its laws
and institutions have been revolutionized, and it lies
crushed in perpetual bondage beneath the Roman
forces."

78. On the basis of votes they resolved that those in-
capacitated for war by age or physical condition must
leave the town and that every expedient should be tried

before resorting to Critognatus' proposal, but that his suggestion would be adopted, if pressure and the delay of reinforcements compelled them to do so, in preference to submitting to surrender and accepting terms. The Mandubii, who had received the Gauls into their town, were forced to leave it with their wives and children. They approached the Roman lines and tearfully and prayerfully begged to be taken in as slaves and fed. But Caesar posted guards on the rampart and denied them admission.

79. Meanwhile Commius and the other leaders entrusted with general command arrived near Alesia in full force, and occupied and encamped on a hill in the outer range not more than a mile from our circumvallation. The next day they brought their cavalry out of camp and filled the whole three-mile plain we have described above; their infantry they posted on high ground a little to the rear of the plain. The town of Alesia commanded a view of the plain, and when the reinforcements were sighted the defenders streamed together and felicitated one another; all were happy and elated. They brought their forces out and took position in front of the town; our nearest trench they covered with hurdles piled with earth, and held themselves ready for a sortie or any other development.

80. Caesar posted his whole force on both lines of fortification so that each man should know and keep his place if occasion should arise, and ordered the cavalry to move out of camp and engage. All of the camps, which occupied the ridges round about, commanded a view of the field, and all the soldiers were intently awaiting the outcome. The Gauls had interspersed their cavalry with individual archers and light-armed infantry to support their comrades if they gave ground and block

our charging cavalry. These were a surprise to our men, many of whom were wounded and retired from the battle. The Gauls saw that our men were being overborne by numbers and were sure that theirs had the upper hand; they cheered their side on with shouts and yells from every direction, both those who were shut in by our entrenchments and those who had come to relieve them. Because the action was taking place in full view so that neither gallantry nor cowardice could remain unseen, eagerness for distinction and fear of disgrace served to stimulate courage on both sides. From noon till almost sunset the issue of the fighting was inconclusive; then the Germans charged with massed squadrons at one point and routed their enemy, and when these had been put to flight the archers were surrounded and killed. From other parts of the field likewise our men pursued the retreating enemy up to their camp without giving them a chance to rally. Those who had come out of Alesia retired into the town, gloomily and almost despairing of success.

81. After an interval of one day, during which they prepared large quantities of hurdles, ladders, and grappling hooks, the Gauls silently stole out of their camp at night and approached our entrenchments in the plain. They raised a sudden shout to signify their approach to the beleaguered town, threw their hurdles down, dislodged our men from the rampart with slingshots, arrows, and stones, and set about other regular assault procedures. At the same time Vercingetorix, who had heard the shout, sounded the signal and led his men out of the town. Our men took the stations which had been assigned them during the preceding day and beat the enemy off with one-pound sling-stones, stakes which had been got ready along the entrenchment, and bullets.

Darkness limited vision, and there were many casualties on both sides. The artillery showered missiles. The legates Mark Antony and Gaius Trebonius, who were in charge of the defense in this sector, sent supports drawn from the remoter redoubts to assist our men where they saw they were hard pressed.

82. So long as the Gauls stood away from our defenses the quantity of their missiles gave them an advantage, but when they came closer they were caught unaware on the "spurs" or fell into the "lilies" and were impaled or were transfixed by artillery pikes from the rampart and towers and perished. Everywhere their casualties were very heavy, but at no point did they breach our defenses, and as dawn approached they retired to their own lines for fear of being surrounded on their exposed flank by a sortie from the higher camps. The besieged lost much time in bringing out the equipment Vercingetorix had prepared for the sortie and in filling up the interior trench, and before they could get near our defenses they discovered that their allies had retreated. And so they returned to the town with nothing accomplished.

83. Twice repulsed with heavy loss, the Gauls planned their next step in consultation with persons familiar with the terrain, from whom they ascertained the position and defenses of the upper camps. On the north there was a hill so broad that our men had not been able to include it within the circumvallation and had been obliged to build their camp on a slight incline which would put them at a disadvantage. The position was held by two legions under the legates Gaius Antistius Reginus and Gaius Caninius Rebilus. The enemy generals reconnoitered the terrain with patrols, and out of their whole host selected 60,000 belonging to the

tribes which had the highest reputation for courage. They agreed in secret on the objective and plan of the operation and timed the attack at noon. Vercassivellaunus, one of the four generals and a kinsman of Vercingetorix, was given command of the operation. He left camp in the first watch and by dawn had almost completed his march; he concealed his soldiers behind the hill and ordered them to rest after their exertions of the night. Upon the approach of noon he advanced on the camp described above, and at the same time the cavalry began to advance on the entrenchments in the plain and the rest of the army to show themselves in force in front of the camp.

84. Vercingetorix sighted the movement from the citadel of Alesia, and moved out of the town with the hurdles, poles, mantlets, siege-hooks, and other equipment prepared for the sortie. There was simultaneous fighting at all points; every expedient was tried, with concentrated attacks upon the weaker sectors. Roman strength was thinned by the spread of the defenses and it was not easy to rally at disparate points. The shouts emanating from the fighting behind them served to unnerve our men, who saw that their own safety depended upon the courage of others. What they cannot see usually upsets men most.

85. Caesar found a vantage point from which to observe the action in all quarters and sent supports where they were needed. Both sides realized that this was the moment for supreme effort. The Gauls had nothing to hope for if they could not break through our defenses, and the Romans looked forward to the end of all their troubles if they held their ground. The most critical situation was at the upper entrenchments where, as has been noted, Vercassivellaunus launched his attack.

Here the downward slope was a weighty factor. Some of the enemy discharged missiles, some moved close in "tortoise" formation, and fresh men took the place of the wearied. All hands piled earth over the entrenchment, and this enabled the Gauls to ascend and covered the traps which the Romans had hidden in the ground. Soon our men were short of both weapons and energy.

86. When he became aware of this situation Caesar sent Labienus with six cohorts to support the distressed garrison. His instructions were, if he could not hold the ground, to regroup his men and fight his way out, but only as a last resort. Caesar himself visited the other sectors and urged the men not to give in to the pressure, pointing out that the prize of all their previous efforts depended on that day and on that hour.

On the town side the enemy gave up hope of forcing the defenses on the plain, because of their size, and made an attempt to scale a sheer sector, where they brought the implements they had prepared. They dislodged the defenders on the towers with showers of missiles, filled the trenches with earth and hurdles, and pulled down rampart and breastwork with grappling hooks.

87. Caesar first sent young Brutus with some cohorts in support, and then the legate Gaius Fabius with others; finally, as the fighting grew fiercer, he himself brought fresh reinforcements up. When the action was normalized and the enemy repulsed Caesar proceeded to the sector to which he had dispatched Labienus. He withdrew four cohorts from the nearest redoubt and ordered part of the cavalry to follow him and part to circle the outer entrenchments and attack the enemy from the rear. Labienus had luckily been able to withdraw eleven cohorts from nearby posts when neither ramps nor trenches proved capable of withstanding the enemy

onset, and sent messengers to inform Caesar of his intentions. Caesar hurried forward to participate in the action.

88. The color of the cloak which Caesar habitually wore in battle apprised the enemy of his approach, and from their higher ground they could see, in the depressions, the squadrons of cavalry and cohorts of infantry which he had ordered to follow him. The enemy joined battle, and the shout raised on either side was taken up on the rampart and the whole line of defense. Our men dropped their javelins and plied their swords. Suddenly cavalry appeared at the enemy's rear, and new cohorts advanced against them. The enemy turned tail, but their flight was blocked by the cavalry. There was a great slaughter. Sedulius, general and chief of the Lemovices, was killed; Vercassivellaunus the Arvernian was taken alive in flight; seventy-four military standards were brought to Caesar. Out of that great host few got back to their camp alive. When the men in Alesia saw the slaughter and rout of their allies they recalled their forces from the entrenchments in despair. As soon as this became known the Gauls fled from their camp, and if our men had not been exhausted by frequent supporting movements and a whole day's fighting, the entire enemy force might have been wiped out. About midnight the cavalry was sent forward to overtake their rear guard; a great number were captured and killed, and the survivors went off to their respective tribes.

89. On the following day Vercingetorix summoned a council. He had not undertaken the war for his personal ends, he declared, but for the sake of their common liberty, and since they must now yield to fortune he would submit to either of two fates to appease the Romans: they could either kill him or surrender him to the Romans. Representatives were dispatched to treat of this

question with Caesar, and Caesar ordered them to surrender their arms and produce their leading personages. Caesar himself occupied a seat in front of the entrenchments, where the leaders were brought, Vercingetorix handed over, and the arms thrown down. With the exception of the Aedui and Arverni, through whom he hoped to recover those states, he distributed the remainder of the captives as prizes to his soldiers, one captive to each man.

90. After completing these arrangements Caesar proceeded to the Aedui and received their submission. There representatives from the Arverni promised to submit to his orders, and he exacted a large number of hostages. His legions he sent to winter quarters. To the Aedui and Arverni he restored some 20,000 prisoners. He ordered Titus Labienus to proceed to the Sequani with two legions and cavalry, and assigned Marcus Sempronius Rutilus as his aide. The legate Gaius Fabius, with Lucius Minucius Basilus and two legions, he stationed among the Remi, to protect them from injury at the hands of their neighbors the Bellovaci. Gaius Antistius Reginus he sent to the Bituriges and Gaius Caninius Rebilus to the Ruteni, each with a legion. Quintus Tullius Cicero and Publius Sulpicius he stationed at Chalon and Mâcon, on the Saône, in the Aeduan country, to collect grain. He himself decided to winter at Bibracte. When news of these operations was communicated to Rome a thanksgiving of twenty days was celebrated.

VIII 51-50 B.C.

The final book of the Gallic War *was written not by Caesar but by Aulus Hirtius, who was one of his officers and who, as consul in 43 B.C., died along with his colleague Pansa fighting against Mark Antony at Mutina.*

In a deprecatory preface the author sets forth his intention to supply the link between the end of the Gallic *and the beginning of the* Civil War. *The major campaign of 51 was against the Bellovaci, who were the center of the last organized resistance. After their subjugation (1-23) punitive expeditions were directed against other recalcitrants (24-47). At 48 the author explains that, whereas Caesar had devoted a book to each year's campaign, he would write none for 50 B.C. because no major operations were carried out that year. He closes (48-55) with an account of the enthusiastic welcome given Caesar on his return to Italy and a brief statement of the political situation in Rome, which makes a transition to the* Civil War. *On almost the last page we are told that Labienus, who had been Caesar's loyal and efficient lieutenant, was being approached by Caesar's opposition. In the* Civil War *we shall find him fighting at Pompey's side against Caesar.*

CIVIL WAR

I 50-49 B.C.

1. A letter from Caesar [offering to resign if Pompey would also resign] was handed to the consuls, and only after extreme exertion could the tribunes prevail upon them to have it read in the senate. But the consuls refused to put Caesar's proposal on the agenda, and limited debate to questions of general policy. The consul Lentulus delivered an inflammatory speech. "I shall support the government fully," he promised, "if you will express your views with courage and energy; but if you are concerned for Caesar's reactions and show complaisance to him as you have done on previous occasions, I shall make my own plans without bowing to the senate's authority. I too can protect myself by currying favor with Caesar."

Scipio spoke to the same effect. Pompey, he said, would stand by the government if the senate would back him, but if it proved dilatory and irresolute, no solicitations could procure his support in future crises.

2. Scipio's speech had the effect of coming from Pompey himself, for Pompey [was holding a military command and] could not attend a session inside the city.

A more moderate view also found expression. Marcellus, for example, urged that discussion be postponed until soldiers could be drafted throughout Italy and an army mobilized; then the senate could freely and securely venture upon any desired measures. Marcus Calidius moved that Pompey should retire to his own province and so avert armed violence. Caesar had been deprived of two legions, he said, and was afraid that Pompey was retaining them near the city [instead of sending them to his province] as a weapon against himself. Marcus Rufus echoed Calidius almost verbatim.

But Lentulus excoriated these moderates. He categorically refused to entertain Calidius' motion, and so terrified Marcellus that he abandoned his proposal. The consul's language and the proximity of Pompey's army and the threats of his adherents compelled most of the senators, reluctantly and under pressure, to adopt Scipio's proposal "that Caesar must disband his army by a specified date, or else be considered a traitor." The tribunes Mark Antony and Quintus Cassius intervened, and debate on the intervention followed. Extreme positions were taken, and Caesar's enemies applauded vigorously in the degree that the speeches were intransigent and ruthless.

3. Towards dark the session was adjourned and the members were summoned by Pompey [outside the city]. Pompey thanked his partisans and made sure of their continued support; the reluctant he castigated and put pressure upon. From all parts veterans of Pompey's former armies were attracted by the prospect of pay and promotion, and others were summoned from the two legions which Caesar had handed over. The whole city, the very comitium, was filled with tribunes, centurions, reserves. The senate was packed with friends of the consuls, connections of Pompey, and all who bore Caesar a

grudge; their shouts and scurrying terrified the weak, settled the doubtful, and robbed the majority of independent decision. Lucius Piso the censor offered to go to Caesar, as did the praetor Lucius Roscius, to inform him of the situation; they requested six days for this mission. Others suggested that commissioners be sent to communicate the senate's pleasure to Caesar.

4. All these proposals were blocked; the consul, Scipio, and Cato spoke in opposition. Cato's motives were his longstanding personal grudge and his resentment of his defeat [in the consular elections of 51]. Lentulus was actuated by his enormous debts; he expected to become general and governor and so be able to command huge fees for conferring royal titles. Among his friends he boasted that he would prove a second Sulla and attain absolute power. Scipio was instigated by a similar hope of a governorship and generalship; as Pompey's father-in-law he expected a full share of power. At the same time he was apprehensive of prosecution for bribery, and gloried in the adulation of the millionaires who were then at the height of their power in politics and the law. Pompey himself was instigated by Caesar's enemies and by his unwillingness to tolerate an equal. He had turned from friendship with Caesar completely and become reconciled with the enemies they had in common—with most of whom he himself had caused Caesar to break when he was Caesar's son-in-law. He was also irked by his discreditable diversion of the two legions from their march to Asia and Syria to serve his own ambitious designs for power. He was therefore eager for open conflict.

5. Hurry and confusion were the keynote. Caesar's supporters were allowed no time to apprise him of the situation, nor was opportunity afforded the tribunes to

protest against the threatened violation of their sacro-
sanct privileges or to exercise the basic right of veto
which even Sulla had left them. In the seventh day of
their term they were compelled to take thought for their
safety; in former days even the most turbulent of tribunes had not needed to be apprehensive about what they
had done before at least eight months had gone by. Recourse was had to the most extreme measure of which
the state is capable, the declaration of martial law; never
had this measure been resorted to unless the city itself
were ablaze and the audacity of malefactors had
brought universal despair of survival. On 7 January the
senate recorded the decree: "Consuls, praetors, tribunes,
and such proconsuls as are near the city shall see to it
that the state incur no harm." On the first five days during which the senate could transact business from Lentulus' accession to the consulship (there were two election days) measures most severe and hostile were taken
affecting Caesar's constitutional prerogatives and the
solemn privileges of the tribunes. The latter at once fled
the city and joined Caesar at Ravenna. There he had
been awaiting a reply to his very moderate demands, in
the hope that a decent sense of fair-play might bring a
peaceable settlement.

6. On the days following the senate met outside the
city, and Pompey himself delivered the arguments he
had transmitted through Scipio. He commended the
firmness of the senate and listed his own resources. He
had ten legions ready for action, and had ascertained
that Caesar's troops were disaffected and would refuse
to uphold or follow him. Other proposals were debated:
that soldiers should be conscripted throughout Italy;
that Faustus Sulla should be dispatched to Mauretania
forthwith; that Pompey should be subsidized from the

treasury. It was also proposed that King Juba should be designated Ally and Friend, but this Marcellus refused to allow for the present; and Faustus' appointment was vetoed by the tribune Philippus. The other motions were passed. The provinces, two consular and the rest praetorian, were assigned to private individuals. Syria was allotted to Scipio and Gaul to Lucius Domitius. Philippus and Cotta were passed over; by private arrangement their names were omitted from the lots. To the remaining provinces praetors were assigned, contrary to the practice of former years, they did not wait for confirmation by the popular assembly, but put on their uniforms, pronounced the customary prayers, and departed. In the face of all precedent, the consuls left the city, and in defiance of all tradition, private individuals were attended by lictors in the city and the capital. Levies were raised throughout Italy, matériel was requisitioned, money was exacted from municipalities and confiscated from temples, all rights sacred and profane were confounded.

7. Upon intelligence of these events Caesar addressed his troops. He mentioned the wrongs his enemies had inflicted upon him over a long period; it was through them, he complained, through their envy and denigration, that Pompey, whose prestige and distinctions he had always promoted, had been alienated and corrupted. He protested at the revolutionary innovation which branded tribunician intervention a crime and suppressed it by force of arms. Though Sulla had stripped the tribunes of all other prerogatives he left their right of intercession untouched; but Pompey, who claimed credit for restoring what they had lost, had rifled them of the privileges they had retained. Heretofore martial law, whereby the magistrates are directed to safeguard

the state, had been declared only in constitutional crises when the tribunes used violence and the people mutinied and seized temples and strategic terrain; and the fate of Saturninus and the Gracchi showed that past resorts to such a declaration required expiation. But in the present instance no such radical proceedings had been carried out or even contemplated. Finally Caesar exhorted his men to defend from his enemies the honor and reputation of the general under whose leadership they had brilliantly served the state for nine years, had fought many a successful battle, had subdued all Gaul and Germany. The men shouted (they were the Thirteenth Legion, which he had summoned at the beginning of the disturbance; the rest had not yet assembled) that they were ready to defend their general and the tribunes from harm.

8. Assured of the soldiers' morale, Caesar advanced with the Thirteenth to Rimini and there met the refugee tribunes. The other legions he ordered to leave their winter cantonments and follow him. Young Lucius Caesar, whose father was an aide to Caesar, arrived, and after the usual preambles indicated that the purpose of his visit was to convey a personal message from Pompey: Pompey desired to exculpate himself and hoped that Caesar would not regard as a personal affront the steps he had taken for the country's sake. Always, he said, he himself had put the welfare of the state above personal considerations; and Caesar too owed it to his position to sacrifice partisanship and resentment to the public interest and not be so intent upon hurting his enemies as to work injury to the state. Lucius added remarks to the same effect and made excuses for Pompey. The praetor Roscius made a similar plea, and his use of virtually identical language showed that the speech was Pompey's.

9. Though these intercessions did nothing to diminish Caesar's grievances, here were opportune men to carry a message from him to Pompey, and he begged each of them to consent to convey his wishes to Pompey as they had conveyed Pompey's to him; a little exertion might wipe out momentous disagreements and relieve all Italy from fear. "To me," he said, "the prestige of the state has always been a primary consideration, weightier than life itself. It has pained me that the gift of the Roman people should be insolently wrested from me by my enemies; six months of my term have been snatched away, and I am being dragged back to the city when the people had voted that I might stand in the next election *in absentia*. This affront I bore with patience for patriotic reasons; but when I proposed to the senate in writing that *all* armed forces should disband, I could not obtain even so much. All Italy is being mobilized, the two legions enticed from me on the pretext of a Parthian war are being retained, the state is on a war footing. What other purpose can this have than to destroy me? Still I am prepared to demean myself and submit to humiliation for the public good. Let Pompey proceed to his own governorship, let us both disband our armies, let all Italy be demobilized; let the state be released from fear, let free elections and control of the government be put into the hands of the senate and Roman people. To facilitate these measures and guarantee them by exchange of oaths I invite Pompey to approach my headquarters or allow me to approach his. Surely all our differences can be settled by a conference."

10. Roscius and Lucius Caesar agreed to carry the message, and found the consuls and Pompey at Capua, where they delivered Caesar's proposals. After some discussion they drafted a reply and dispatched it to Caesar

by the same messengers. The substance of their message
was this: Caesar must return to Gaul, evacuate Rimini,
disband his army; this done, Pompey would proceed to
Spain. Meanwhile, until Caesar supplied guarantees that
he would perform his promises, the consuls and Pompey
would not relax their mobilization.

11. It was unfair of Pompey to demand that Caesar
evacuate Rimini and retire to his province while he himself retained his two provinces and legions to which he
was not entitled, to call upon Caesar to disband his army
while he himself continued to mobilize, to promise that
he would proceed to his province without specifying a
date, so that if he waited until Caesar's consulship was
finished he would not be chargeable with overt decep-
tion. By refusing to negotiate at his own headquarters
or Caesar's he generated general despair of peace. Accordingly Caesar with two legions remained at Rimini,
and arranged to raise a levy there. He dispatched Mark
Antony to Arezzo with five cohorts and secured Pesaro,
Fano, and Ancona with one each.

12. Meanwhile Caesar was informed that the praetor
Thermus was holding Gubbio with five cohorts and fortifying the place, but that the inhabitants all strongly
favored himself; accordingly Caesar sent Curio with
three cohorts which he was holding at Pesaro and
Rimini. Learning of Curio's approach and mistrusting the
town's attitude Thermus withdrew his cohorts and
levanted, but the soldiers deserted him on the way, and
went home. Gubbio gave Curio an enthusiastic welcome.
News of this emboldened Caesar to rely upon the good
will of the municipalities; he withdrew the cohorts of
the Thirteenth from their garrisons and marched towards
Osimo. This town was being held by Attius; he had in-

troduced his cohorts into it and had sent senators
throughout Picenum to draft troops.

13. When the commissioners of Osimo learned of Caesar's approach they waited upon Attius in a body and
explained that it was not for them to judge the case but
that neither they nor other municipalities could exclude
from their town walls such a general as Gaius Caesar,
who had served the state so well and wrought such great
deeds; Attius must therefore take thought for the future
and for his own safety. These representations moved
Attius to withdraw the garrison he had introduced and
flee. A detachment of Caesar's shock troops overtook
him and forced him to halt, and in the ensuing engagement his men deserted Attius. Part of his soldiers went
home and the rest made their way to Caesar. Among
them was Lucius Pupius, a senior centurion who had
held the same rank in Pompey's army; he was arrested
and brought before Caesar. Caesar commended the deserters, released Pupius, thanked the people of Osimo,
and promised to remember what they had done.

14. News of these events created panic in Rome.
When the consul Lentulus came to open the treasury in
order to deliver to Pompey the money which the senate
had decreed, he fled the city before he could open the
vault, for there was an unfounded report that Caesar
was nearing the city and that his cavalry had already arrived. Lentulus was followed by his colleague Marcellus
and most of the magistrates. Pompey had started the
day before, and was en route to the legions which he had
received from Caesar and billeted in Apulia for the winter. Conscription came to a standstill in the neighborhood of Rome; it was generally believed that nothing
this side of Capua was safe. It was only at Capua that

they rallied and collected themselves. They instituted a levy of the colonists who had been settled in Capua by the Julian law. The gladiators whom Caesar kept in training at Capua Lentulus brought into the forum, promised freedom, presented with horses, and ordered to fall in after him. Subsequently his own friends pointed out that such an action was reprehensible, and so he assigned the men to the corporations of Capua for safe-keeping.

15. From Osimo Caesar moved swiftly through the entire region of Picenum; here all the prefectures welcomed him with enthusiasm and provided his army with full supplies. From Cingulo too, a town which Labienus had founded and built up at his own expense, emissaries came to Caesar to promise eager obedience to all his bidding. He bade them send soldiers, and they did so. In the meanwhile the Twelfth Legion had joined Caesar, and with it and the Thirteenth he marched to Ascoli in Picenum. Lentulus Spinther was holding that town with ten cohorts, but when he heard of Caesar's approach he fled; he tried to take the cohorts with him, but the greater part deserted him. Left with a handful on the road, he was met by Vibullius Rufus, whom Pompey had sent to secure the allegiance of the Picene territory. Vibullius was informed of the situation by Spinther, took over his soldiers, and dismissed him. He also mustered what cohorts he could from Pompey's levy in the neighboring regions, and took over Lucilius Hirrus' six cohorts which had comprised the garrison of Camerino, from which they were fleeing. These brought Vibullius' total to thirteen cohorts. With these he proceeded by forced marches to Domitius Ahenobarbus at Corfinium and informed him that Caesar with two legions was close at hand. Domitius himself had raised about twenty

cohorts of Marsi and Peligni from the neighboring districts.

16. Caesar recovered Fermo and ordered that the soldiers who had deserted Lentulus when he was driven from Ascoli should be rounded up and levies be raised. After pausing one day for replenishing the commissary he hurried to Corfinium. About three miles from the town five cohorts sent for the purpose by Domitius were dismantling a bridge; these were quickly repulsed from the bridge in an engagement with Caesar's outriders and retired to the town. Caesar marched his legions across, halted, and pitched camp near the town wall.

17. Realizing his situation, Domitius procured messengers well acquainted with the area to carry a dispatch, for a large reward, to Pompey in Apulia and beg and beseech him for support. The narrow defiles, he wrote, made it easy for two armies to blockade Caesar and prevent him from foraging. If Pompey would not cooperate, then he, with more than thirty cohorts and a large number of senators and equestrians would be endangered. Meanwhile Domitius gave his men encouragement, posted artillery on the walls, and assigned individual sectors for defense. In a harangue he promised each man four acres of land out of his own property, with a proportionate increase for centurions and veterans.

18. Caesar received intelligence that the people of Sulmo, about seven miles distant from Corfinium, were eager to comply with his wishes but were prevented from doing so by the senator Quintus Lucretius and Attius the Pelignian, who had occupied the town with seven cohorts. Caesar dispatched Mark Antony with five cohorts of the Thirteenth Legion, and as soon as the people of Sulmo saw our standards they opened their

gates, townspeople and soldiers in a body, and came out
to welcome and felicitate Antony. Lucretius and Attius
jumped from the wall. Attius was brought to Antony
and asked to be sent to Caesar, and Antony returned
with the cohorts and Attius on the same day he marched
out. Caesar absorbed the cohorts in his own army, and
let Attius go free. During the next three days Caesar
fortified his camp with extensive works, brought grain in
from the neighboring municipalities, and awaited the
remainder of his forces. He was joined by the Eighth
Legion, twenty-two cohorts newly recruited in Gaul, and
about 300 horse from the Noric king. Upon their arrival
he pitched a second camp at the opposite side of the
town, under the command of Curio, and in the days
following he began to encircle the town with earthworks
and redoubts. The greater part of this work was completed when Pompey's messengers returned.

19. Domitius read the dispatches but his public announcement falsified their contents. He declared that
Pompey would bring speedy supports and urged the
people to keep their spirits up and make necessary preparations for defending the town. But in a secret conference with a few intimates he resolved to flee. But the
facts could not long be concealed or dissembled; his
face belied his words, his conduct was more petulant
and timid than had been his wont, he met with his intimates in frequent and unaccountable clandestine conferences, and avoided public meetings and encounters.
What Pompey had actually written was that he would
not imperil their cause: it was not by his advice or consent that Domitius had thrown himself into Corfinium;
if he could manage it he should join Pompey with all his
forces. But this he could not do because of Caesar's circumvallation.

20. When Domitius' intentions had become common knowledge the soldiers at Corfinium held an unauthorized meeting with their military tribunes, centurions, and respected representatives of the rank and file. They were blockaded by Caesar, whose siege-works were almost completed; their general Domitius had betrayed the confidence which kept them loyal and was contemplating flight; they must take thought for their own safety. At first the Marsians objected, and seized what seemed to be the most defensible part of the city; wrangling reached the point of impending armed hostility. But soon exchanges of messages enlightened their ignorance of Domitius' intended escape. With one accord, then, they brought Domitius out, surrounded and guarded him, and sent their representatives to Caesar to declare their readiness to open their gates, obey his orders, and deliver Domitius into his power alive.

21. Caesar considered it important to take possession of the city as promptly as possible and transfer its garrison to his own camp, for there was danger that lavish bonuses, effective propaganda, or lying rumors might shift the balance: in war trifling causes often exert great influence. Yet he feared that soldiers entering at night might turn disorderly and plunder the city, and so Caesar thanked the emissaries and sent them back to the city with orders to keep guard over the walls and gates. He personally posted his soldiers at the unfinished earthworks, not at regular intervals as had been his earlier practice, but in a continuous line of pickets around the whole circumvallation, close enough together to touch one another. He urged the officers patrolling the circuit to watch out not only for sorties but also for individuals stealing out. Not a man was so slack or indifferent as to indulge in sleep. All were on the *qui vive,*

according to their several interests: What would happen to the Corfinians? To Domitius? To Lentulus? To the garrison? What would the outcome be for each side?

22. About five in the morning Lentulus Spinther hailed our pickets from the wall, and requested the privilege of an interview with Caesar. Permission was given; Domitius' troops escorted him, and did not leave him until he was brought into the presence of Caesar. His plea was for his own safety. He begged and implored mercy, mentioned their long-standing friendship, rehearsed the very great favors Caesar had conferred upon him—membership in the pontifical college, governorship of Spain after his praetorship, support of his candidacy for the consulship. Caesar interrupted this plea to remark that he had not quitted his provinces for any mischief but to protect himself from the malice of his enemies, to restore the tribunes who had been wrongfully expelled to their proper dignities, and to vindicate his own and the Roman people's liberty which had been subverted by a small clique. This speech encouraged Lentulus to ask permission to return to the town. Impunity granted to him, he suggested, would give comfort and hope to others who were so terrified as to plan suicide. He received his permission and departed.

23. At daybreak Caesar ordered all senators, sons of senators, military tribunes, and Roman equestrians to be brought before him. There were fifty; those of senatorial rank included Lucius Domitius, Publius Lentulus Spinther, Lucius Caecilius Rufus, Sextus Quintilius Varus the quaestor, Lucius Rubrius, and also Domitius' son and many other young men. There were also a large number of Roman equestrians and aldermen whom Domitius had summoned from the municipalities. When these were brought forward Caesar protected them from the

insults and catcalls of the soldiers, and addressed them
briefly, complaining of their total ingratitude for his
numerous kindnesses to them. Then he dismissed them
without punishment. The commissioners of Corfinium
delivered to Caesar the six million sesterces which
Domitius had brought with him and deposited in their
treasury; this sum Caesar restored to Domitius, in order
not to show less abstinence in money matters than in
taking life. It was perfectly plain that the money
belonged to the state and had been disbursed by Pompey
to pay the soldiers. Domitius' soldiers Caesar swore in as
part of his own army. On the same day he struck camp
and completed a full day's march. From Corfinium,
where his total stay amounted to seven days, he
marched through the territory of the Marrucini, Frentani, and Larinates down into Apulia.

24. When Pompey learned what had transpired at
Corfinium he moved from Luceria to Canosa and thence
to Brindisi, where his new recruits from all quarters
were ordered to concentrate. From slaves and shepherds
whom he equipped and supplied with horses he acquired some 300 cavalry. The praetor Lucius Manlius
was flying from Alba with six cohorts and the praetor
Rutilius Lupus from Terracina with three, but when
they caught sight of Caesar's cavalry under the command of Vibius Curius they deserted the praetors, transferred their standards to Curius, and changed to his side.
Similarly on the rest of the march sundry cohorts joined
Caesar's column and others his cavalry. Pompey's chief
engineer, Numerius Magius of Cremona, was captured
on the road and brought to Caesar. Caesar sent him
back to Pompey with the following message: "So far you
have denied me an interview. I shall shortly arrive in
Brindisi and it is to the interest of the state and the com-

mon welfare that we confer. Personal discussion is more
effective than negotiations at a distance through third
parties."

25. This message dispatched, Caesar arrived at Brindisi with six legions, three of veterans and the remainder
of the new levy and the men he recruited on the march.
The Domitian cohorts at Corfinium he sent directly to
Sicily. Caesar discovered that the consuls had proceeded
to Durazzo with a large part of the army, leaving Pompey at Brindisi with twenty cohorts. He could not ascertain whether Pompey had stayed back to defend
Brindisi and secure easier control of the Adriatic from
the heel of Italy and the Greek lands, or whether lack of
shipping kept him. Apprehending that Pompey might be
resolved to retain a hold on Italy, Caesar determined to
block Brindisi's communications and cripple its harbor.
This was the plan of his operations: Where the mouth
of the harbor was narrowest and its waters shallow, he
laid down a mole heaped with earth at either side of the
entry. Farther out, where the water was too deep for
the mole to hold, he placed floats thirty feet square at
the end of each mole; to steady them against the waves
each of the floats was anchored down at each of its four
corners. To these, when they were finished and in place,
he attached others of like size, and the whole was
covered with earth to form a causeway and make access
for defense easy. The front and sides were protected
with wicker screens, and every fourth float carried a two-
story tower, for convenient defense against naval and
incendiary attacks.

26. As a countermeasure Pompey fitted large freighters, which he had seized in the harbor of Brindisi, with
three-story towers, armed them with artillery and missiles of all kinds, and drove them against Caesar's works

to penetrate the line of floats and upset his arrangements. Daily there was long-range fighting, with slings, arrows, and other missiles. But even in the midst of these operations Caesar did not despair of negotiation. It was surprising that Magius brought back no reply to the message he had sent Pompey, but though the repeated efforts to negotiate hampered energetic action and planning, Caesar nevertheless thought he should exhaust every approach. Accordingly he sent his aide Caninius Rebilus to talk with Scribonius Libo, who was a close connection of Caninius'. Caninius was enjoined to urge Libo to work for reconciliation, for which the first requisite was that Caesar should talk with Pompey. Given such an opportunity, Caesar was confident that peace could be made on honorable terms. A great part of the credit for such a consummation would redound to Libo if his initiative and efforts produced a cease-fire. After talking with Caninius, Libo went to Pompey, and shortly thereafter brought back word that no settlement could be discussed without the consuls present. Caesar at last decided to abandon attempts which had so often proved fruitless and to concentrate on war.

27. After nine days' work, when nearly half his dam was completed, the flotilla which had ferried the first contingent to Durazzo and had been sent back by the consuls returned to Brindisi. Whether actuated by Caesar's operations or because his original plan had been to evacuate Italy, Pompey prepared for departure. He feared that Caesar's troops might break into the city while his men were embarking, and in order to delay such an attack he barricaded the gates, walled up streets and lanes, dug trenches across highways, embedded stakes and pointed blocks in them, and leveled them with light hurdles and earth. The two avenues of ap-

proach to the harbor outside the walls he blocked by
planting huge beams sharpened to a point. These preparations made, he ordered his troops to embark in silence. At intervals on the wall and towers he posted light-
armed veterans, slingers and archers, to be recalled at a
signal when all the soldiers were on board; oar-propelled
galleys were left for them at an accessible spot.

28. The Brindisi townfolk had been annoyed by the
outrages of the Pompeian soldiery and the contempt of
Pompey himself and favored Caesar's cause. When they
became aware that Pompey was withdrawing, therefore,
and while his men were busily scurrying about, they
signaled to Caesar from their rooftops. Not to lose the
opportunity for action, Caesar ordered his men to fall in,
and scaling ladders to be readied. Pompey weighed anchor at nightfall; the rear guard on the wall were recalled by the signal prearranged and ran down to their
ships as they had been directed. Caesar's men mounted
the wall on their scaling ladders, but, warned by the
Brindisians against the road-blocks and blind trenches,
they waited to be guided to the harbor by circuitous
routes. Using skiffs and dinghies they did overtake and
capture two troopships which had grounded on Caesar's
mole.

29. Caesar's best plan for finishing the business was
to collect shipping and follow Pompey across the sea before he could build his forces up overseas; but this, he
feared, would involve a long delay, for Pompey had interdicted pursuit by commandeering all shipping. The
alternative was to wait for shipping from the remote regions of Gaul and Picenum and from the Sicilian straits,
and the season of the year made this a slow and difficult
task. In the meanwhile Pompey would confirm the allegiance of the two Spains (one of which was under

heavy obligations to him), procure auxiliaries and cavalry, and, in Caesar's absence, subvert Gaul and Italy.

30. Accordingly, for the present, Caesar abandoned the plan of following Pompey and resolved to proceed to Spain. The commissioners of all municipalities were directed to requisition ships and have them brought to Sicily. One legion was sent to Sardinia under the command of Valerius, two others to Sicily under Curio as propraetor; Curio had orders to transport his army to Africa as soon as he had recovered Sicily. Sardinia was governed by Marcus Cotta and Sicily by Marcus Cato; Africa had been allotted to Tubero. Cotta was ejected from Cagliari as soon as its people heard of Valerius' appointment, before he quitted Italy. Terrified by the realization that the whole province was united against him Cotta fled from Sardinia to Africa. Cato was refitting old battleships in Sicily and requisitioning new ones from the communities. He showed great zeal in his task. His agents were recruiting levies of Roman citizens in Lucania and Calabria, and he exacted quotas of cavalry and infantry from the Sicilian townships. He had almost finished these preparations when he learned of the arrival of Curio. In a public harangue he complained that he had been sacrificed and betrayed by Pompey, who had embarked on an unnecessary war without the least preparation and had insisted, when questioned by himself and other senators, that he had got everything needed for war ready for service. With these public protestations Cato fled the province.

31. Valerius and Curio found their provinces without governors, and brought their armies to Sardinia and Sicily respectively. As to Africa, when Tubero arrived in the province he found Attius Varus in control. When his troops deserted him at Osimo, as has been noted

above, Attius had fled directly to Africa and on his own initiative usurped the vacant governorship. By conscription he mustered two legions. His knowledge and experience of the populace and terrain (he had been governor of the province a few years before, after his praetorship) enabled him to undertake these measures. When Tubero approached Utica with his fleet, Attius kept him from the harbor and would not even allow his ailing son to be landed. Tubero was compelled to weigh anchor and sail away.

32. These steps taken, Caesar quartered his men in the neighboring towns to afford them a respite for the remainder of the season, and himself proceeded to the capital. He convoked the senate and rehearsed the wrongs inflicted upon him by his enemies. He explained that he sought no unconstitutional office: he had waited for the legitimate term for the consulship and would have been content with what any Roman might aspire to. In Pompey's own consulship the ten tribunes had passed a law that Caesar might stand *in absentia,* though his enemies opposed it strenuously and Cato had tried his customary filibuster. If Pompey objected, why did he allow the law to pass? If he did not, why did he prevent Caesar from taking advantage of the people's kindness? Caesar then set forth his own forbearance in urging the disbanding of both armies; this he had done on his own initiative, though it involved sacrifice of prestige and rank. He expatiated on the prejudice of his enemies, who refused him what they demanded for themselves and preferred anarchy to loss of power and military authority. He spoke of their injustice in robbing him of his legions and of their high-handed insolence in curtailing the tribunes' prerogatives. He listed the offers he had made, the interviews he had solicited and been denied.

In view of this history he urged and charged them to take up the burdens of state and cooperate in administering it. If timidity made them hesitate, he would not burden them further but administer the state himself. Envoys should be sent to Pompey to negotiate a settlement, he said: he was not afraid of Pompey's recent remark in the senate to the effect that the dispatch of envoys signified authority for the recipients and fear for the senders. Such a position argued a petty and timid spirit. He himself was no less eager to surpass in justice and equity than he had been to excel in action.

33. The senate approved the proposal to send envoys, but none were found to send; everyone refused the assignment, mainly out of fear; on his departure from the capital Pompey had declared in the senate that he would hold those who remained in Rome equally guilty with those who joined Caesar. Wrangling and excuses dragged on for three days; the tribune Lucius Metellus was suborned by Caesar's enemies to obstruct this and any other proposal Caesar might make. When this design had become clear and several days had been frittered away, to waste no more time Caesar left what he had intended to do undone, quitted the capital, and arrived in Transalpine Gaul.

34. There he learned that Vibullius Rufus, whom he had captured and released at Corfinium a few days before, had been sent by Pompey [to Spain]; that Domitius had gone to seize Marseilles, with seven oar-propelled galleys requisitioned from private owners at Igilium and Cosannum and manned with his own slaves, freedmen, and tenants; and that Pompey had sent some young Massilian aristocrats back to Marseilles as envoys, with an injunction not to allow Caesar's recent services to obliterate the memory of his own earlier bene-

factions to the city. On receipt of these injunctions the
Massilians closed their gates against Caesar, and summoned to their assistance the Albici, a barbarian tribe
who lived in the hills above Marseilles and had long
been a dependency of the city. They brought into the
city stores of grain from neighboring districts and all
their fortresses, set arms factories up in the city, and put
their walls, gates, and fleet in a state of repair.

35. Caesar summoned fifteen of the leading citizens
and pleaded with them not to let hostilities begin at
Marseilles. They ought to follow the example of all of
Italy rather than bend to the will of one man. He detailed other arguments which he thought might make
them see reason. The envoys reported Caesar's speech
to the city and brought back an official answer: "We
understand that the Roman people is split into parties,
and it is not in our discretion or power to decide which
is in the right. Of these parties the leaders are Gnaeus
Pompey and Gaius Caesar, both patrons of our state;
one has formally granted us lands among the Volcae
Arecomici, the other has given us lordship over the
Sallyes, whom he vanquished, and has increased our
revenues. Since their services to us have been equal, it is
our duty to show them equal good will; we will aid
neither against the other nor receive either in our city
or harbor."

36. While these negotiations were in progress Domitius' fleet sailed into Marseilles. He was welcomed,
put in charge of the city, and made supreme commander. At his orders the Massiliot fleet was ordered to
scour the sea and seize merchant ships and bring them
into harbor; the bolts, timbers, and rigging of those inadequately fitted they used for repairing and equipping
the others. Any grain that was found was stored in the

public granaries, and other wares and provisions were reserved for use in the event of blockade. These hostile measures moved Caesar to march three legions to Marseilles. He began to erect towers and mantlets for an assault on the city and to build twenty warships at Arles. These were completed and equipped within thirty days of felling timbers for them. Caesar put Decimus Brutus in command of the flotilla when it was brought to Marseilles, and left his lieutenant general Gaius Trebonius to besiege the city.

37. While these preparations and dispositions were in progress, Caesar sent his legate Gaius Fabius with three legions, which had been quartered for the winter in Narbonne and its vicinity, ahead to Spain, with orders to seize the passes of the Pyrenees at once. These were garrisoned at this time by Pompey's deputy Lucius Afranius. The remaining legions, which were wintering in remoter parts, he ordered to follow. In obedience to his orders Fabius moved quickly and expelled the garrison from the pass; then he advanced towards Afranius' army by forced marches.

38. At the arrival of Lucius Vibullius Rufus (it has been mentioned above that Pompey sent him to Spain) the country was held by three of Pompey's deputies, Afranius, Petreius, and Varro. Afranius held eastern Spain with three legions, Varro western Spain from the Sierra de Segura to the Guadiana with two legions, and Petreius Lusitania and the region from the Guadiana to the Douro with two. They divided their duties as follows: Petreius was to march with all his forces from Lusitania towards Douro to join Afranius, while Varro was to protect all the western provinces with the legions he had. Pursuant to these arrangements Petreius requisi-

tioned cavalry and auxiliaries from the whole of Lusitania, and Afranius from Castile, the Asturias, and the
barbarian tribes on the northern seaboard. When their
increments were collected Petreius hurried westward to
Afranius and both agreed to base their operations on
Lerida because of strategic advantages.

39. Afranius' strength, as was mentioned above, was
three legions, Petreius' two, and there were besides
about eighty cohorts of auxiliaries, those from the east
armed with wooden shields and those from the west with
leather, and also about 5,000 cavalry from either province. Caesar had sent into Spain six legions, 5,000 auxiliary infantry and 3,000 cavalry which had served under
him in all his previous wars, and an equal number from
Gaul (which he had himself subdued) made up by en-
listing the bravest and most distinguished men of every
state by name; the finest were from Aquitania and the
mountains adjacent to Gaul. Caesar had heard that Pompey and his legions were marching into Spain through
Mauretania and would soon arrive. At the same time he
borrowed money from the military tribunes and centurions and distributed it to the soldiers. This achieved
two results: the stake fixed the loyalty of the centurions,
and the largesse purchased the good will of the troops.

40. Fabius was attempting to sway the neighboring
peoples through writings and messengers. He built two
bridges over the Segre four miles apart, and used them
for foraging parties, because he had exhausted the supplies this side the river in the days preceding. At
the same time and for the same reason the Pompeian
generals were doing the same thing, and cavalry skirmishes were frequent. Fabius customarily sent two legions to protect the foragers. Once when they crossed
the nearer bridge, with their transport and cavalry fol-

lowing behind, the bridge suddenly collapsed as a result of high winds and rushing waters, and a large force of cavalry was isolated. Petreius and Afranius were apprised of what had happened by the earth and debris swept downstream; at once Afranius marched four legions and all his cavalry across the bridge by which he had linked his camp to the city and advanced towards the two Fabian legions. Informed of his approach Lucius Plancus, who was in command of these legions, met the emergency by occupying higher ground and formed his line to face two fronts to prevent its being surrounded by cavalry. Thus, though outnumbered, he withstood powerful charges of foot and horse. When the cavalry were in action each side sighted the standards of two legions at a distance. Suspecting that the enemy generals would exploit their lucky chance to crush our men, as they actually did, Fabius had sent these legions to support our men by the farther bridge. Their arrival ended the battle, and each general retired to camp with his own legions.

41. Two days later Caesar reached camp with 900 cavalry which he had retained as a bodyguard. Repairs on the bridge which had collapsed in the storm were well advanced; he ordered them completed at night. After reconnaissance he left all his baggage in camp with six cohorts to guard it, and on the next day marched to Lerida in triple column. He halted near Afranius' camp and remained under arms to offer battle on level ground. Afranius availed himself of the opportunity to lead his forces out and post them halfway down the hill from his camp. But when Caesar realized that he would not fight a pitched battle, he resolved to make camp about 400 paces from the foot of the hill. To forestall surprise charges of the enemy while his men

were at work, which might set them in panic and prevent its completion, he forbade the erection of a rampart, whose height would necessarily make it visible from a distance, and instead ordered a fifteen-foot trench dug on the side facing the enemy. The first two lines remained under arms, as they had originally been posted, and screened the third line which was the working party. The camp was finished before Afranius was aware one was being made. Towards evening Caesar withdrew his legions to the shelter of the trench and rested there for the night.

42. The next day he kept the whole army inside the trench. Material had to be fetched from a distance, so for the present he followed a similar plan: he ordered trenches of the same size for the other three sides of the camp, and assigned a legion for the construction of each; the other legions he posted under arms to face the enemy. To alarm our men and impede their work Afranius and Petreius brought their troops down to the very foot of the hill to provoke an engagement, but Caesar trusted the defenses of the three legions and the trench and refused to interrupt the work. The enemy did not advance beyond the foot of the hill and after a short while retired to their camp. On the third day Caesar built a rampart about the camp and ordered the baggage and cohorts which he had left in the old camp to join him.

43. Between Lerida and the nearest hill, on which Petreius and Afranius had their camp, there was about 300 feet of level ground with a mound rising at about the middle. Caesar believed that if he seized and fortified this mound he could cut his adversaries off from the bridge and the town, where all their supplies were stored. With this in view he led three legions from his camp and

formed them in a suitable position; the shock troops of
one legion he ordered to charge and seize the mount.
When the stratagem was discovered Afranius sent
the cohorts stationed in front of his camp to occupy the
same position by a shorter route. In the battle which followed our men were repulsed, because the Afranians
had reached the mound first, and upon the arrival of
enemy reinforcements they were compelled to turn and
retreat to the standards of the legions.

44. The enemy's mode of fighting was first to charge
at full speed and boldly seize their objective; they were
not careful to keep rank but scattered and fought singly,
and when hard pressed were not ashamed to retire and
give ground. Long experience against the Lusitanians
and other barbaric peoples had accustomed them to
this type of warfare; when a soldier has acclimated himself in a given region, almost invariably he is affected
by local practices. Our men were not used to this sort of
fighting, and it threw them into confusion. Individual
enemy charges convinced them they were being out-
flanked, while they themselves thought it correct to keep
ranks, not to stray from their standards, not to yield a
position they had once taken unless absolutely necessary.
And so when the shock troops were thrown into confusion the legion in that sector could not stand its
ground and retreated to the nearest hill.

45. Panic seized almost the whole of Caesar's line, a
development unforeseen and virtually unprecedented;
Caesar shouted encouragement and brought the Ninth
Legion up for support. He checked the enemy's insolent
and furious pursuit and forced him to turn in retreat to
Lerida and halt under its wall. The men of the Ninth
were fired with zeal to repair the setback and their pursuit rashly carried to unfavorable terrain close under the

hill upon which Lerida was situated. When they wished
to withdraw, the enemy pressed hard upon them from
higher ground. There was a sheer drop on either side of
the spot, which would hold only three cohorts in formation; support from the flanks was impossible nor could
cavalry assist our hard-pressed infantry. From the town
the ground sloped in an easy grade for a distance
of about 400 paces; it was to this spot that their reckless
zeal had carried our men, and this was their rallying
point and here they fought. The terrain was against
them; it was narrow and exposed to adjoining hills, so
that every missile found its mark. The enemy added to
his strength; fresh cohorts sent from the camp through
the city constantly relieved the wearied. Caesar was
forced to the same course of relieving the exhausted by
ordering fresh cohorts to take their place.

46. After five continuous hours of such fighting under
grievous odds, when our men had exhausted their ammunition, they drew their swords and charged the cohorts up the hill; a few they overwhelmed and the rest
they forced to retreat. When the enemy cohorts were
pushed to the wall, and some frightened into the city, our
men were able to retreat, and their withdrawal was fa-
cilitated and protected by our cavalry. Though they had
been posted at the foot of the sheer hill they struggled
gallantly to the top, where they rode up and down between the opposing lines. So the battle fluctuated. In the
first encounter about seventy of our men fell, including
Quintus Fulginius, a man whose outstanding courage
had raised him from the lower ranks to the first centu-
rionship of the Fourteenth Legion; above 600 were
wounded. On the Afranian side five centurions, including
Titus Caecilius, a first centurion, and more than 200
of other ranks were killed.

47. The impression left by the day's fighting on either side was that it had come off best. The Afranians could claim that though they were generally considered inferior, they had stood their ground in close combat for so many hours, had withstood our charge, had clung to the mound which was our objective, and had forced our men to retreat in the first engagement. Our men could claim that they had kept up the battle for five hours on unfavorable ground and with inferior numbers, had forced their way up a hill with drawn swords, had compelled their adversaries to retreat from a higher position, and had driven them into the town. The Afranians heavily fortified the mound they had defended and posted a garrison on it.

48. Within two days of these events an unforeseen disaster befell us. Torrential rain caused flooding unprecedented in that country; it washed the snow down from the mountains so that the river flooded its banks and in a single day destroyed both the bridges Gaius Fabius had built. This caused Caesar's army serious difficulties. As has been shown above, the camp was situated between the rivers Segre and Cinca, thirty miles apart; since neither of these could be crossed all were necessarily confined to these narrow limits. States which had formed ties with Caesar could not deliver grain; parties which had gone some distance to forage could not return; large convoys en route from Italy and Gaul could not reach the camp. The time of year was the most difficult: there was no grain stored in the winter reserves and the harvest was not quite ripe. The native states were depleted because Afranius had carried almost all their grain into Lerida before Caesar arrived, and Caesar himself had used up any that was left during the days preceding. Their cattle, which might have served our

need in an emergency, the neighboring states had removed to a distance because of the war. Any of our men
who went out to find fodder or grain were overtaken by
light-armed Lusitanians and Spanish targeteers who
knew the country: for them it was easy to swim across
the river because it is their general custom to include
swimming-bladders in their equipment.

49. But Afranius' army was abundantly supplied.
Quantities of grain had been provided and brought in
beforehand, and quantities were being delivered from
the whole province; the supply of fodder was ample.
These resources were available to Afranius and involved
no danger, for he had a bridge at Lerida, and the untouched area across the river was inaccessible to Caesar.

50. It was several days before the floods subsided.
Caesar attempted to repair the bridges but the river was
too high and the enemy cohorts posted on the bank did
not allow work to proceed. For them it was easy to prevent our working: concentrated in one spot and hampered by strong current and high water, we were an
easy target for missiles from the length of the river bank;
it was hard to work against the current and simultaneously dodge missiles.

51. Afranius received intelligence that the large convoys en route to Caesar had halted at the river. These included archers from the Ruteni and cavalry from Gaul
with carts and loads of baggage, after the Gallic manner.
There were also some 6,000 assorted civilians, with their
slaves and children. But there was no system and no
centralized authority; everyone did as he chose and all
traveled without fear, as they had freely done on
earlier days and earlier journeys. There were a number
of upper-class youths, sons of senators and equestrians;
there were embassies from native states; there were some

of Caesar's own ambassadors. All of these were held up
by the river. Afranius set out at night with three legions
and all his cavalry, to overwhelm them, and caught
them off their guard with a cavalry attack. The Gallic
cavalry readied themselves very quickly, however, and
gave battle. So long as the engagement was confined
to cavalry the Gauls withstood a much larger enemy
force, but when the legionary standards began to approach they betook themselves to nearby hills, leaving
a few dead. The duration of this battle contributed sub-
stantially to the security of our side, for they had space
in which to retire to higher positions. Losses on that day
amounted to about 200 archers, a few cavalry, and no
great quantity of camp followers and baggage.

52. But these events did raise the price of grain; prices
regularly rise not only in actual scarcity but when there
is apprehension for the future. Now it reached fifty de-
narii the peck; the dearth was affecting the soldiers'
health, and their troubles were increasing daily. Within
so short a time the situation had altered completely;
fortunes had so shifted that our men were laid low by
serious shortages, while the enemy enjoyed great abundance and seemed to hold the upper hand. Because
grain was in short supply Caesar requisitioned livestock
from the states which had entered into relations with
him, sent sutlers to the remoter states, and sought to relieve the present dearth by every possible resource.

53. Afranius and Petreius and their friends wrote detailed and exaggerated reports of these events to their
connections at Rome. Rumor embroidered the tale, and
the war seemed virtually finished. When the letters and
messages reached Rome crowds congregated at Afranius' house and congratulations poured in. Many left
Italy to join Pompey, some to be the first with the good

news, and some not to seem to have awaited the outcome of the war or to be the last to come.

54. When the situation was reduced to such a strait,
when all the roads were blocked by Afranius' infantry
and cavalry and it was impossible to make the bridges
serviceable, Caesar ordered his soldiers to build boats
of a type he had learned in his earlier British experience.
The keels and ribs were made of light timber; the body
of the ship was of wicker-work covered with hides. The
finished boats he carted in pairs of wagons at night to a
distance of twenty-two miles from camp, and used them
to ferry soldiers over the river and occupy a hill adjoining the bank without being observed. This hill he fortified quickly, before his adversaries could take notice,
and then brought a legion in and set about building a
bridge from either bank; in two days it was finished.
Now he could safely recover the supplies and the
stranded foraging parties and begin to expedite the grain
supply.

55. On the same day he threw a large part of his cavalry across the river. These attacked unwary enemy foragers who were scattered in complete security and cut
off a large number of men and pack-animals. When cohorts of targeteers were sent in support, our cavalry
skillfully separated into two troops, one to guard the
booty and the other to resist and drive off the attackers.
One cohort which rushed forward from their main body
was cut off, surrounded, and annihilated. The cavalry
returned safe to camp by the same bridge with a quantity of booty.

56. Such were the operations at Lerida. At Marseilles,
upon the advice of Lucius Domitius, the Massilians
fitted out seventeen warships, of which eleven were

decked. To these they added many smaller boats so that sheer numbers should frighten our fleet. They put on board large numbers of archers and of the Albici (who have been described above) and egged them on with bonuses and promises. Certain ships Domitius demanded for himself; these he manned with the tenants and shepherds he had brought with him. Fully equipped and confident, the fleet advanced against our vessels, which were stationed at the island opposite Marseilles under the command of Decimus Brutus.

57. In number of ships Brutus was far inferior, but Caesar had assigned to the fleet the bravest men chosen from all the legions, shock troops and centurions who had volunteered for this duty. They had got ready grappling irons and harpoons and supplied themselves with large quantities of pikes, flying darts, and other weapons. Apprised of the enemy's approach, they put to sea and fought with the Massilians. Valor and dash was exhibited on both sides, nor did the Albici yield much to our men in courage; they were rough, mountain-bred, and used to weapons, and they remembered the promises the Massilians made them when they sailed out. And Domitius' shepherds were stimulated by the prospect of liberty and were eager to demonstrate their handiwork before their master's eyes.

58. The Massilians themselves relied on the speed of their ships and the skill of their pilots to dodge our men and sustain their rush. So long as they were free to use wide space they tried to surround our vessels with their extended line or to attack single ships with several, or to shear oars off by running alongside. But when they were forced to close quarters, the tricks and skill of the pilots made way for the prowess of the mountaineers. Our men not only had to depend on untrained rowers and inex-

pert pilots who had suddenly been drafted from mer-
chantmen and had not yet learned the technical terms
used on men-of-war, but they were further hampered
by the sluggishness and dead weight of their ships.
These had been built hurriedly of unseasoned timber
and did not possess requisite maneuverability. Consequently, when there was a chance for hand-to-hand
fighting they blithely took on two ships with one. They
would make the enemy ships fast to theirs with grappling irons, fight at both port and starboard, and board
the enemy ships, and when they had killed a large number of Albici and shepherds they sank some of the enemy,
captured some with their crews, and drove the rest into
port. On that day the Massilians lost nine ships, including those captured.

59. Caesar received the news at Lerida, as he completed his bridge. Fortune shifted rapidly. The enemy
was cowed by the prowess of our cavalry and no longer
roamed about so freely and openly. Sometimes they advanced a short space from the camp, to secure a speedy
retreat, and foraged within narrow limits; sometimes
they avoided our outposts and cavalry pickets by taking
a roundabout way, but if they suffered the least reverse
or sighted our cavalry at a distance, they dropped their
loads wherever they were and fled. In the end they suspended daytime foraging for several days and, contrary
to all custom, went foraging by night.

60. Meanwhile the Oscenses and their tributary Calagurritani sent emissaries to Caesar and promised
to do his bidding. These were followed by emissaries
from Tarragona, the Jacetani, the Auretani, and a few
days later by the Illurgavonenses, who live near the Ebro.

He asked all of them to assist him with grain. This they
promised to do, and collected all available pack-animals to bring it into camp. One Illurgavonensian cohort
went over to Caesar, when they learned their government's intention, and moved their standards from their
post. The situation changed markedly and rapidly. The
bridge was built, five powerful states had joined us, the
food supply was organized, the rumors that Pompey was
on his way through Mauretania with auxiliaries for the
legions proved false, and many of the more distant states
had defected from Afranius and taken Caesar's side.

61. These events threw the enemy into panic. To
avoid always having to send his cavalry across the bridge
by a long detour Caesar found a suitable site where he
decided to dig several trenches thirty feet wide, which
would divert part of the Segre to make it fordable at that
point. When these were nearly finished Afranius and
Petreius were alarmed at the prospect of being cut off
from grain and fodder, since Caesar was very strong in
cavalry. They determined to quit the area and move the
war to Aragon. Contributory to this decision was the circumstance that two different classes were attached to
Pompey: the states that had sided with Sertorius in the
late war feared the name and power of their conqueror
Pompey even in his absence; and those that had remained loyal were devoted to him for his signal favors
to them. Caesar's name was little known among the barbarians. The Pompeians counted on large reinforcements of cavalry and auxiliaries from these states and
planned to protract the war into the winter in friendly
territory. Pursuant to this plan they ordered all ships
that could be found on the Ebro to concentrate at
Mequinenza, a town on the Ebro about thirty miles

from their camp. At this spot they ordered a bridge made of a chain of boats, moved two legions across the Segre, and built a camp with a twelve-foot rampart.

62. His scouts brought Caesar intelligence of this operation. His soldiers worked feverishly day and night at the task of diverting the river, and had proceeded so far that the cavalry, albeit with great difficulty and exertion, could venture to ford the river, but for the infantry it was impossible because the water was up to their chests and shoulders and its current was rapid. Nevertheless, virtually at the same instant they learned that the bridge over the Ebro was nearly finished, they had located a ford in the Segre.

63. Now the Pompeians thought it more urgent to speed their departure. They crossed the Segre in full force, leaving two cohorts to garrison Lerida, and encamped with the two legions which had crossed over a few days earlier. Caesar's only recourse was to harass and wear down the enemy column with his cavalry; his own bridge involved a long circuit, whereas the enemy could reach the Ebro by a direct route. Petreius and Afranius had decamped after midnight; suddenly the cavalry which Caesar sent across the river showed themselves at the rear of their column. They swarmed around them in numbers and began to slow them down and block their progress.

64. At dawn the high ground near Caesar's camp afforded a view of our cavalry in action. They pressed hard upon the enemy rear guard, and sometimes held the end of the column up or even separated it from its main body; sometimes they charged our men in full force and drove them off, but when they wheeled forward our men could again take the offensive. Throughout Caesar's camp knots of soldiers complained that the

enemy was being allowed to slip out of their hands and that the war was being needlessly prolonged. They approached their centurions and tribunes and begged them to assure Caesar that he need not spare them effort or danger: they had the strength and courage to cross the river where the cavalry had crossed and were ready to do so. Caesar had hesitated to expose his army to the violence of the river, but he was roused by the men's clamorous enthusiasm and decided the attempt was worth making. Men whose morale or physique seemed unequal to the effort he ordered culled from all the centuries; these he left, together with one legion, to garrison the camp. The other legions he led out in light equipment and marched them across the river between lines of pack-animals that he had placed above and below the ford. The few soldiers who were swept off their feet by the current were caught and supported by cavalry; not one drowned. When the army was safely across Caesar marshaled them and led them forward in three columns. So intent were the soldiers that though they were delayed by six miles of detour and the river crossing, before three in the afternoon they came up with men who had started soon after midnight.

65. When Afranius, with Petreius, caught sight of them at a distance he was astonished and dismayed. He called a halt on rising ground and formed his line. Caesar rested his army in the plain, not to expose it to battle while it was fatigued; but when the enemy attempted to advance he followed and checked them, and they were forced to pitch camp sooner than they had planned. Near by were mountains, and five miles on there were difficult and narrow roads. The enemy was eager to gain the mountains; then he could escape Caesar's cavalry, block his advance by posting detachments in the narrow

roads, and cross the Ebro in complete security. This was an essential procedure, to be carried out at all costs; but the men were worn out by the day's fighting and marching, and postponed its execution to the next day. Caesar pitched camp on the nearest hill.

66. About midnight an enemy watering party which had gone some distance from their camp were taken prisoner by our cavalry; from them Caesar learned that the enemy generals were silently marching their forces out of the camp. At this news Caesar ordered the signal to be sounded, with the usual shouted orders to pack up. The enemy heard the noise and were afraid they might have to fight at night while carrying packs or be caught by Caesar's cavalry in the defiles; they canceled their march and kept to their camp. Next day Petreius stole out with a few horsemen to reconnoiter. Caesar's army made a similar move: Lucius Decidius Saxa was dispatched with a few men to study the terrain. Each gave his side the same information: after five miles of prairie the terrain was wild and mountainous, and it would be easy for whoever occupied the defile first to keep the enemy out.

67. The question of the best time for departure was debated in a council of war convoked by Petreius and Afranius. The majority were of the opinion that they should march by night; this would enable them to gain the defiles before their departure was discovered. Others argued that the alert in Caesar's camp the night before was proof that a clandestine departure was impractical. "Caesar's cavalry," they maintained, "operates in force at night and is blocking every sector and every egress. Night engagements must be avoided because in civil war a soldier who is frightened is apt to be guided by fear rather than duty, whereas in daylight he is shamed

by the crowd of witnesses and by the presence of tribunes and centurions; these are the factors that discipline soldiers and hold them to their duty. Every consideration, therefore, dictates a sortie by daylight; some loss may be suffered, but our objective can be gained without serious risk to the army as a whole." This was the view adopted by the council; their decision was to set out the following dawn.

68. On the basis of his reconnaissance Caesar marched his forces out of camp as soon as daylight showed and led the army in a wide circuit where there was no clearly marked path, for the roads to Mequinenza and the Ebro were barred by the situation of the enemy's camp. He had to negotiate deep and difficult valleys, and in many places rocks so sheer blocked the path that weapons had to be passed from hand to hand while the men made their way unarmed, boosting one another up. But not one objected to the hardship, for they believed that if they could manage to block the enemy and keep him from grain supplies all their work would be finished.

69. At first the Afranian soldiers ran out of their camp to enjoy the spectacle and shouted insults at our men, to the effect that starvation was forcing them to levant and go back to Lerida. Our route did indeed diverge from our objective and seemed to head in the opposite direction. Their generals congratulated themselves on their sagacity in sticking to their camp. Their delusion was supported by our starting out without pack-animals or baggage: surely it was because shortages were too much for us. But when they saw our column gradually veer to the right and noticed that our vanguard had passed the area covered by their camp, then even the stupidest and laziest realized that they must leave camp at once

and go to meet the enemy. Orders to fall in were
shouted and the whole force, with only a few cohorts
left for a garrison, marched out on the direct route to the
Ebro.

70. The whole issue was now reduced to a race to see
which could first seize the mountain defiles. Caesar's
army was slowed by the difficulty of its road, Afranius'
by the harassment of Caesar's cavalry. But the Afranians
had been forced into a situation where even if they won
the race to the mountains and secured their own safety
they could not save any of their baggage or the cohorts
they had left in camp, for Caesar's army shut them off
from any possibility of support. Caesar was the first to
reach the goal, and drew his battle line up to face the
enemy on a plain at the foot of high cliffs. When Afranius saw the enemy in front and his rear harassed by cavalry he found a hill on which to halt. From there he dispatched four cohorts of targeteers at the double quick to
the highest mountain in sight with orders to occupy it;
his plan was to follow with his whole forces and then
change his route and make his way to Mequinenza
through the highlands. The targeteers were making for
the mountain by zigzags, but Caesar's cavalry sighted
them and attacked. The targeteers could not withstand
their charge even for an instant, but were surrounded
and all killed in the sight of both armies.

71. This was an opportunity for a telling stroke. Caesar knew very well that no army demoralized by witness-
ing such a reverse could hold up, especially when it was
surrounded by cavalry and the fight was on level and
open ground; and pressure was put upon him from all
sides to attack. Legates, centurions, tribunes beseeched
him to join battle without hesitation; our men's morale,
they urged, was at its highest, whereas the Afranians had

betrayed fear by many signs: they had failed to support their men, they were not coming down from their hill, they scarcely held against our cavalry thrusts, and though they were packed close with standards bunched in one place they did not keep lines or formations. If it was the uphill terrain that he feared, they said, he would soon have an opportunity to fight elsewhere, for Afranius could not perch on his hill without water and would have to come down.

72. It was Caesar's hope that he could finish the business without fighting or casualties because he had cut his adversaries off from food supply. Why lose men, even for victory? Why expose soldiers who deserved so well of him to wounds? Why even tempt fortune? Victory through policy is as much a mark of the good general as victory by the sword. Caesar was also actuated by compassion for fellow Romans, who would inevitably be killed; it was better to gain his point with them safe and sound. But the majority did not agree with Caesar's reasoning; indeed, among themselves the soldiers openly declared that since such an opportunity for victory was being wasted they would not fight even when Caesar wanted them to. But Caesar persevered in his opinion, and withdrew a little to lessen his opponents' fears. Petreius and Afranius took the opportunity offered to return to camp. Caesar blocked every access to the Ebro by posting detachments in the hills and made his own camp as near as possible to the enemy's.

73. The enemy generals lost all hope of reaching their food supply or the Ebro, and in their alarm met the next day to take counsel on alternatives. There was one road to take if they wished to return to Lerida, another if they made for Tarragona. While they were deliberating they received word that their watering parties were being at-

tacked by our cavalry. Upon this intelligence they stationed posts of cavalry and auxiliary cohorts at frequent
intervals, with legionary cohorts in between, and began
to build a rampart from the camp to the water supply,
to be able to fetch water under shelter, without fear and
without escort. This task Petreius and Afranius shared,
and themselves advanced a considerable distance to over-
see the work.

74. Their absence afforded the soldiers an opportunity
to stroll about and talk with our men; any that had
friends or fellow-townsmen asked after them and called
them out. First they thanked all hands for having spared
them the day before when they were in panic, and said
they owed them their lives. Then they asked whether the
general was an honorable man to whom they could
safely entrust themselves, and said they regretted they
had not done so at the start instead of taking arms
against kith and kin. So far had fraternization gone that
they solicited the general's word of honor to guarantee
the lives of Petreius and Afranius, so that it should not
appear that they had surreptitiously conspired to betray
their commanders. Reassured on this point, they agreed
to transfer their standards at once and sent their first centurions to treat with Caesar. Meanwhile some in our
camp were entertaining their acquaintances, and some
went to theirs to visit, so that the two camps seemed to
have become one. A number of their tribunes and centurions called on Caesar to win his good opinion, and
so did a number of Spanish chiefs whom the Pompeians
had called up and were keeping in camp as hostages.
These looked for acquaintances and connections who
might introduce them to Caesar and say a word for
them. Even Afranius' young son asked Sulpicius to intercede for his own and his father's safety. Joy and felicita-

tions were general: among the Pompeians because they
thought they had escaped a critical predicament, and
among our men because they thought they had won a
decisive victory without scathe. Caesar, all agreed,
reaped the harvest of his traditional leniency, and his
policy was universally applauded.

75. At tidings of this development Afranius abandoned the work he had started and returned to camp,
prepared to bear whatever chance should bring with
calm resignation. But Petreius kept his spirit. He armed
his domestic staff, and with them, the official cohort of
targeteers, and a few mounted barbarian retainers whom
he always kept as a personal guard, he flew unannounced
to the rampart, broke off the fraternization, drove our
men back from his camp, and killed those he caught.
The others, dismayed by the sudden hostility, gathered
in a body, wrapped their cloaks about their left arms
and drew their swords, and so defended themselves
against the targeteers and horsemen in the knowledge
that their camp was close by. The cohorts posted at the
gates protected them, and they made their way in.

76. After this melee Petreius went from squad to
squad, buttonholing the men and beseeching them not
to deliver him nor their general Pompey to the enemy's
vengeance. Men quickly assembled at the command post
where Petreius demanded that all take an oath not to
desert or betray the army and its leaders and not to look
out for their individual safety without regard to the rest.
He himself took the lead in swearing to this formula and
made Afranius do likewise; next came the tribunes and
centurions, and then the soldiers were brought up company by company to take the oath. A general order required everyone harboring a soldier of Caesar's to bring
him forward, and those produced were publicly executed

at the command post; but many were concealed by their hosts and sent across the rampart at night. And so the generals' resort to terrorism, their savage executions, and the constraint of the new oath frustrated hope of surrender for the present; the temper of the soldiers changed, and the situation reverted to a war footing.

77. Caesar ordered a careful search for enemy soldiers who had come over during the fraternization and sent them back, but a number of the tribunes and centurions voluntarily opted to remain with Caesar, and these he subsequently promoted; centurions he restored to their former rank, and Roman equestrians to tribunician posts.

78. Foraging became impossible for the Afranians and they got water with difficulty. The legionaries had some grain, for they had been ordered to bring twenty-two days' supply from Lerida, but the targeteers and auxiliaries had none; they had had little opportunity to get any, and were not inured to carrying burdens. Consequently large numbers deserted to Caesar every day. Such was their plight. The simpler of the two plans which had been proposed was to return to Lerida, where they had left a little grain. Once there they were sure they could work out further plans. Tarragona was too far, and in so long a journey accidents might be expected. They adopted the former plan, therefore, and marched out. Caesar sent his cavalry ahead to harass their rear and himself followed with the legions. There was no intermission in the fighting between their rear guard and our cavalry.

79. This is how it was done. Their rear guard was composed of light-armed cohorts, of which several would make a stand on level ground. If there was a hill to climb, the terrain itself averted danger, for the van in its higher position could cover those still ascending. But

in valleys or downgrades the van could not assist the
stragglers and our cavalry could shoot from above and
behind. In such cases their position was critical, and all
they could do, when they came to terrain of this kind,
was to halt their legions, charge vigorously against our
cavalry, and when it had fallen back descend the valley
in a body at a run, and when they had crossed it halt
again on the next height. Their own cavalry, of which
they had a large number, was not only unable to help
them but actually had to be received into the center of
the column and sheltered, so demoralized had it become
in earlier engagements; none could stray from the road
without being caught by Caesar's cavalry.

80. Progress is slow and difficult with fighting of this
kind; frequent halts must be called to give the rear support. So on this occasion, when they had gone four miles
under the steady harassment of our cavalry, they occupied a height, and, without unloading their pack-animals,
entrenched only on the front facing the enemy. When
they observed that Caesar had made camp, pitched
tents, and sent his cavalry to forage, they made a quick
start, about midday, in the belief that the absence of
our cavalry would afford them a respite, and resumed
their march. Upon observing this Caesar followed, his
legions somewhat refreshed. He ordered the foragers
and cavalry recalled and left a few cohorts to guard the
baggage, with instructions to resume the march about
four o'clock. The cavalry quickly returned to its normal
assignment on the march, and the fighting at the enemy's
rear guard was so intense that they almost turned tail,
and a number of soldiers, including some centurions,
were killed. Caesar's column was pressing on and threatened their entire body.

81. Without a chance to find a suitable place for a

camp or advance further they were obliged to halt and
pitch their camp on ground that was unfavorable and
far from water. But Caesar refrained from attacking, for
the reasons set forth above; but on that day he forbade
the pitching of tents, so that all hands should be ready
to give chase if the enemy should attempt a break, day
or night. When the enemy realized how badly their camp
was situated they carried their entrenchments forward
all during the night to shift to a better position; all the
next day, beginning at dawn, they continued at the same
task. But the better they worked and the farther they
pushed their camp, the farther were they from water; the
remedy had only aggravated the disease. The first night
none went out for water; on the following day all went
on the march in a body, leaving a guard for the camp,
but none were sent to forage. Rather than fight Caesar
preferred to leave them to the torments which must force
them to surrender. But because he believed they would
inevitably try a sudden sortie Caesar endeavored to surround them with a rampart to forestall them. For lack of
fodder and to increase mobility they ordered all their
pack-animals killed.

82. These operations and decisions consumed two
days; on the third a large part of Caesar's works were
well advanced, and to prevent their completion the enemy marched their soldiers out, about three o'clock, and
formed a line near the camp. Caesar recalled the legions
from their work, ordered all the cavalry to assemble, and
formed his line. Avoiding battle was a blow to Caesar's
reputation with the soldiers and his general credit, but
his unwillingness to fight was motivated by the considerations already mentioned and by the further circumstance that the space between the two camps was so
slight that even a rout of the enemy would not contrib-

ute much to final victory. The interval was not more
than 2,000 paces, of which two thirds were occupied by
the lines and only one third left for charge and attack.
In the event of battle, the defeated could quickly retreat into their camp. For this reason Caesar resolved to
resist any advance but not himself to take the offensive.

83. Afranius formed a double line of five legions, with
a third composed of auxiliary cohorts as a reserve. Caesar's was a triple line of five cohorts, and so the next also
of four, three, and three cohorts respectively, the cohorts
for each line being drawn from different legions. Archers
and slingers were placed within the line, and the cavalry
outside the flanks. The lines formed, each general
achieved his purpose: Caesar, not to engage unless compelled to do so, and Afranius to retard the entrenchment.
The positions were maintained until sunset, and then
each retired to his own camp. On the following day Caesar set about completing the entrenchment he had begun, and the enemy attempted to ford the Segre. Caesar
took note of this and threw the light-armed Germans and
part of the cavalry across the river and posted detachments at short intervals along the bank.

84. And now hedged in on every hand, their animals
unfed for three days, short of water, wood, and grain,
they asked for a parley, to be held if possible, out of the
soldiers' sight. This Caesar refused, but offered a public
interview if they wished it. Afranius' son was delivered
to Caesar as a hostage, and the meeting took place at a
spot of Caesar's choosing. Afranius spoke, with both
armies listening: "You must not be angry with us or our
men for wishing to keep faith with our general Gnaeus
Pompey. But now by suffering total privation we have
discharged our duty and been sufficiently punished. We
are penned in like animals and cut off from water and

movement; we cannot bear the pain and the ignominy, and we confess ourselves beaten. We beg and beseech you, if any room is left for mercy, do not feel obliged to proceed to the extreme penalty."

85. To this speech, delivered with groveling humility, Caesar replied: "No one could be a less appropriate spokesman for querulous complaints or pity. Every man else has done his duty; I, when I refused to fight when time and place were right and conditions favorable because I would not prejudice the chances of peace; my army, when they shielded and protected the men in their power though they had been grievously offended and their comrades murdered; and lastly your army, when they tried to arrange an armistice on their own initiative in the thought that it was their duty to save the lives of their comrades. Men of all ranks stood out for compassion: it was you, the generals, who shrank from peace. You have disregarded the laws of truce and armistice and have barbarously murdered innocent men beguiled by a truce. What generally happens to obstinate and arrogant men has happened to you—you run back to beg and importune what you just now contemned. But I do not expect to augment my resources by your humiliation and my advantageous situation; I wish only that the armies which have been maintained to oppose me for many years be disbanded. It was only to destroy me that six legions were sent to Spain and a seventh recruited here, that so many fleets have been fitted out, that the ablest commanders were chosen. There was no need of such measures for pacifying Spain or protecting it; the province had long been at peace and required no armed assistance. It was against me that these long preparations have been made; against me a novel system of government has been set up, which enables one man to

control Rome from outside its gates and at the same time
act as absentee governor over two warlike provinces
for years on end. It was against me that the rights of
magistracies have been subverted; the men sent to provincial governorships are not retiring consuls or praetors but
the appointees of a small clique. It was against me that
the privileges of age were canceled and veterans who
had served their time called to make up armies. It was
against me that the invariable usage of allowing successful generals to come home with honor or at least without
ignominy, and there disband their armies, was abrogated.
All these indignities I have borne patiently, and will continue to do so. I do not contemplate taking your army
over and retaining it for myself, though I could easily
do so; my only wish is that you do not have it for use
against me. As I have said, then, leave the province and
disband your army; if you do this I shall harm no one.
This is my sole and final condition of peace."

86. The soldiers were overjoyed, as was obvious from
their reactions; they had expected some form of the punishment they deserved, and now they were being rewarded with a discharge. While the discussion of time
and place of disbanding was in progress, all shouted and
gesticulated from the rampart where they stood that they
should receive discharges at once; no pledges could assure that they would do so if the business were postponed. The final decision, after brief arguments pro and
con, was that all who had homes or property in Spain
should be discharged at once, and the rest at the river
Var. Caesar engaged that they should suffer no harm or
be compelled to swear allegiance to anyone.

87. Caesar promised to supply them with grain from
that point until they should reach the Var, and provided
that property they had lost during the war which had

come into the possession of his men should be restored
to the original owners; he compensated his men on the
basis of cash evaluation. Any disagreement between
the soldiers they voluntarily brought to Caesar for ad-
judication. The enemy soldiers demanded their pay
and were on the point of mutiny when Petreius and
Afranius said that it was not yet payday; there was a
demand that Caesar should examine the case, and both
parties were content with his decision. Within two days
about a third of the army was discharged. Caesar
ordered two of his own legions to lead the way and the
rest to follow, so that their camps should not be separated by too great an interval. He made Quintus Fufius
Calenus his deputy to supervise this arrangement. In
accordance with his instructions they marched from
Spain to the river Var, and there the remainder of the
army was disbanded.

II   49 B.C.

1. During the operations in Spain Caesar's deputy Gaius
Trebonius, whom he had left behind for the purpose,
was engaged in the siege of Marseilles. He had started
the construction of earthworks, sheds, and towers on two
sides of the town, one near the harbor and docks, and
the other near the gate leading to Gaul and Spain, adjacent to the mouth of the Rhone. Only a fourth of Marseilles is accessible by land; almost all the remaining
three fourths is washed by the sea. Even on the land
side, the section connecting with the citadel, a deep val-

ley, provides a natural defense, and this necessitated a long and difficult siege. To complete his works Trebonius had summoned large numbers of men and beasts from all the province and had ordered quantities of osiers and timber brought up. With this material he erected an earthwork to a height of eighty feet.

2. But from the earliest times Marseilles had stockpiled enormous stores of material of every description, and possessed such a quantity of artillery that no sheds of wicker-work could withstand their power. The enormous catapults hurled beams twelve feet long and tipped with iron points with such force that they passed through four layers of hurdles and buried themselves in the ground. Shelters were therefore constructed wholly of foot-square beams, under which material for the earthwork could be passed from hand to hand. In front was a movable shed sixty feet long, for leveling the ground; this too was made of stout timbers and covered with anything that could afford protection against firebrands and other projectiles. But the scale of our works and the height of their walls and towers and their abundant artillery slowed our operations. The Albici made frequent sorties from the town, and fire was applied to our works and towers; but these our soldiers repelled with ease and even inflicted losses on the attackers as they drove them back into the town.

3. In the meanwhile Pompey had sent Lucius Nasidius with a fleet of sixteen ships, some with brazen beaks, to support Lucius Domitius and the Massilians. Nasidius coasted along the Sicilian strait without Curio being aware of or suspecting his presence, descended suddenly on Messina, where the frightened chiefs and senate fled in panic, and seized a ship from their docks. With his fleet thus enlarged he finished his voyage to Marseilles

and sent a boat to inform Domitius and the Massilians of his arrival, and to urge them strongly to take advantage of their enlarged forces to attack Brutus' fleet once more.

4. After their previous losses the Massilians had rebuilt an equal number of old vessels lying in their docks and armed them carefully; they had ample crews and pilots to man them. They also manned a number of fishing vessels with archers and artillery and decked them over to protect the rowers from missiles. When the fleet was ready the older men and matrons and maidens tearfully implored the crews to save their country in its great peril, and the men embarked with no less spirit and confidence than they had shown in the earlier battle. It is a quirk of human nature that the unusual and unfamiliar evokes extremes of confidence or anxiety, and so it was then. The arrival of Nasidius had filled Marseilles with high hopes and optimism. A fair wind carried them out of the harbor and they joined Nasidius at their fort Taurois; there they shared their plans, heartened one another, and stripped for action. The right was assigned to the Massilians, the left to Nasidius.

5. Brutus made for the same spot. His fleet was increased, for he had added six captured Massilian ships to those Caesar had had built at Arles. These he had overhauled and refitted during the days preceding. He encouraged his men to despise an enemy they had already beaten when his strength was intact, and then full of good hope and enthusiasm advanced to the charge. Trebonius' camp and the surrounding heights afforded an easy view into the city. All the young people who had remained in the city, all the older people with their wives and children, could be seen stretching their hands to heaven from the streets and watchtowers and walls, or

flocking to the temples of the immortal gods and prostrating themselves before the images in prayer for victory. One and all were convinced that all their fortunes depended on that day's outcome. The young aristocrats and the respected persons of every age had been called upon by name and entreated to serve in the fleet; in case of failure, then, there would be no wherewithal for another effort, while if they won they were confident the city could survive by its own resources or by assistance from abroad.

6. And when the battle began the Massilians' courage left nothing to be desired; they remembered the precepts lately impressed upon them and fought like men who would never have a second chance. If they should fall now, they believed, they would anticipate the fate of their fellow citizens only by a little, for when the city was taken all would suffer the same fortune of war. As our ships were gradually drawn apart, the skill of their pilots and the maneuverability of their vessels had free play, and they ran in from all sides to support any we had been able to catch and hold fast with our grappling irons. Nor were the Albici found wanting when it came to hand-to-hand fighting, but proved nearly as brave as our men. Showers of missiles fired at a distance from smaller vessels inflicted many wounds upon our men, who could not guard against them and were otherwise occupied. Two enemy triremes sighted Brutus' ship, which its standard made conspicuous, and attacked from port and starboard. But Brutus grasped the situation and with a burst of speed got clear. The triremes collided so violently that both were seriously damaged; one had its beak broken off and was a total wreck. The nearest vessels of Brutus' fleet attacked the triremes they saw crippled and promptly sank them both.

7. Nasidius' flotilla was of no use and quickly retired from the fight, without the loss of a single vessel; there was no fatherland in sight, no kin to implore them to risk their lives. Of the Massilian ships five were sunk, five captured, and one escaped with Nasidius' flotilla, which headed for eastern Spain. Of the surviving ships, one was sent ahead to bring word to Marseilles, and when it approached the city all the populace poured out to hear the news. Their lamentations, when they heard it, made it seem as if the city had been taken on the spot. Nevertheless the Massilians began to make other energetic preparations for defense.

8. The legions charged with fortifications on the right realized that a brick shelter and tower near the wall would afford them great protection against the frequent enemy sorties. The first they made was small and low, to meet sudden emergencies. To it they retired and fought when the enemy outnumbered them, and from it they dashed forward to repel and pursue. The area of the redoubt was thirty feet square, but its walls were five feet thick. Experience is the best teacher, and native wit showed them that the tower could be very useful if it were raised to a height.

9. The plan they followed was this. When the structure reached the height of a story they built the studs into the wall and covered them with its masonry, not to leave projections for the enemy's incendiaries to set afire. Above this woodwork they laid small bricks as high as the sheds and screens could give protection. On this masonry they laid two horizontal joists, not quite reaching the main walls; these were to hold the flooring which would eventually become the roof. Over the joists they laid others at right angles and fastened them with tie-beams; these were long enough to project beyond the

outer walls, so that they could hang screens from them to ward missiles off from the men who would build the outer wall up from below. The top of this woodwork they paved with mud and bricks to make it impervious to fire, and on top they spread mattresses to prevent artillery projectiles from piercing the woodwork or shattering the brick. From the joists projecting beyond the walls of the tower, on the three sides facing the enemy, they hung mats, woven out of anchor ropes, four feet wide and the breadth of the walls. Experience elsewhere had taught them that this was the only serviceable protection against missiles and projectiles. When the finished part of the tower was covered and shielded from every kind of blow they removed the sheds for use elsewhere, and they hoisted the roof by leverage from the first floor to a height at which the hanging mats would protect the masons building the outer wall, and then hoisted them again to let them build higher. When the time came for another story, they sank the studs as they had done before in the outside wall, and again used the floor to raise the roof-platform with its hanging mats. In this way they built six stories, without casualties or danger, leaving portholes for artillery at appropriate places in the masonry.

10. Confident that the tower would afford protection for work in its vicinity, they decided to carry a mining gallery, sixty feet long and built of timber two feet square, from their brick tower to a tower in the enemy's wall. The plan was as follows. First they laid on the ground two beams of equal length four feet apart, and upon them fixed posts five feet high. Pairs of posts were connected by rafters, with a slight pitch, to hold the roofing of the gallery, and upon the rafters were placed two-foot beams fastened with plates and nails. The ga-

ble ends of the gallery and the lower ends of the rafters
were fitted with shingles four finger-breadths square to
hold the tiles for the roof. When the roof was finished
with a regular pitch and the beams placed on the rafters,
the gallery was covered with tiles and mortar to protect
it against fire thrown from the city wall. Over the tiles
were spread hides, to protect them from being washed
away by water from hoses, and the hides in turn were
covered by mattresses to shield them from fire and
stones. The whole structure was finished under sheds
near our brick tower, and when the enemy were off
guard it was moved up on rollers by a naval winch to
touch the enemy tower.

11. The townspeople were alarmed by this sudden
reverse; they moved the largest boulders they could up
to their wall with crowbars and rolled them down on
the gallery, but the sturdy structure withstood the impact, and whatever fell upon its roof rolled off because
of the pitch. Thereupon the enemy adopted a different
tactic; they set fire to barrels filled with resin and tar and
rolled them on to the gallery from the wall. These too
slid off, and were removed from the structure by poles
and forks. In the meanwhile, from the shelter of the gallery soldiers were prying loose the foundation stones of
the enemy tower; men in our brick tower covered their
operation with missiles and artillery. The enemy were
dislodged from their wall and towers, and could no
longer freely defend their wall. When a number of stones
had been pulled out next the gallery a part of the tower
collapsed and the rest listed forward. Thereupon the
enemy was terrified at the prospect of their city being
sacked and in a body rushed out the gate, unarmed and
bearing fillets, and stretched their hands out to our officers and men like suppliants.

12. At this strange phenomenon all military activity ceased; the soldiers were curious to hear what would happen, and turned from battle. When the enemy drew near they all prostrated themselves at the feet of our officers and men and begged them to wait for Caesar. They realized, they said, that their city had fallen, for our offensive works were finished and their tower undermined; they were therefore abandoning the defense. Our men could plunder their city from top to bottom at once if, on Caesar's arrival, they did not obey his every nod. If the tower should collapse entirely, they explained, the soldiers could not be prevented from rushing into the city to find booty and destroying it utterly. These and similar arguments their trained pleaders proffered with pathos and tears.

13. Our officers were so far moved that they recalled the soldiers from the works, at which they left sentries, and abandoned the siege. They made a kind of truce, out of pity, and waited for Caesar to come. Not a shot was fired from the wall, and none by our men; all vigilance was relaxed, as if the business were finished. Caesar's dispatches had impressed it upon Trebonius that he must not allow the city to be taken by storm, for the soldiers were bitter because of the city's high-handedness, its contempt of them, and their own tedious labor, and might slaughter all adults. This they actually threatened to do, and were barely kept from rushing into the town and were indignant because Trebonius apparently stood in the way of their taking possession of it.

14. But the unscrupulous enemy were only seeking an opportunity for treachery. After a few days one noon when our men were inactive and relaxed, some away from the line and some taking a nap, after their long exertions, in the siege-works themselves, with their arms

stacked out of sight, the Massilians suddenly sallied out
and with a stiff wind favoring them, set fire to our siege-
works. So quickly did the fire spread that earthwork,
screens, shed, tower, and artillery were ablaze before
anyone realized how it had happened. Stung by the
sudden misfortune, our men seized what weapons they
could and others dashed out of the camp. They charged
the enemy, but were prevented from following their attack up by archers and artillery on the wall. The enemy
retired under the wall, where they were free to set fire
to the gallery and the brick tower. The perfidy of the
enemy and the violence of the wind destroyed many
months' work in an instant. The next day there was the
same wind, and the enemy made a similar attempt, with
greater confidence, against the other tower and earthwork. They made a sortie and carried much fire against
their objective, but though our men had relaxed their
earlier intensity the lesson of the previous day had taught
them to take adequate precautions. They killed many
of the enemy and drove the rest back without accomplishing their purpose.

15. Trebonius took the repair of the damage in hand,
and the soldiers set to with good will. They had seen
their ingenious and laborious work treacherously ruined,
and they were stung at the insult delivered to their manhood by the scoundrelly violation of the truce. The
whole countryside around Marseilles had been stripped
of timber and there was no other source of material for
a rampart; they therefore decided to construct masonry
works on a novel and unprecedented pattern. They built
a pair of walls, each six feet thick, with beams of approximately the same length as in the earlier structure
laid across them to make a floor. Where space or the
weakness of the material necessitated additional support,

posts carrying crossbeams made the structure solid. The
portion roofed was covered with wicker-work and mortar. The soldiers were shielded by masonry on the right
and left, and in front by screens, and so were able to
bring necessary materials up in safety. The work proceeded swiftly; the long labor lost was quickly made
good by the wit and energy of the soldiers. Sally-ports
were left in the wall at suitable points.

16. The enemy had not expected that their damage
could be repaired even over a long period; now they
saw that a few days' work had put the siege-works into
such a condition that there was no chance for force or
treachery nor any way open for hurting our men with
missiles or our works with fire. They realized that a similar technique could so encircle the whole city on its land-
ward side with wall and towers that they could keep
no footing on their own redoubts. Our works seemed
near enough to tie into their very walls, which were
within range of hand-thrown missiles. This proximity
made their artillery, by which they set such great store,
quite useless; and they knew they could not equal the
prowess of our men in a fight from wall and towers on
equal terms. Accordingly they returned to the same terms
of capitulation.

17. Marcus Varro was in western Spain when he heard
of the events in Italy. At first he mistrusted Pompey's
success and spoke of Caesar in the friendliest terms.
Holding an appointment from Pompey, he said, he was
obligated to him; but an equally strong tie bound him
to Caesar. He knew the duty of a deputy in a trusted
post, and he knew too what his own resources were and
how the whole province was disposed to Caesar. This
was the burden of all his conversations, but he took no

steps in either direction. But later, when he learned that Caesar was detained at Marseilles, that Petreius' forces were united with Afranius' army, that quantities of auxiliaries had collected and quantities more were expected, and that all eastern Spain was pro-Pompeian; when he heard too of subsequent events and our food shortage at Lerida, which Afranius enlarged upon and exaggerated in his letters—he began to veer with fortune's breeze.

18. By conscription throughout the province Varro raised two full legions and about thirty auxiliary cohorts. He requisitioned quantities of grain to send to Marseilles and also to Afranius and Petreius. He ordered Cadiz to build ten warships and contracted for several others at Seville. All the money and treasures from the shrine of Hercules he deposited in Cadiz; to garrison Cadiz he sent six cohorts from the province. The government of the town he entrusted to Gaius Gallonius, a Roman equestrian and friend of Domitius, who had sent him there to settle an estate; all weapons public and private were laid up in Gallonius' residence.

Varro himself delivered harangues against Caesar. Frequently he issued communiques to the effect that Caesar had been defeated in battle and that large numbers of his soldiers had gone over to Afranius, alleging that this information rested on unimpeachable authority. From the Roman citizens in the province, whom he had frightened by his assertions, he exacted promises to deliver eighteen million sesterces, 20,000 pounds of silver, and 120,000 measures of wheat. Upon such states as he thought were friendly to Caesar he imposed heavier burdens and posted garrisons in them; he brought individuals to trial on the charge of speaking against the state, and declared their property forfeit. He compelled the whole province to swear allegiance to himself and Pompey. When he learned what had happened in eastern Spain he prepared for war. The plan of his campaign was to retire to Cadiz with two legions and to concentrate shipping and grain there, for he knew that the province as a whole favored Caesar's cause. With food and shipping concentrated in the island he thought it would not be difficult to hold out.

Urgent business demanded Caesar's return to Italy, but he was resolved to leave no part of the war in the Spanish peninsula unfinished, for he knew that Pompey had conferred lavish benefits on the western province and had many retainers there.

19. Accordingly he dispatched two legions under the tribune of the people Quintus Cassius to western Spain, and himself with 600 cavalry pushed on to Cordova by forced marches, having promulgated an edict that the magistrates and senators of all states should meet him there on a specified day. This edict was published throughout the province, and not a state failed to send part of its senate to Cordova by the appointed day, nor did any Roman citizen of any position fail to attend. At the same time the corporation of Cordova closed its gates against Varro of its own accord, posted guards and pickets upon its towers and walls, and retained for its protection two cohorts called colonial which chanced to be in the town. At this same period Carmona, far the strongest state in the whole province, of its own accord ejected the three cohorts which Varro had assigned to garrison the town and barred its gates.

20. This spurred Varro to hasten to Cadiz with his legions as quickly as possible to avoid being stopped on the march or in crossing to the island, for he found the province enthusiastically in favor of Caesar. When he

had gone a little way he was handed a dispatch from
Cadiz informing him that as soon as Caesar's edict was
published the leaders of the city had conspired with
the officers of the cohorts garrisoned there to expel Gallonius and hold the city and island for Caesar. They had
then notified Gallonius to leave Cadiz voluntarily while
he could do so safely; if he failed to do so they would
take appropriate steps. Gallonius was intimidated and
left. When Varro's army heard this news one of the two
legions called native moved its standards while Varro
stood by and looked on, and marched to Seville, where
they bivouacked in the forum and colonnades without
doing any harm. The Roman corporation in the town
approved their action so heartily that they invited them
and entertained them in their homes. Varro was dismayed and, changing his route, sent word that he was
coming to Italica; but his friends there informed him
that its gates were closed against him. Cut off, then, on
all sides, he sent Caesar word that he was ready to turn
his legion over to whomever Caesar should designate.
Caesar sent Sextus Caesar to receive the surrender. After
he surrendered his legion Varro presented himself to Caesar at Cordova, gave him a true account of the public
funds, turned over the cash in his possession, and indicated the quantities and locations of the grain and
shipping in his charge.

21. At Cordova Caesar delivered a public address in
which he thanked the various groups—the Roman citizens for their efforts to keep the city under his control,
the Spaniards for driving the garrison out, the people
of Cadiz for having nipped the enemy attempts and secured their liberty, and the tribunes and centurions of
the garrison for having strengthened the resolution of
the Cordovans by their own courage. The money which

the Roman citizens had promised Varro for public use he remitted, and he restored the property which he understood had been confiscated from individuals for speaking too freely. To certain peoples he awarded public and private honors and to others he gave assurances of future benefits. After a stay of two days at Cordova Caesar proceeded to Cadiz, where he ordered the money and dedications which had been removed from the shrine of Hercules to a private house to be restored to the temple. He gave Quintus Cassius command over the province and assigned him four legions. With the ships that Marcus Varro had built, and those built at his order by the people of Cadiz, Caesar arrived at Tarragona in a few days, where embassies from almost the whole of eastern Spain awaited his arrival. There he awarded private and public honors as he had done at Cordova, and then traveled overland first to Narbonne and then Marseilles. There he learned that a dictatorship had been declared [at home] and that he himself had been nominated to the office by the praetor Marcus Lepidus.

22. The Massilians had suffered every species of disaster. They were reduced to starvation rations, they had twice been defeated at sea, their numerous sorties had been routed, they were afflicted by pestilence by reason of their long confinement and unaccustomed diet (they had been living on stale millet and rotten barley which had been stored in public granaries for a very long time against such an emergency as this), their tower had collapsed and a large part of their wall was tottering. They could hope for no reinforcements from provinces and armies which they knew had come into Caesar's power, and so they resolved upon unconditional surrender. Lucius Domitius had divined their intentions a few days

before; he procured three ships, embarked his friends
upon two of them and himself on the third, and when
the weather was foul sailed out. The ships which maintained a daily patrol of the harbor at Brutus' orders
sighted them and weighed anchor to give chase. Domitius' own ship persisted in its course and was helped by
the storm to get out of sight; the other two were frightened by our ships gathering against them and put back
to harbor. The Massilians brought their weapons and
artillery out of the town, their shipping out of the harbor
and docks, their money out of the treasury, and surrendered them all. When this was done Caesar spared
them, for their name and antiquity rather than their deserts, and left two legions as a garrison. The rest of the
legions he sent to Italy and himself set out for the capital.

23. During this same period Gaius Curio set out from
Sicily for Africa. From the beginning he scorned the
strength of Publius Attius Varus and took only two of
the four legions he had received from Caesar and 500
horses. After a voyage of two days and three nights he
landed at a place called Anquillaria. This is twenty-two
miles from Kalibia; it is enclosed by two promontories
and has a fairly good anchorage in summer. To oppose
him young Lucius Caesar had ten ships near Kalibia;
these had been laid up at Utica after the pirate war and
had been refitted for the present war upon the orders of
Publius Attius. Lucius was alarmed at the great fleet sailing in from the high seas, beached and abandoned his
own decked trireme on the shore nearby, and escaped
overland to Hadrumetum, which Gaius Considius
Longus held with a garrison of one legion. Upon Lucius'
flight the rest of his ships took themselves to Hadrume-

tum. Curio had brought twelve ships from Sicily to escort the transports; when the quaestor Marcius Rufus, who commanded this flotilla, saw the trireme abandoned on the shore he dragged it off in tow and rejoined Curio's fleet.

24. Curio sent the fleet under Marcius ahead to Utica, and himself set out with the army. Two days' march brought him to the river Bagrada, where he left Caninius Rebilus with the legions while he himself rode ahead with the cavalry to explore Castra Cornelia, which was considered an ideal position for a camp. The site is a straight ridge projecting into the sea, sheer and rugged on both sides, but with a somewhat gentler slope in the direction of Utica, which is a little more than three miles away in a straight line. But here there is much marshy ground because the sea comes inland to overflow a stream; avoiding the marsh involves a detour of six miles.

25. His reconnaissance showed Curio that Varus' camp adjoined the town wall at the gate called Baal's. The position was very strong: on one side was the town and on the other a theater outside the wall whose massive substructures made access to the camp difficult and narrow. Curio also noticed heavy traffic on the roads, for property and livestock were being brought into the city for fear of sudden disorders. Curio sent his cavalry to plunder and bring back the property, and at the same time Varus sent 600 Numidian horse and 400 infantry from the city to protect it. Juba had sent these reinforcements to Varus a few days before; he had hereditary ties with Pompey and bore a grudge against Curio who, as tribune, had proposed confiscation of Juba's kingdom. When the cavalry engaged, the Numidians could not withstand our first charge but fled to their camp by the

town, leaving about 120 dead. Meanwhile Curio's fleet
had arrived and he promulgated an order to the some
200 freighters stationed at Utica that he would treat as
an enemy any who did not at once transfer their ships to
Castra Cornelia. Immediately upon this announcement
all weighed anchor and sailed from Utica as they were
bidden. This afforded our army ample supplies.

26. After this success Curio returned to the camp at
the Bagrada, where the whole army acclaimed him as
"Imperator," and on the next day marched to Utica and
encamped near the town. Before the entrenchment was
completed the cavalry reported from their stations that
large reinforcements of foot and horse sent by King Juba
were approaching Utica; simultaneously, a great cloud
of dust was seen, and in an instant the van came into
view. Curio was disturbed by this unexpected development and sent his cavalry to meet the first onset and
retard the march, while he himself recalled the legions
from their work and formed his line. Before the legions
could be fully marshaled the cavalry engaged and
routed all the king's reinforcements, who had been
marching in disorder and without apprehension. Their
cavalry got to the city almost intact by hurrying along
the shore, but their infantry suffered heavy losses.

27. The following night two Marsian centurions with
twenty-two of their men deserted from Curio's camp to
Attius Varus, and assured him that Curio's army was disaffected and that he must by all means show himself to
the army and afford them an opportunity to talk. It may
be that they believed what they said, or it may be they
said what he would wish to hear—we are very ready to
believe what we wish, and expect others to think as we
think. The report moved Varus to lead his legions out of

camp the following morning. Curio did the same, and the lines faced each other across a small valley.

28. Serving in Varus' army was Sextus Quintilius Varus; he had been at Corfinium, as was related above, and when Caesar released him, had gone to Africa. The legions Curio brought over were those Caesar had earlier recovered at Corfinium; except for a few centurions the organization of the personnel was unchanged. Quintilius took advantage of this circumstance to speak to the soldiers up and down Curio's line and beg them not to forget their original oath of allegiance to Domitius and to himself as quaestor, not to bear arms against comrades who had suffered with them in the siege, and not to fight for those who had insulted them as deserters. He added promises of the bounty they might expect if they followed him and Attius. Curio's army showed no reaction to this speech, and each general led his army back.

29. But in Curio's camp everyone was disquieted, and ordinary gossip quickly aggravated their apprehensions. Individuals imagined things and added some of their own fear to what they heard from others. One man's apprehensions filtered down to several, and as man repeated it to man the thing seemed to have many vouchers . . . [*The text of the lines following is too imperfect to admit of translation.*]

30. In view of this situation Curio convoked a council to deliberate on what course was best. Some were of the opinion that an all-out attempt should be made to storm Varus' camp. They argued that the morale of the soldiers being what it was, inaction was the worst course; it was in any case better to try the fortune of war by fighting bravely, they said, than to be deserted and overreached

by their own comrades and be subjected to severe penalties. Others were of the opinion that they should withdraw to Castra Cornelia near midnight; this would give
the soldiers time to come to their senses, and if a crisis
should occur the naval facilities would afford a safer and
easier retreat to Sicily.

31. Curio disapproved of both proposals, on the
grounds that one was as rash as the other was timid, for
one contemplated cowardly flight and the other would
give battle even on unfavorable ground. "On what as-
surance can we be confident of storming a camp so
strongly fortified by nature and art," he asked, "or what
good will it do us if we retire from the assault with
heavy losses? It is success that wins an army's devotion,
and failure its hatred. What else does a change of camp
signify but cowardly flight, general despair, and the
alienation of the army? The dutiful soldiers ought not
be made to suspect that they are not trusted, or the mu-
tinous to know that they are feared, for a show of fear
will increase the willfulness of the latter as it diminishes
the zeal of the former. If we had full corroboration of
the alleged alienation of the army—I myself am sure
that the reports are false or at least greatly exaggerated
—how much better it is to dissemble and cover the reports than ourselves to confirm them! Should not an
army's reverses, like a body's wounds, be concealed from
the enemy, so as not to heighten his morale? The added
proposal of starting at midnight is only calculated to give
the malefactors greater license. The restraining factors
of shame and fear are minimized by night's darkness.
Hence I am neither so rash as to propose a hopeless
assault in the camp, nor yet so timid as to despair. I believe we should first try every other means, and am con-

fident that together we shall reach an advantageous decision."

32. When the council was adjourned Curio convoked a meeting of the soldiers. He reminded them of their zeal in Caesar's cause at Corfinium: their example had served to make a great part of Italy Caesar's. "It was you and your action," said he, "that all the municipalities followed, and it was not without reason that Caesar's judgment of you was so friendly and the Pompeians' so severe. It was your decision, and not a defeat in battle, that determined Pompey to quit Italy. It was to your loyalty that Caesar entrusted me, his very dear friend, and the province of Sicily and Africa, which are essential to the safety of Italy and the capital. There are some who urge you to defect from us: what dearer wish could they have than at one stroke to overreach us and involve you in treason? What worse fortune could they wish for you than that you should betray the side which acknowledges an enormous indebtedness to you and come into the power of the side which attributes its disasters to you? Have you not heard what Caesar accomplished in Spain, how he routed two armies, defeated two generals, recovered two provinces, and all within forty days of sighting the enemy? Can those who could not withstand him with their strength intact withstand him when it has been ruined? When victory was still uncertain you followed Caesar; now that the issue of the war has been determined, shall you follow the vanquished when you ought to be collecting the rewards of your good services? They say that you deserted them and speak of the earlier oath: did you desert Lucius Domitius or did Domitius desert you? Did he not abandon you when you were ready to endure fortune's worst? Did he not

slink away to seek his own safety? And when he betrayed you, was it not Caesar's kindness that preserved you? How could a man hold you to an oath when he had thrown his fasces aside, laid his command down and become a civilian, and passed, a captive, into another's authority? A strange notion of obligation that would require you to ignore the oath by which you are bound and respect that which was canceled by the surrender and degradation of the general! But perhaps, if you approve of Caesar, it is I whom you balk at. I shall not boast of my services to you; as yet they fall short of my wishes and your expectations. But it is upon the outcome of a war that soldiers seek the rewards of their toil, and what the outcome will be none of you can doubt. My efficiency and luck, as far as we have gone, I may speak of. Can you find fault with my bringing the army over safe and sound without the loss of a single ship, with my having routed the enemy fleet on my very arrival, with my having won two cavalry battles in two days, with my having abstracted 200 loaded ships from inside the enemy's harbor, thereby cutting him off from supplies by land and sea? Will you reject this consistently successful leadership and commit yourselves to the debacle of Corfinium, the flight from Italy, the surrender of Spain, the odds of the African campaign? For myself I was content to be called Caesar's soldier; you have given me the title Imperator. If you regret your gift I return it to you; do you give me back my old name, and let it not appear that you conferred an honor only to insult me."

33. The soldiers were deeply affected by this speech and interrupted frequently to show how distressed they were that their loyalty was suspect. As Curio left the meeting all urged him to take heart and never hesitate

to try their loyalty and their courage in battle. Now the general mood and temper was changed, and all supported Curio's resolution to join battle at the first opportunity. The next day he deployed his soldiers in battle formation in the position he had taken during the previous days. Varus promptly led his troops out also, to seize any opportunity that might offer either for propaganda or for a fight on equal terms.

34. Between the two lines there was a valley, as has been pointed out, not very large but sheer and difficult to climb. Each side waited to see whether the enemy forces would attempt to cross and thus gain the advantage of position. On the left the whole of Varus' cavalry with light-armed troops interspersed was observed descending into the valley. Against them Curio sent his cavalry and two cohorts of Marrucini. The enemy horse broke at their first charge and scampered back to their own lines full tilt, leaving behind the light-armed foot who had advanced with them; these our men surrounded and killed. Varus' whole line faced the spectacle of their men fleeing and being cut down. At this point Rebilus, a legate of Caesar's whom Curio had brought with him from Sicily because of his extensive military experience, said, "Curio, you see the enemy in panic: why hesitate to exploit the opportunity?" All that Curio said to the soldiers was to remember their promises of the day before; then he ordered them to follow, and himself charged at their head. So difficult was the valley that the front-line men could clamber up only with those behind boosting them, but Varus' soldiers were so demoralized by the rout and slaughter of their comrades that they made no effort to resist. They thought they were already being surrounded by our cavalry, and before a missile could be discharged or our men could come any nearer

Varus' whole line turned tail and betook themselves to
their camp.

35. A Pelignian of the lowest rating named Fabius
was the first to catch up with the column of fugitives in
this rout, and kept shouting for Varus by name, to make
it seem that he was one of Varus' men and had some
advice or suggestion to offer. Hearing his name repeatedly called, Varus saw the man and stopped to ask
him who he was and what he wanted, whereupon Fabius struck Varus' unprotected shoulder with his sword
and came near killing him; Varus met the danger by
raising his shield to the blow. Fabius was surrounded
and killed by the nearest soldiers.

The disorderly throng of fugitives crowded the gates
of the camp and blocked the road, and more perished
at that point without a wound than had died in the battle or flight. It wanted but little for them to be driven
out of their camp, and some headed straight for the town
without stopping. But the terrain and entrenchment of
the camp prevented access, and when Curio's soldiers
had marched out to battle they did not bring the equipment required to assault a camp. And so Curio returned
to his camp with Fabius his only casualty; about 600
of the enemy were killed and a thousand wounded. On
Curio's withdrawal all of these and many others who
feigned wounds retreated from the camp into the town
in terror. Observing this and realizing that his army was
in panic, Varus left a trumpeter and a few tents for appearance's sake and silently led his army into the city
soon after midnight.

36. On the next day Curio determined to besiege the
city and surround it with earthworks. The populace of
Utica had no experience of war because there had long
been peace; the Uticans were friendly to Caesar because

of certain benefits he had conferred upon them, and the Roman corporation consisted of various classes. The earlier battles had caused great alarm, and there was general and open talk of surrender. People pleaded with Varus not to allow his stubbornness to bring disaster to all. While the question was still under discussion messengers sent forward by King Juba arrived to say that Juba would soon bring large forces to their support and to urge them to guard the city and defend it. These tidings restored their morale.

37. The same intelligence reached Curio also, but so confident was he of success that for a time he could not believe it. Dispatches had brought word of Caesar's victory in Spain, and in his elation he could not imagine that the king would try measures against him. But when he was reliably informed that Juba was less than twenty-five miles from Utica he abandoned his earthworks and retired to Castra Cornelia. Here he began to gather grain, entrench a camp, and assemble timber, and immediately sent to Sicily for two legions and the remainder of his cavalry. His situation was ideal for protracted war: terrain and entrenchment made the camp strong, the sea was near and there was ample water and salt (there was a stock pile from nearby saltworks on hand), and the abundance of trees and of field crops guaranteed against shortage of timber or grain. With the unanimous agreement of his staff, therefore, Curio prepared to wage defensive war while awaiting the rest of his forces.

38. When this resolution had been duly approved, Curio heard from certain deserters from Utica that Juba had been recalled by a quarrel with the people of Leptis and had stayed behind to fight in his kingdom, and that it was his lieutenant Saburra who had been sent ahead, with only moderate forces, and was now approaching

Utica. Rashly believing these informants, Curio changed his plans and resolved upon a pitched battle. His youth, his gallantry, his earlier success, his confidence of victory contributed largely to this decision. Prompted by such incentives he sent all his cavalry at nightfall to the enemy camp at the river Bagrada. Saburra, of whom he had heard, was indeed in command, but the king with all his forces was close behind and had halted six miles from Saburra. The cavalry reached their objective at night and surprised the enemy off their guard. The Numidians had bivouacked at random, after a barbarian fashion, with no regular order. A large number of them were killed, while they were heavy with sleep, and many fled in panic. Their mission accomplished, the cavalry returned to Curio, bringing captives with them.

39. Curio had marched out about three A.M. in full force, leaving five cohorts to guard the camp. When he had gone six miles he met the returning cavalry and learned of their success. He asked the prisoners who was in command of the camp at the Bagrada, and was told Saburra. In his eagerness to complete his march he neglected to interrogate them further but turned to the nearest standards and said: "Do you see, men? The prisoners' story agrees with the captives'. The king is not there; he has sent a small force, which cannot stand up to a few horsemen. On with a will to plunder and glory; we have now to think of rewarding and thanking you." The achievement of the cavalry was indeed notable, especially in view of their small number as compared with the great Numidian host. But they had exaggerated their story in their telling of it, as men are apt to do in describing their own prowess. Furthermore, they had booty to display and men and horses to bring forward, so that any lapse of time seemed only a postponement of victory. The soldiers' eagerness, then, matched Curio's high hopes.

He ordered the cavalry to fall in and quickened his pace with the intention of attacking while the enemy was still demoralized by their flight. But the cavalry were weary with a whole night's marching and could not keep up, and one after another fell behind. Not even this dampened Curio's expectations.

40. When Juba heard of the night engagement from Saburra he sent to his support 2,000 Spanish and Gallic cavalry which he habitually kept as a bodyguard, the part of his infantry on which he most relied; he himself followed with the remainder of his forces, including sixty elephants. Saburra suspected that Curio himself would follow the cavalry he had sent ahead; he drew up his forces, foot and horse, and ordered them to give ground as if frightened and retreat step by step, promising that he himself would give the signal for battle at the proper time and issue such other directions as in his judgment the situation required. Curio's earlier hopes were strengthened by the present impression that the enemy was in retreat, and so he led his forces down from higher ground to the plain.

41. When he had advanced a considerable distance and his army was tired out by twelve miles of marching, he halted. Saburra gave the signal, marshaled his line, and began to circulate among the ranks to encourage them. But his infantry he used only for show, at a distance; it was his cavalry he sent into action. Curio did not falter but urged his men to set all their hopes on courage. Nor were fighting spirit and valor wanting in the infantry, weary though they were, nor in the cavalry, exhausted as they were and few in number; there were, indeed, only 200, the rest having fallen out on the march. Wherever they charged they forced the enemy to give ground, but they could not press pursuit or drive their mounts too hard. But the enemy cavalry

began to surround our line on both flanks and to wear them down from the rear. When our cohorts charged forward from their line the fresh Numidians nimbly avoided their onset and then regrouped to surround our men and cut them off from their line. To stand and keep rank or to charge and be exposed was equally unsafe. The enemy was constantly reinforced by new units sent by the king, and our men were steadily weakened; the wounded could not leave the line or be carried to safety because the whole army was hemmed in by the enemy cavalry. Despairing of survival they lamented their own death, as men are wont to do in the last moments of life, or commended their parents to any whom fortune might preserve from the disaster. Terror and grief were everywhere.

42. When Curio realized that his terror-struck men were not accessible to exhortation or prayers he saw that their sole hope in the calamity was for the whole army to occupy the nearest hills, and ordered the standards to move in that direction. But here too Saburra's cavalry anticipated them. Then indeed did our men plumb the depths of despair; some were cut down by the cavalry as they fled, some collapsed without a wound. Cnaeus Domitius, his cavalry commander, urged Curio to flee for safety with the few horsemen with which he surrounded him and to push on to the camp, promising that he would never leave his side. But Curio declared that he would never return to face Caesar after losing the army entrusted to him, and so died fighting. A handful of the cavalry got safe out of the battle; those who had halted at the rear of the column to refresh their mounts, as has been noted above, observed the rout of the army from a distance and got safely back to camp. The infantry were killed to a man.

43. On hearing the news the quaestor Marcus Rufus, who had been left in charge of the camp by Curio, urged his men not to lose heart. They begged and besought him to take them back to Sicily by sea; he promised to do so, and ordered the skippers to have their launches on the beach early in the evening. But in the great and widespread panic some said that Juba's forces were close by, others that Varus was ready to pounce with his legions and that the dust was already visible (none of this was true), and others suspected that the enemy fleet would fly to the attack. With panic universal, every man looked out for himself. Those in the fleet hastened their departure, and their flight goaded the captains of the transports; only a few small craft met their obligation and awaited orders. But on the swarming beach the competition to get aboard was so great that some of the boats sank under their excessive weight of passengers, and this frightened the others from approaching too near.

44. The result was that a few soldiers and heads of families who could use influence or arouse pity or had the strength to swim to the ships got back safe to Sicily. The remainder made the centurions their emissaries to Varus that night and surrendered to him. When, on the following day, Juba saw the men of these cohorts before the town, he claimed them as his booty; the larger part he executed, some he selected to be sent back to his kingdom. Varus protested that his parole was being violated, but did not venture to resist. Juba himself rode into Utica attended by a number of senators, among whom were Servius Sulpicius and Licinius Damasippus. He gave brief orders on what he wanted done, and after a few days withdrew to his own kingdom with all his forces.

III 49-48 B.C.

1. As dictator Caesar presided over the elections, in
which himself and Publius Servilius were made consuls;
it was the year in which Caesar could legally hold the
office. This done, since credit was constricted throughout
Italy and debts were being left unpaid, Caesar decided
that assessors be appointed to evaluate real and personal
property at pre-war standards and that creditors should
be paid at these rates. This he considered the best measure for removing or diminishing the creditors' fear of a
moratorium (which frequently follows upon war or civil
conflict) and at the same time for preserving the standing of the debtors. Likewise he restored to their rights,
upon motions introduced by the praetors and the tribunes of the people, persons who had been condemned
on charges of bribery when Pompey had troops quartered in the city; their trials had been finished in a single
day, with one set of judges hearing the cases and another
passing sentence. Since these persons had offered their
services to Caesar at the beginning of the civil conflict
if he should wish to avail himself of them in his operation, he regarded their making themselves available as
tantamount to actual service. He resolved that the res-
toration should be effected by the decision of the people
rather than by an apparent act of grace on his own part,
for he did not wish to seem either ungrateful in repaying

a kindness nor arrogant in usurping the people's privilege to confer favors.

2. On these measures, the celebration of the Latin festival, and the supervision of elections, he spent eleven days; then he resigned from the dictatorship and left Rome for Brindisi, where he had ordered twelve legions and all his cavalry to assemble. But he found shipping only barely sufficient to transport 15,000 legionaries and 600 cavalry; this one factor prevented a speedy conclusion to the war. Even the forces embarked were below full strength; many had been exhausted in the numerous Gallic campaigns, the long march from Spain had reduced their numbers further, and after the salubrious climate of Gaul and Spain the unwholesome autumn in Apulia and round Brindisi had affected the health of the whole army.

3. Pompey had gained a whole year free of war and of hostile operations to muster his forces. He had assembled a great fleet from Asia and the Cyclades, from Corfu, Athens, Pontus, Bithynia, Syria, Cilicia, Phoenicia, and Egypt, and had contracted for massive shipbuilding at many centers. He had requisitioned large sums from Asia and Syria and from the kings, potentates, and tetrarchs and the free peoples of Achaea; and he had compelled the tax-farming corporations under his control to make large contributions.

4. He had formed nine legions of Roman citizens: five that he brought over from Italy; one of veterans from Cilicia (this was made up of what had been two, and he named it the Twin Legion); one from Crete and Macedonia, consisting of veterans discharged by former commanders who had settled in those provinces; and two from Asia, which Lentulus had recruited as consul. Among these legions, moreover, he distributed a large

number of supplementary troops from Thessaly, Boeotia, Achaea, and Epirus, and with these he mixed men who had served under Antonius. Besides these legions, he expected two from Syria under Scipio. He had 3,000 archers from Crete, Lacedaemon, Pontus, Syria, and other states; two cohorts of slingers of 600 men each; and 7,000 cavalry. Of these Deiotarus had brought 600 from Gaul, and Ariobarzanes 500 from Cappadocia; Cotys had sent the same number from Thrace with his son Sadala; and there were 200 from Macedonia under Rhascypolis, an outstanding soldier. Pompey's son transported 500 Gauls and Germans from the army which Aulus Gabinius had left in Alexandria as a garrison for King Ptolemy. Pompey had enrolled 800 of his own slaves and shepherds. Tarcondarius Castor and Domnilaus contributed 300; one of these came with his contingent, the other sent his son. From Syria, Antiochus of Commagene sent 200, among them many mounted archers; Pompey rewarded him generously. He further procured Dardani and Bessi, partly for hire and partly through conscription and influence, and added to them men of Macedonia, Thessaly, and other tribes and states to make up the number cited above.

5. Grain he obtained in large quantities from Thessaly, Asia, Egypt, Crete, Cyrene, and other regions. He resolved to winter at Durazzo, Apollonia, and all the maritime towns in order to prevent Caesar from crossing the Adriatic, and to the same end he posted his fleet along the whole coast. The Egyptian flotilla was commanded by Pompey's son, the Asiatic by Decimus Laelius and Gaius Triarius, the Syrian by Gaius Cassius, the Rhodian by Gaius Marcellus along with Gaius Coponius, the Liburnian and Achaean by Scribonius Libo and Marcus Octavius. The chief command of naval op-

erations was entrusted to Marcus Bibulus; he adminis-
tered the whole and held supreme authority.

6. Upon arriving at Brindisi Caesar addressed his
troops and asked them, since they were nearing the end
of their toils and danger, to leave their slaves and baggage in Italy without misgivings and board ship with
light equipment to leave room for more men; victory
and Caesar's generosity would ensure their reimburse-
ment. The men shouted for him to give whatever orders
he liked: they would carry them out with confidence.
On 4 January he weighed anchor, with seven legions, as
has been stated, on board, and on the day following he
made land. Between the Ceraunian Rocks and other
dangerous points he found a quiet roadstead, and because he was afraid that all the harbors were in the
hands of the enemy, he disembarked at the place called
Palaeste, without damage to a single ship.

7. Lucretius Vespillo and Minucius Rufus had eighteen Asiatic ships at Oricum, where they had been
posted by Decimus Laelius, and Marcus Bibulus had
110 at Corfu. But though Caesar had only twelve galleys
(four of them decked) to convoy his transports, Vespillo
and Rufus dared not leave harbor, and Bibulus was too
slow. His ships were disorganized and his rowers dispersed, because Caesar was sighted near the mainland
before any rumor of his approach had reached that area.

8. When the soldiers were disembarked Caesar sent
the ships back to Brindisi that same night, to be in position to transport the remaining legions and the cavalry.
The legate Fufius Calenus was put in charge of this operation, with orders to use all speed. But the ships sailed
too late to catch the night breeze and got into trouble on
the return voyage. Bibulus at Corfu had been informed
of Caesar's arrival and hoped to encounter some of his

ships loaded; but they were empty, and he vented upon
them the fury of his negligence and regret. The thirty
ships he found he set afire, burning crews and captains
with their vessels, in the hope that such terrible punishment would deter the rest. This done, Bibulus occupied
every roadstead along the whole extent of the shore,
from Saseno to Veglia, with his fleets; he himself dili-
gently attended to posting the stations, passing his nights
aboard in bitter winter and shirking no task or exertion
nor waiting for support if only he could get within reach
of Caesar [*text imperfect*].

9. On the departure of the Liburnian flotilla from
Illyricum, Marcus Octavius brought the ships he had to
Salonae. There he agitated the Dalmatian and other
native tribes and subverted Vis from its ties with Caesar.
The corporation of Salonae he could sway neither by
promises nor threats, and so decided to besiege the town.
Its situation on a hill protected the town, and the Roman citizens quickly constructed wooden towers for
their defense. When the effectiveness of their resistance
was reduced by reason of their numerous casualties, they
resorted to the extreme measures of liberating their adult
slaves and cutting their women's hair off to make catapults. Aware of their determination, Octavius surrounded the town with five camps and began to subject
it to the pressure of siege and assault simultaneously.
The townsfolk were ready to endure any trial; their acut-
est difficulty was shortage of food. To relieve this they
sent emissaries to Caesar to ask his assistance; their other
inconveniences, they said, they would survive through
their own resources. When, after a long interval, the duration of the siege had made the Octavians careless, the
people of Salonae took advantage of the enemy's dis-
persal at the noon hour, placed their boys and women

on the wall to make the appearance of normal activity complete, and themselves formed into a band with the newly liberated slaves, and overran the nearest of Octavius' camps. With the same dash they attacked the second, after they secured the first, and then the third and fourth and last. When they had driven them all from their camps and killed a large number they forced the remainder, including Octavius himself, to fly to their ships. This was the outcome of the siege. Now winter was approaching; his heavy losses made Octavius despair of taking Salonae, and so he betook himself to Pompey at Durazzo.

10. We have shown that Pompey's prefect Lucius Vibullius Rufus had twice fallen into Caesar's power and been released by him, once at Corfinium, and again in Spain. In view of these benefits conferred upon Rufus, Caesar judged him a suitable emissary to carry a dispatch to Pompey, whose good opinion Caesar knew Rufus enjoyed. The substance of the dispatch was as follows: Each party should call a halt to his obstinacy, lay down his arms, and no longer tempt fortune. The losses each had suffered were a sufficient lesson to fear further disasters: Pompey had been driven from Italy and had lost Sicily, Sardinia, and both Spains, and 130 cohorts of Roman citizens in Italy and Spain; Caesar's losses included the death of Curio, the destruction of a large army in Africa, and the capitulation of Antonius' men at Veglia. In view of such demonstrations of what the fortunes of war might bring they should show consideration to themselves and the state. This was precisely the time to discuss peace, when each leader was confident and both seemed on a par; if fortune favored one contestant even a little his apparent superiority would not suffer him to consent to terms or to be satis-

fied with an equal share when he was sure he could win all. Since agreement had so far proved impossible, conditions should be sought at Rome from the senate and people. Meanwhile the state and the two parties should be content if each would publicly swear an oath that he would disband his army within the next three days. If both would lay down the arms which made them bold, they must perforce be content with the decision of the senate and the people. To make it easier for Pompey to consent Caesar said he would disband all his land forces [*text imperfect*].

11. It was at Corfu that Rufus received this message; the step he considered most essential was to inform Pompey of Caesar's arrival so that he could make plans accordingly before the question of the message should be broached. And so he pushed on to apprise Pompey of Caesar's presence, traveling night and day, with change of horses at every town. At the moment Pompey was in Candavia, on his way to winter quarters in Apollonia and Durazzo. The upsetting news spurred Pompey to make for Apollonia by longer stages, for fear Caesar might occupy the cities of the seacoast. But Caesar set out for Oricum the same day he disembarked his troops. Upon his arrival Pompey's commander Lucius Torquatus, who was holding Oricum with a garrison of Parthini, closed the gates and attempted to defend the town. He ordered the Greeks to mount the walls and take arms, but they declared they would not fight against the authority of the Roman people, and the townsfolk on their own initiative attempted to receive Caesar. Despairing of support Torquatus opened the gates and surrendered himself and the town to Caesar, who gave him protection.

12. With Oricum in his power Caesar set out for Apollonia, without delay. Hearing of his approach Lucius Staberius, who was in command, began to stock the citadel with water, fortify it, and draft hostages. But the Apolloniates refused to deliver any and said they would not shut their gates against a consul or take a decision contrary to that of Italy and the Roman people. When he realized their determination Staberius stole out of Apollonia. The populace sent emissaries to Caesar and received him within their town. Their example was followed by Byllis, Amantia, and the other neighboring cities and all of Epirus; they all sent emissaries to Caesar and promised to do his bidding.

13. When Pompey heard what had transpired at Oricum and Apollonia he feared for Durazzo and marched day and night to reach it. At the same time there was a report that Caesar was approaching, and so great a panic struck Pompey's army, which had been marching continuously without respite, that almost all the men from Epirus and the adjacent regions deserted their standards; many threw their weapons away, and the march looked like a rout. The army was still in panic when Pompey halted near Durazzo and ordered a camp measured out; at this point Labienus came forward and swore that he would never desert Pompey but share whatever fate fortune would bestow. The other legates took the same oath, then followed the tribunes and the centurions, and finally the whole army swore the oath. Caesar stopped his rapid advance when the road to Durazzo was occupied and pitched camp near the river Apsus in the territory of the Apolloniates, to afford protection to the state which deserved well of him. He decided to winter under canvas and await the arrival of

his remaining legions from Italy. Pompey followed suit; his camp he pitched on the other side of the Apsus, and brought all his forces and auxiliaries there.

14. Pursuant to Caesar's orders Calenus embarked the legions and cavalry at Brindisi, to the extent that his shipping sufficed, and weighed anchor. He had gone but a little way when he received a dispatch from Caesar informing him that all harbors and the entire seacoast were occupied by enemy fleets. Upon this intelligence Calenus returned to port and recalled all ships. One disregarded Calenus' order because it carried no soldiers and was under private management; this vessel was carried to Oricum, where Bibulus seized it and executed every last man on it, slave or free, including boys. Thus the safety of the whole army hung upon the momentous chance of a few seconds.

15. Bibulus, it has been mentioned above, was with his fleet near Oricum, and just as he was keeping Caesar from the sea and harbors so he was himself being kept from the mainland in that area. Caesar had occupied the whole coast by posting detachments at strategic points, and there was no opening for Bibulus to procure wood or water or moor his vessels to the shore. So difficult was his situation and so pressing his shortages of all necessaries that he was forced to fetch not only food but wood and water from Corfu by merchant transport. Once when the weather was foul they were compelled to catch the night's dew from the skins with which the ships were covered. But they bore these hardships calmly and patiently and were determined not to leave the shore undefended or abandon the harbors. While Bibulus was in such straits he was joined by Libo, and both men from shipboard hailed Caesar's legates Marcus Acilius and Statius Murcus; one was in command of the

town walls, the other of the land detachments. The Pompeians said they wished to discuss weighty matters with Caesar if they were given an opportunity to do so. A few remarks they added strengthened the impression that they would discuss terms. In the meanwhile they asked for a truce, and this was granted. The proposal seemed significant, and Caesar's officers knew that he was very eager for such a development; apparently Rufus' mission was producing results.

16. At this point Caesar had set out with one legion to receive the submission of the remoter communities and expedite the grain supply, which was short. At Buthrotum, a town opposite Corfu, dispatches from Acilius and Murcus advised him of the request of Libo and Bibulus. He left the legion and returned to Oricum, where he invited the Pompeian leaders to a conference. Libo came forward and made excuses for Bibulus: Bibulus was a passionate man and had been at odds with Caesar from the days of their aedileship and praetorship; he was avoiding a confrontation with Caesar for fear his hot temper might prevent highly desirable and advantageous results. His own wish was and had always been, Libo asserted, to come to terms and lay down arms, but the decision of their council had been to entrust supreme control of all questions pertaining to the war to Pompey. Yet if he knew Caesar's demands, he said, he would forward them to Pompey, who would make the final decision according to his officers' prompting. Libo asked that the truce continue, with neither side injuring the other, until word came back from Pompey. He then added a few remarks about the issues and the strength of his own forces.

17. At the time Caesar judged that these remarks called for no reply, nor do I now regard it worth while

to record them. He asked safe conduct for his envoys:
they might themselves receive or escort them. In regard
to the truce Caesar said that their strategy was to block
his shipping and reinforcements with their fleet, and his
to keep them from water and land. If they wished him
to relax his blockade, they must relax theirs also; if they
maintained theirs he would maintain his also. But even
without such relaxation negotiations could nevertheless
proceed; one factor need not block the other. Libo
neither received Caesar's envoys nor guaranteed them
safe-conduct, but referred the whole matter to Pompey.
The one point about which he was most eager and in-
sistent was the continuation of the truce. When Caesar
realized that the whole enterprise was a device to avoid
their present danger and famine and that it brought no
proposal or prospect of peace he returned to his own
plans for the war.

18. Bibulus had been kept from land for many days
and had fallen seriously ill of cold and overwork; he
could not be cured and would not leave the duty he had
undertaken, and so succumbed to his disease. After his
death the supreme command devolved upon no single
individual, but each admiral directed his own fleet separately, at his own discretion.

Vibullius Rufus chose an opportune moment, when
the excitement caused by Caesar's arrival had subsided,
to deal with Caesar's proposals, inviting Libo, Lucius
Lucceius, and Theophanes (whom Pompey regularly
consulted on his most important business) to be present.
Pompey interrupted Rufus before he had well started
and forbade him to say more. "What use of life or country," he said, "if I appear to hold them by grace of Caesar? Such an impression will be ineradicable if, after myself leaving Italy, men think I was brought back by Cae-

sar's victory." This episode Caesar learned from persons who were present; nevertheless he persisted in other attempts to negotiate a peace through conferences.

19. Between Pompey's and Caesar's camps there was only the river Apsus; the soldiers talked together frequently, and there was an understanding that no shots would be fired in the meanwhile. Caesar sent his legate Publius Vatinius to the very bank of the river to present arguments which might be conducive to peace. Repeatedly and loudly he called out: "Cannot citizens send representatives to their fellow citizens? Even fugitives in the forests of the Pyrenees, even pirates have been permitted to do so; but now the issue is to keep citizens from fighting against fellow citizens." He begged and pleaded, as a man should when his and the general safety is at stake, and was heard in silence by both sides. The reply from the other side was that Aulus Varro agreed to a conference on the day following, where they could together consider how emissaries might have safe-conduct to express their views, and a time was arranged for the discussion. At the meeting on the following day there was a great crowd from either side, and eagerness for peace was generally evident. Titus Labienus stepped forward from the crowd and began to argue and bicker with Vatinius, but said nothing at all about peace. Missiles suddenly flying from both directions interrupted his speech in the middle; Vatinius was shielded by the arms of his soldiers and was unhurt, but a number of men were wounded, including Cornelius Balbus, Marcus Plotius, Lucius Tiburtius, and several centurions and soldiers. Then Labienus cried: "Away with this talk of a settlement then; there can be no peace unless Caesar's head is brought us."

20. At Rome during this time the praetor Marcus

Caelius Rufus made himself champion of the debtors.
At the beginning of his magistracy he placed his tribunal near the chair of the city praetor Gaius Trebonius
and announced that he would support any appeal
against valuations and payments fixed by an assessor in
accordance with the arrangement Caesar had made
when he was in Rome. But Trebonius believed that at
such a time justice should be tempered with mercy, and
as a result of the fairness and humaneness of his decrees
none could be found to institute an appeal. No great
spirit may be required to plead poverty or to complain
of ruin and hard times and set forth the difficulties of
forced sales; but what brazen effrontery it is to confess
indebtedness and yet cling to one's entire possessions!
No such persons could be found; Caelius, it turned out,
was harsher than the people whom harshness would
benefit. In order not to appear to have embarked on a
shameful course to no purpose, he proceeded to pro-
mulgate a law that debts should be carried without interest for six years.

21. The consul Servilius and the other magistrates opposed this measure, whereupon finding his expectations
of arousing enthusiasm had miscarried, Caelius revoked
his first law and promulgated two others: one making a
free gift of a year's rent to house tenants, and the other
canceling debts. The crowd rushed upon Trebonius and
drove him from his tribunal; some persons were injured.
The consul Servilius reported the affair to the senate,
which voted to remove Caelius from office. Pursuant to
this vote the consul excluded Caelius from the senate,
and when he attempted to speak from the rostrum had
him removed. Stung by shame and resentment Caelius
pretended in public that he was going to Caesar, but
secretly he sent messengers to recall Milo, who had been

found guilty of the murder of Clodius; Milo had given many gladiatorial shows and still had the remnants of his troupe. The two joined forces and Caelius sent Milo to the Thurine region to agitate among the shepherds. As Caelius reached Casilinum his military standards and arms were seized at Capua and the band of gladiators, who were preparing to betray the town, were seen at Naples. His designs detected, Caelius was shut out of Capua, whose corporation declared him a public enemy and took up arms. Caelius took fright, abandoned his plan, and moved off in another direction.

22. Meanwhile Milo sent letters to the municipalities round about saying that he was acting upon the instructions of Pompey, delivered to him by Vibullius Rufus. People he thought plagued by debts he tried to win over. When he could make no headway he loosed some slaves from their barracks and began to attack Cosa in the Thurine district, where the praetor Quintus Pedius had a legion. Milo was struck by a stone from the wall and was killed. Caelius, still advertising that he was going to join Caesar, arrived at Thurii. When he tried to subvert members of that municipality and to bribe Caesar's Gallic and Spanish cavalry which had been sent to garrison the place, they killed him. This was a quick and easy ending for a movement which, in a critical juncture when the magistrates were preoccupied, had kept all Italy disturbed.

23. Libo sailed from Oricum, with the fleet of fifty ships which he commanded, to Brindisi and occupied the island which faces its harbor, thinking it better to hold the one point our shipping would necessarily have to pass than to blockade the whole coast and its harbors. Arriving unexpectedly, he came upon and burned a number of transports and terrified our men by towing

off one loaded with grain. At night he disembarked his soldiers and archers and routed our cavalry outpost. So well had he exploited his opportunity that he sent Pompey a dispatch telling him that he might beach and refit his other ships if he liked; he himself could blockade Caesar with his own fleet.

24. Antony was in Brindisi at the time. Relying on the valor of his soldiers, he covered about sixty ships' boats with wicker and screens, manned them with picked soldiers, and stationed them at several points along the shore; then he ordered two triremes, which he had had built at Brindisi, to advance to the mouth of the harbor for training exercise. Libo hoped he could intercept them when he saw them advance so boldly, and sent five quadriremes against them. When they drew near our veterans retreated to the harbor, and in their excitement the pursuers unwarily followed. At a signal Antony's boats drove against the enemy from all points and at their first charge took one of the quadriremes with its crew and marines and drove the rest to disgraceful flight. This loss was aggravated by Antony, who posted cavalry along the shore to keep them from fresh water. Driven by shortage and shame, Libo abandoned his blockade and left Brindisi.

25. Months had passed and winter was hurrying on but no ships or legions reached Caesar from Brindisi. It seemed to Caesar that several opportunities had been missed, for there had often been steady winds which they should have trusted. And as time went on the vigilance of the enemy commanders increased, as did their confidence in their blockade. In numerous chiding letters Pompey had told them that since they had not prevented Caesar's first landing they must at least block the rest of his army, and every day they expected worse

weather for sailing as the winds grew slacker. These considerations moved Caesar to write his people in Brindisi a sharp note bidding them not miss the opportunity of a suitable wind; they could steer for Apollonia or its vicinity and run aground there. These places were generally clear of sea patrols, which did not venture too far from their ports.

26. Acting with boldness and resolution, with Mark Antony and Fufius Calenus directing operations and the soldiers themselves encouraging them and refusing no danger in behalf of Caesar's safety, they weighed anchor with a south wind and the next day coasted past Apollonia. When they were sighted from the mainland, Coponius, who commanded the Rhodian fleet at Durazzo, put to sea and drew near our ships as their breeze slackened. But then the south wind freshened again and saved them. Coponius did not give up his attempt, however, but hoped that the toil and perseverance of his sailors could overcome the force of the gale; though the strong wind swept us past Durazzo he followed nevertheless. Though fortune was favoring our men, they were still fearful of an attack if the wind should drop. They made a harbor called Nymphaeum, three miles beyond Lissus, and brought their ships in; this harbor was protected from the southwest but not from the south, but they were less concerned with the weather than with danger from the enemy fleet. By incredible good luck, as soon as they entered the harbor the wind which had blown from the south for two days turned to a southwester.

27. This is an illustration of the sudden shifts of fortune. Those who had been afraid were now secure in a safe harbor, and those who were menacing our ships were now forced to be anxious for their own. By virtue

of the change the weather protected our ships and so
battered the Rhodians that every last one, sixteen
decked vessels in all, were shattered and foundered. Of
the large number of rowers and marines, part were
dashed to death on the rocks and part pulled off by our
men; these Caesar saved and sent home.

28. Two of our ships that sailed more slowly were
overtaken by night, and since they did not know where
the others had gone, dropped anchor opposite Lissus.
Otacilius Crassus, who was in command there, sent a
number of launches and lesser boats to seize them; at
the same time he parleyed with them and promised their
lives if they would surrender. One of the ships carried
220 men of the legion of new recruits, the other something under 200 of a veteran legion. This shows how a
resolute spirit begets safety. The tyros were frightened
by the swarm of ships and exhausted by the rolling and
by seasickness; they accepted the enemy's promise that
he would do them no harm and surrendered to Otacilius.
All were brought forward and cruelly butchered in his
sight despite his solemn oath. The soldiers of the veteran
legion had been equally afflicted by storm and bilge
water but were resolved not to relax their courage. The
first part of the night they spun out by arguing about
terms and pretending to surrender, then they forced the
skipper to run the ship aground and found a good spot
to spend the rest of the night. At early dawn Otacilius
sent against them some 400 horse who patrolled that
part of the shore, and these were followed by other
armed men from the garrison. The veterans defended
themselves, killed some of their assailants, and made
their way safe to our forces.

29. Thereupon the corporation of Roman citizens
which held Lissus (Caesar had assigned them the town

in the past and seen to its fortification) opened their gates to Antony and helped him in every way. Otacilius feared for his safety; he fled the town and made his way to Pompey. Antony disembarked all his forces, consisting of three legions of veterans, one of recruits, and 800 cavalry, and sent most of his ships back to Italy to bring over the remaining soldiers and cavalry. The boats of the Gallic design called pontoons he left at Lissus, his purpose being that if Pompey should cross back to Italy in the thought that it was undefended (there was a widespread rumor that such was his intention) Caesar might have facilities for following him. Antony promptly sent messengers to inform Caesar what forces he had brought over and where he had disembarked them.

30. This intelligence reached Pompey almost as soon as Caesar. They had themselves seen the convoys as they coasted past Apollonia and Durazzo and had marched by land in the same direction, but for the first few days they did not know where they had made land. When Antony's whereabouts were known each adopted a different plan, Caesar to join Antony as soon as possible, and Pompey to meet his opponents on the march and surprise them from ambush if possible. Each led his army out from his permanent camp on the Apsus on the same day, Pompey surreptitiously at night, Caesar openly by day. But Caesar had to make a long detour upstream to reach a ford; Pompey had no river to cross and could move quickly. He pushed on towards Antony by forced marches, found a suitable spot to post his forces when he learned Antony was approaching, and kept them within the camp and forbade them to light fires to keep his presence concealed. But some Greeks promptly informed Antony, who sent word to Caesar and kept his men in camp for a day. On the next day

Caesar joined him. When Pompey learned of Caesar's arrival he quitted the place, to avoid being caught between two armies, and moved in full force to Asparagium near Durazzo and there pitched camp in a suitable place.

31. During this period Scipio, having suffered sundry defeats near Mt. Amanus, styled himself Imperator and proceeded to requisition large sums from states and principalities, and at the same time exacted from the tax-farmers of his provinces the arrears for two years and an advance for the year following. He also requisitioned cavalry from the whole province. When he had collected his forces he led legions and cavalry out of Syria—leaving behind him on the frontier of Syria the hostile Parthians who a short while before had killed the Roman general Marcus Crassus and had kept Marcus Bibulus under siege. The province was greatly alarmed by the threat of a Parthian war, and there was murmuring among the soldiers to the effect that they were ready to march against an enemy but would not bear arms against a fellow citizen and a consul. But Scipio took the legions to Pergamum, quartered them for the winter in luxurious cities, gave them huge bonuses, and to improve their morale allowed them to plunder the native states.

32. Meanwhile the moneys requisitioned were being ruthlessly exacted throughout the province. Avarice devised novel kinds of imposts. A poll tax was imposed on slaves and children, and taxes were collected on columns, doors, grain, soldiers, weapons, rowers, artillery, carts: anything for which a name could be found was deemed appropriate for collecting taxes on. Officials with military authority were placed not only over cities but

over hamlets and individual castles, and those who acted with the greatest sternness and cruelty were looked upon as the best men and the best patriots. The province was filled with catchpolls and commissioners, crowded with inspectors and bailiffs, and besides the exactions authorized all of them were busily lining their own pockets. To cloak their disgusting behavior with an honest title, they kept saying that they had been driven from home and country and were completely destitute. The situation was aggravated by exorbitant interest rates, a familiar phenomenon in war when capital is levied; a mere extension was referred to as a donation. In that two-year period, consequently, the indebtedness of the province increased manifold. Nevertheless the Roman citizens in the province were forced to pay through separate corporations and communities, on the pretext that these were loans exacted in accordance with a decree of the senate. As was done in Syria, the tax-farmers were forced to advance the proceeds of the year following.

33. At Ephesus, moreover, Scipio ordered that the ancient deposits in the temple of Diana be removed. On a day appointed he came to the shrine attended by several persons of senatorial rank whom he had invited, but was handed a dispatch from Pompey informing him that Caesar had crossed the Adriatic with his legions and directing him to drop other business and hurry to join him with his army. On receipt of this dispatch he dismissed his suite and prepared to leave for Macedonia. In a few days he started, and this was the salvation of the treasury of Ephesus.

34. After Caesar joined his army with Antony's he withdrew the legion he had posted at Oricum to guard the seacoast, with a view to proceeding inland to win the

provinces over. Envoys arriving from Thessaly and Aetolia promised that those peoples would do his bidding if he sent garrisons to protect them. Caesar sent Lucius Cassius Longinus to Thessaly with a legion of recruits (called the Twenty-seventh) and 200 cavalry, and Gaius Calvisius Sabinus to Aetolia with five cohorts and a few horsemen. Since these regions were near by he gave particular instructions to arrange for food supplies from them. Cnaeus Domitius Calvinus with two legions, the Eleventh and Twelfth, and 500 cavalry was ordered to proceed to Macedonia. Menedemus, the principal personage in the part of Macedonia called Free, came as an envoy to give assurances of the complete loyalty of his people.

35. Of these officers Calvisius was enthusiastically welcomed by the Aetolians; he expelled the enemy garrisons from Calydon and Lepanto and gained control of all Aetolia. Cassius, who brought his legion to Thessaly, met with good will or the reverse according as the communities favored one or the other of two factions; Hegesaretus, a man of long-established power, favored the Pompeian cause, while Petraeus, a young man of the highest nobility, staunchly supported Caesar with his own and his followers' resources.

36. At the same time, Domitius had arrived in Macedonia and was receiving numerous deputations from the states when word reached him that Scipio and his legions had come. Rumor exaggerated his strength, as is natural with unexpected news. Without halting anywhere in Macedonia Scipio marched towards Domitius at full speed, and when he was within twenty miles of him suddenly wheeled towards Cassius Longinus in Thessaly. So quick was this maneuver, that news of his coming and his arrival were brought simultaneously. To

expedite his march he left his legions' baggage with eight
cohorts under Marcus Favonius to guard it at the river
Aliacmon, which divides Macedonia from Thessaly, and
ordered a stronghold built there. At the same time King
Cotys' cavalry, whose regular haunt was Thessaly,
swooped down to Cassius' camp. Cassius was terrified.
He knew Scipio was approaching and thought the cavalry he saw was Scipio's, and so turned to the mountains
which encircle Thessaly and chose Ambracia as his objective. Scipio hurried in pursuit but was overtaken by
a dispatch from Favonius informing him that Domitius
with his legions was close by and that he could not hold
his assigned position without Scipio's help. Upon this
intelligence Scipio changed his plan and his route; he
gave up his pursuit of Cassius and hurried to relieve
Favonius. By marching without pause day and night he
arrived so opportunely that the dust of the Domitian
army and the outriders of Scipio's were sighted simultaneously. Thus Domitius' promptness saved Cassius,
and Scipio's speed Favonius.

37. For two days Scipio remained in the permanent
camp at the Aliacmon, which flowed between it and
Domitius' camp. On the third day he forded his army
across at dawn and pitched camp, and on the following
morning marshaled his forces in front of this camp.
Domitius thought it advisable to bring his legions out
promptly and fight a pitched battle. Between the two
camps there was a plain of some two miles; Domitius
brought his line right up to Scipio's camp, but Scipio
persisted in clinging to his rampart. Domitius' soldiers
were hard to restrain; the factor which mainly prevented
a battle was a stream just under Scipio's camp whose
steep banks blocked the advance of our men. When
Scipio realized how enthusiastic our men were and how

keen for a fight he foresaw that on the next day he
would either have to fight against his will or suffer the
disgrace of keeping to his camp. He had come with high
hopes, but his rash advance had an ignominious sequel;
without even giving the signal for breaking up camp he
crossed the river at night, returned to the spot whence
he had come, and pitched camp on a natural elevation
near the river. A few nights later he posted a cavalry
ambush where our men had regularly been foraging for
several days, and when, following the routine, Quintus
Varus, Domitius' cavalry commander, came up, the am-
bushers rose to attack. But our men withstood their assault bravely, quickly fell into their ranks, and seized
the initiative in a counterattack. They killed about
eighty and routed the rest, and then returned to camp
with the loss of two men.

38. After these operations Domitius pretended that
shortage of grain was forcing him to move camp, in the
hope that Scipio could be enticed to fight. He gave the
usual military signal for breaking camp and advanced
three miles to a suitably concealed spot where he posted
his whole army and cavalry. Scipio prepared to pursue
and sent a good part of his cavalry ahead to explore
Domitius' route and determine his position. When they
had advanced so far that the first squadrons were within
the ambuscade, the neighing of our horses made them
suspicious and they began to retire to their main body,
and those behind them halted when they saw their hasty
withdrawal. With the ambush discovered it was futile
for our men to wait for the main body; they caught and
cut off two squadrons, among whom was the cavalry
commander Marcus Opimius. The rest they killed or
took prisoner and brought to Domitius.

39. When Caesar withdrew the patrols from the sea-coast, as shown above, he left three cohorts at Oricum to protect the town, and assigned them the custody of the warships which he had brought from Italy. In charge of this duty and of the town was the legate Acilius Caninus. He brought the warships into the inner harbor behind the town, moored them to the shore, sank a merchantman to block the channel to the harbor, near it anchored another upon which he built a tower to face the harbor's entry, and manned it with soldiers for the event of sudden emergencies.

40. The younger Cnaeus Pompey, who was in command of the Egyptian fleet, learned of these arrangements and sailed to Oricum. The sunken ship he hoisted up with a winch and numerous ropes, and the other, which Acilius had stationed as a guard, he attacked with a number of boats fitted with towers. These were built to a height calculated to give his men the advantage, and he constantly relieved the weary with relays of fresh men. At the same time he divided his adversaries' strength by attacking the town walls in several places, on land with scaling ladders and by sea with his fleet. His energy and the masses of his missiles overwhelmed our men, and when he had dislodged its defenders (all of whom escaped in boats) he took the guard ship. At the same time he seized the natural breakwater on the other side of the harbor, which almost made an island of the town, put four triremes on rollers, and pried them across into the inner harbor with crowbars. This enabled him to attack the empty warships moored to land from either side; he towed four off and burned the rest. This accomplished, he left Decimus Laelius, detached from the Asiatic fleet, to prevent supplies from Byllis and

Amantia from being imported into the town. He himself proceeded to Lissus, attacked thirty transports left inside the harbor by Antony, and burned them all. He attempted to storm Lissus itself, but the Roman citizens of the corporation and the soldiers Caesar had sent to garrison the place defended it, and so after wasting three days and losing a few men in the assault he departed without achieving his purpose.

41. When Caesar learned that Pompey was at Asparagium he set out for that place with his army. On the march he stormed the stronghold of the Parthini, where Pompey had posted a garrison, and on the third day came up with Pompey and pitched camp nearby. On the following day he led his troops out and formed them in line to offer battle, but when he saw that Pompey would not leave his position Caesar marched his army back to camp and resolved to adopt a different plan. On the next day, accordingly, he set out with all his forces by a circuitous, difficult, and narrow road for Durazzo, hoping that Pompey could either be shut into Durazzo or kept out of it, for he had stored all his stocks of provisions and supplies in the town. So it turned out. At first Pompey was unaware of Caesar's intentions, for the road he saw him take went in a different direction and he thought that shortages of food had forced him to leave. Then, upon his scouts' intelligence, he shifted his camp the next day, hoping he could confront Caesar by taking a shorter route. This is what Caesar foresaw he would do; he urged his soldiers to be patient in their exertions and took only a small part of the night for rest, and in the morning arrived at Durazzo. As soon as he saw Pompey's column in the distance he pitched camp.

42. Pompey was cut off from Durazzo, and since he had failed of his objective he adopted the next best

plan and entrenched a camp on an elevation called Petra, which had a serviceable anchorage for ships and sheltered them from certain winds. He ordered part of his war fleet to concentrate there and made it the depot for food and supplies from Asia and the other regions under his control. Caesar thought the war would be long drawn out and could hope for no supplies from Italy because the Pompeians were keeping vigilant watch over the whole coast; moreover his own fleet, which he had had built during the winter in Sicily, Gaul, and Italy, was slow in coming. He therefore sent Quintus Tillius and the legate Lucius Canuleius into Epirus to procure provisions, and because the distance was great he established granaries at certain points and assigned the neighboring states the duty of carting the grain. He also ordered a search for whatever grain might be found at Lissus, among the Parthini, and in the various strongholds. The amount was very slight, not only because the region is naturally unproductive, being rough and mountainous and itself dependent upon imported grain, but also because Pompey had foreseen Caesar's step and during the days preceding had treated the Parthini as legitimate spoils, had ransacked and dug the floors of their houses up in the search for grain, and had used his cavalry to carry it off.

43. When he learned of this Caesar adopted a plan suggested by the terrain. Around Pompey's camp were many high and rugged hills; these he first occupied with detachments and built redoubts upon them. Then he proceeded to invest Pompey by drawing a line of fortifications from one redoubt to the next as the nature of the ground required. His objectives were the following: his own provisions were scant and Pompey had a great advantage in cavalry, which enabled him to supply his

army with grain and stores from all directions with little danger; then, if he could keep Pompey from foraging he would render his cavalry useless for service; and thirdly, he would diminish the prestige among foreign nations upon which Pompey seemed to rely if the rumor should be broadcast throughout the world that Pompey was invested by Caesar and dared not fight a pitched battle.

44. Pompey was unwilling to quit the sea and Durazzo because he had deposited all his matériel there —weapons, armor, artillery—and because the food supply for his army depended on shipping. But neither could he prevent Caesar's works except by fighting a pitched battle, and this he decided he could not then do. The only course left was the strategy of crisis: occupy as many hills as possible and keep the widest possible stretch garrisoned and so split Caesar's forces up as much as possible. This is what he did. He built twenty-four redoubts in a circuit of fifteen miles; in this protected area he foraged, and the field crops in many segments of it were sufficient to feed his animals in the intervals. By a continuous line of fortifications our men took care that the Pompeians should not break through at any point and take us in the rear, and in the same way their men made a continuous line in a smaller circle to prevent our men from entering at any point and taking them in the rear. But they beat us at the job because they had more men and the interior circuit was smaller. Though Pompey had determined not to fight a pitched battle in full force he did send his archers and slingers, of whom he had a great number, to harass Caesar's men whenever they had to occupy a position, and many were wounded. Our men were in terror of the arrows, and almost all of them made tunics or padding of felt or quilting or hides as protection against missiles.

45. Every new position was contested with the utmost energy, Caesar endeavoring to confine Pompey within the narrowest limits, and Pompey to take the largest number of hills in the widest possible circuit, and in consequence there were many skirmishes. Once when Caesar's Ninth Legion had occupied a certain hill and had begun to fortify it, Pompey occupied a neighboring hill facing it and began to keep our men from their work. On one side the position had an almost level approach. First Pompey threw archers and slingers around the hill, then sent in a mass of light-armed men and brought up his artillery. Our fortifications were being impeded, for it was not easy for the men to work and defend themselves at the same time. When Caesar saw that his men were being wounded from all sides he ordered them to retire and yield the position. Their path was downhill, but the enemy pressed on and blocked our withdrawal because it seemed that it was fear which made us abandon the position. It was at this juncture that Pompey is said to have boasted to his friends that he would not mind being thought a worthless commander if Caesar's legions got back without disastrous casualties from an advance which it was rash for them to make.

46. Concerned for the recovery of his men, Caesar ordered screens brought up to the edge of the hill facing the enemy, and while the men were thus shielded, a ditch of moderate width dug and obstacles planted all about. He posted slingers at strategic points to protect our men in their retreat. With these preparations made he ordered the legion to withdraw. Thereupon the Pompeians began to press and thrust upon our men with greater insolence and audacity, and threw down the screens set up as a defense to make their way across the trench. On observing this Caesar feared that his men would seem

not to have withdrawn but to have been thrown back and thus suffer greater hurt. Through Antony, who commanded the legion, he encouraged the men, who were about halfway down the hill, and ordered a trumpet call and a charge against the enemy. The soldiers of the Ninth with a single spirit hurled their pikes and charged uphill from the lower level at the double quick and drove the Pompeians headlong and made them turn tail. Their retreat was much impeded by the overturned screens and the stakes planted as obstacles and the excavated trenches. Our men were content to leave without loss; when they had killed many of the enemy and lost only five of their own they retired quietly and occupied and fortified other hills this side of that position.

47. The large number of forts and the extent of the circuit they covered, the scope of the contravallation, the system of blockade, and other factors made this a novel and unprecedented type of warfare. Normally a blockade is attempted only against a demoralized and weakened enemy which has been defeated in battle or disconcerted by other reverses, and only when the blockader has superior numbers of foot and horse; and the usual object of a blockade is to keep the enemy from provisions. But here Caesar with inferior numbers was containing fresh and untouched forces who were abundantly supplied; every day large convoys of shipping brought provisions in from every direction, nor could any breeze blow but that it favored sailing from some quarter. But Caesar had exhausted the grain over a large area and suffered serious shortages. But his soldiers showed extraordinary patience; they recalled that they had suffered similarly in Spain the year before but had won an important war by their patience and endurance;

they remembered they had endured critical shortages at Alesia and virtual starvation at Bourges, and had come off victors over those powerful peoples. They did not refuse barley when it was offered them, or beans, and they held meat, of which there was a good supply from Epirus, in high esteem.

48. Some who were not on the working shift found a kind of root called *chara* which grew plentifully. Out of this, mixed with milk, they made a kind of bread which greatly relieved their need. When the Pompeians, talking to our men, taunted them as starvelings, our men tossed loaves of this kind over to lessen their hopes.

49. Now the grain began to ripen; the men were sure they would soon have plenty, and this hope sustained them in their need. At their posts and in conversations the soldiers could be heard saying that they would rather live off the bark of trees than let Pompey slip from their hands. They were cheered too by news from deserters that the Pompeians were keeping only their cavalry horses; the rest of their livestock had perished. Also their men's health was affected, not only by the crowding and the foul odor of numerous carcasses and the daily labor to which they were unaccustomed, but also by a serious shortage of water. All the rivers and brooks which flowed down to the sea Caesar had diverted or blocked with extensive works. The country is mountainous and rugged, and Caesar kept the water in narrow valleys by sinking piers in the ground and piling earth about them to make a dam. Necessarily, then, the Pompeians had to keep to the low and swampy ground and dig wells, which aggravated their labors. These wells were at a considerable distance from some of the redoubts, and dried out quickly in the heat. But Caesar's army enjoyed excellent health and an ample supply of

water. They had plenty of provisions of every kind except grain, and could themselves see that harvest was approaching and expectations nearing realization.

50. In this new kind of warfare each side devised new methods of fighting. When the Pompeians observed from our watchfires that our cohorts were bivouacking by their earthworks they crept up in a body, shot their arrows into the mass of men, and then hastily retired to their own side. Experience taught our men a remedy for this tactic; they lighted fires in one place . . . [*There is a considerable break in the manuscript at this point. Parallel accounts indicate that the portion missing described an unsuccessful attack on Durazzo by Caesar, and an attack on Caesar's line by Pompey. The text resumes with the conclusion of this second episode.*]

51. Publius Sulla (whom Caesar had put in charge of the camp at his departure) was informed of the cohort's predicament and came to its assistance with two legions; at his arrival the Pompeians were easily repulsed. They could not withstand the sight or the dash of our men, and when their front ranks broke the rest turned and ran. But when our men started to pursue Sulla recalled them to prevent their advancing too far. Many think that if he had chosen to press his advantage the war might have been finished that day. But his decision must not be criticized. A deputy's role is different from a commander's; he must administer his charge according to instructions, whereas the commander makes decisions of the highest moment on no authority but his own. Sulla had been left in charge by Caesar and was content with liberating his men; he did not choose to fight a pitched battle (whose outcome was in any case uncertain) because he would not give the impression that he had usurped the commander's role.

Their situation made it difficult for the Pompeians to extricate themselves. They had advanced from low ground to an elevated position, and they were afraid of our men pressing on them from above if they should retire downhill; nor was there much daylight left, for in hopes of finishing the business off they had continued in action till almost dark. Pompey was forced to extemporize; his tactic was to seize a hill far enough from our fort to be out of range of our artillery. This ground he occupied in full force and proceeded to entrench.

52. At the same time battles were going on in two other places, for Pompey launched attacks on several redoubts in order to divide our strength and prevent nearby garrisons from sending relief. In one place Volcatius Tullus with three cohorts sustained the attack of a legion and drove it off, in another Germans advanced from our works, killed a few men, and returned safe.

53. In one day, then, six battles were fought, three at Durazzo and three at the earthworks. When an accounting was made we found that about 2,000 of the Pompeians had fallen, including many veterans and centurions (one was Valerius Flaccus, son of the Lucius who had governed Asia as praetor), and that six of their military standards had been brought in. We lost not more than twenty men in all the battles; but in the redoubt every single man was wounded and four centurions of one cohort had lost their eyes. Wishing to produce evidence of their exertion and danger they counted out to Caesar some 30,000 arrows which had been shot into the redoubt, and when the shield of the centurion Scaeva was brought forward 120 holes were found in it. In recognition of his services to himself and the state (it was clear that Scaeva was largely responsible for saving the redoubt) Caesar presented him with 200,000 sesterces,

read a citation for him, and promoted him from the eighth rank to senior centurion. Later Caesar rewarded the cohort generously with double pay, grain, clothing, rations, and military decorations.

54. During the night Pompey strengthened his defenses and on the following days erected towers; he raised his rampart to a height of fifteen feet and shielded the front of his camp with screens. On a cloudy night five days later he barricaded all the gates of the camp, planted obstacles to hinder pursuit, led his army out about midnight, and returned to his former entrenchments.

55. Every day thereafter Caesar marshaled his army and brought the legions forward on the level ground almost to Pompey's camp, in case Pompey should be willing to fight a battle; his front line was so near Pompey's rampart as to be just out of artillery range. To maintain his credit and reputation Pompey also marshaled his line, but so near the camp that his third line touched the rampart and the whole army could be protected by missiles hurled from the rampart.

56. As we have shown above, Aetolia, Acarnania, and Amphilochia had been secured by Cassius Longinus and Calvisius Sabinus; Caesar now thought that a further advance with an attempt upon Achaea was indicated. He therefore dispatched Calenus to that sector and associated with him Sabinus and Cassius with a number of cohorts. When this advance was made known to Rutilius Lupus, who was Pompey's commander in Achaea, he determined to barricade the Isthmus to bar Calenus from Achaea. Calenus secured Delphi, Thebes, and Orchomenus with their own consent and took some cities by storm. Other states he endeavored to win over to

friendship with Caesar through embassies. These projects kept Calenus occupied.

57. While these events were in progress in Achaea and at Durazzo it became known that Scipio had arrived in Macedonia. Consistent with the principle he had long established Caesar sent Scipio their mutual friend Aulus Clodius. It was Scipio who had introduced Clodius to Caesar, and Caesar counted him among his intimate friends. The substance of the letters and instructions which Caesar entrusted to Clodius was this: He had made every effort to obtain peace; his failure he attributed to the fault of the intermediaries he chose, who were afraid of carrying his proposals to Pompey at an inopportune time. Scipio's prestige was such that he could not only give free expression to proposals that he favored but could even put some degree of pressure upon Pompey and guide him when he went astray. Moreover he was in command of an army in his own right and so had power as well as prestige to win compliance. If he did so, he alone would receive mankind's gratitude for the tranquillity of Italy, peace in the provinces, security in the empire. Clodius delivered this message, and during the first few days, apparently, received a friendly hearing; but later he was not admitted to conference, and returned to Caesar with no results. After the war was finished we discovered that Scipio's change of attitude was due to Favonius upbraiding him.

58. In order to contain the Pompeian cavalry at Durazzo and prevent them from foraging, Caesar fortified the two approaches (we have stated above that they were very narrow) with extensive works and strong forts. When Pompey discovered that his cavalry could accomplish nothing he returned them to his own entrenchments by sea after a few days. Shortage of fodder

was so extreme that they fed their horses on leaves
stripped from trees and pounded roots of reeds—the
grain planted within the entrenchments they had used
up. They were forced to import fodder from Corfu and
Acarnania, which meant a long voyage, and because
the supply was inadequate, to supplement it with barley.
By such means they kept their horses alive, but when
barley and hay and shrubs had been cut down everywhere and even the foliage of trees was gone, the horses
were emaciated and Pompey decided that he must attempt to break out somehow.

59. There were two Allobrogian brothers in Caesar's
cavalry, Raucillus and Egus, sons of Adbucillus, who
had been chief of his people for many years. They were
outstanding soldiers and had done Caesar excellent and
gallant service in all his Gallic wars. In return he had
conferred offices of great dignity upon them in their own
country, had procured their election to the local senate
though they were not fully eligible, had bestowed upon
them Gallic estates confiscated from the enemy and large
sums of money, and had raised them from poverty to
wealth. Because of their gallantry they were not only
honored by Caesar but well loved by the whole army.
But in their silly, uncivilized pride they presumed on
Caesar's friendship and despised their own people; they
embezzled the pay of the cavalry and diverted the proceeds to their own uses. The men were indignant and
approached Caesar in a body to lodge open complaint
of this abuse. In addition they charged that the culprits
had falsified the roster of the cavalry in order to appropriate the extra pay.

60. Because he did not think the moment suitable for
severe measures, and was ready to make allowances in
view of their excellent record he deferred the matter,

but reprimanded the men privately for having exploited the cavalry for profit. He reminded them that his friendship was adequate to their fullest expectations and said that his past generosity was an index of what they could hope for. But the affair earned them general indignation and contempt, which they were made sensible of not only by the reproaches of strangers but also by the attitude of their intimates and by their own conscience. Actuated by shame and by the suspicion that they had not been acquitted but only reserved for later punishment they decided to desert and try their luck with different alliances. They discussed the project with those few of their dependents to whom they dared broach such an enormity, and at first tried to murder the cavalry commander Gaius Volusenus (as was discovered after the war was finished) so that they would have some claim upon Pompey when they deserted to him. When this murder seemed too difficult and no opportunity of perpetrating it offered, they borrowed all the money they could, on the pretense that they wished to pacify their comrades and repay their peculations. Then they bought up a quantity of horses and with their accomplices went over to Pompey.

61. Because the men were of noble birth and richly accoutered and had come with a large retinue and many horses, because they had a reputation for courage and had received honors from Caesar, and because such a transfer was strange and anomalous, Pompey paraded them before all his garrisons to show them off. Before this time no one, foot or horse, had gone over from Caesar to Pompey, though men were deserting Pompey for Caesar daily; the men enrolled in Epirus and Aetolia and the regions under Caesar's control came over in a mass. But these men knew and reported all the details

of Caesar's establishment to Pompey—what part of the
fortifications was unfinished, or any other lack that an
experienced eye would notice, the time schedule, the
distance between positions, the relative vigilance of the
pickets according to the temper and devotion of the officers in charge.

62. Pompey, as was shown above, had already
decided on a sortie, and upon this full intelligence he
ordered his soldiers to make wicker coverings for their
helmets and to collect material for filling in trenches.
When these things were ready he loaded a large number
of light-armed troops and archers and all the fill into
boats and tugs at night. About midnight he brought
sixty cohorts from his largest camp and redoubts down
to that part of Caesar's earthworks which extended down
to the sea and was farthest from his camp. To this same
place he sent the boats we said were loaded with
matériel and light-armed troops and also the warships
he had at Durazzo and instructed them on what he expected of them. At that sector Caesar had posted the
quaestor Lentulus Marcellinus with the Ninth Legion;
because Lentulus was in poor health Caesar had sent
Fulvius Postumus to assist him.

63. The sector had a trench fifteen feet wide with an
earthen rampart facing the enemy ten feet high and ten
feet thick. A somewhat lower rampart, facing in the opposite direction, was 600 feet distant. Caesar had built a
twin rampart at this point so that if, as he suspected
some days earlier, our men should be hemmed in by the
fleet they might be able to fight on two fronts. But there
had not been time to finish the work; the size of the operation and the unremitting labor involved in fortifying
a circuit of seventeen miles made it impossible to complete the transverse wall which was to connect the two

ramparts. This circumstance was communicated to Pompey by the Allobrogian deserters, and worked serious injury to our men. At the sea, where two cohorts of the Ninth Legion were on guard, the Pompeians suddenly appeared at dawn, and at the same time soldiers ferried around in boats began hurling their missiles at the outer wall and leveling the trench with fill. At the inner wall Pompey's legionaries brought scaling ladders, artillery, and missiles of every description to terrify the defenders, and a host of archers swarmed around them on every side. Our only weapons were stones, and against these the wicker coverings on their helmets provided considerable protection. When our men were being thus hard pressed and scarcely holding their ground, the flaw in our fortifications mentioned above was noticed and Pompeian soldiers were landed from ships between the two ramparts where the cross wall was not finished. These attacked both ramparts from the rear, dislodged the defenders of each, and forced them to fly.

64. When the commotion was reported to Marcellinus he sent cohorts from the camp to support our men who were in trouble. But when the newcomers saw them flying they could not rally them nor themselves sustain the enemy attack. Similarly every additional reinforcement was demoralized by the terror of the men in flight and aggravated the panic and the danger. Their very numbers impeded their retreat. In that battle an eagle-bearer who was gravely wounded caught sight of our horsemen as his strength ebbed, and said: "This eagle I defended very carefully for many years while I lived, and now when I am dying I return it to Caesar untainted. Carry it to him safe. Do nothing, I beg you, that would open the way for a military blemish which has never happened before in Caesar's army." This encounter saved the eagle,

but every centurion of the first cohort was killed except the senior of the second squad.

65. And now after their great slaughter of our men the Pompeians were approaching the camp of Marcellinus. The other cohorts were in no small terror, when Mark Antony, who commanded the next position and had been informed of the situation, was seen descending from higher ground with twelve cohorts. His arrival checked the Pompeians and gave our men heart to recover from their panic. Not much later Caesar arrived on the scene with cohorts drawn from various redoubts; the message had been carried by smoke signals, according to the practice of earlier times. An inventory of losses showed that Pompey had broken through the line and was fortifying a camp near the sea, which would enable him to forage freely and retain free access for his shipping. Caesar's original purpose having failed, he changed his plan of war and ordered an entrenchment next to Pompey's.

66. When this entrenchment was completed Caesar's scouts noticed that a number of Pompey's cohorts, apparently to the strength of a legion, were moving, behind a wood, towards the disused camp. The nature of the camp was this. Some days earlier when Caesar's Ninth Legion had intercepted the Pompeian forces, as we have shown, and was surrounding them with an earthwork, it had pitched camp at that spot. The camp adjoined a wood and was not more than 300 paces from the sea. Later Caesar found reason to change his plan and moved the camp a little beyond that point; a few days later Pompey occupied the old site, and as he intended to hold several legions there he disregarded the existing rampart and built one on a larger radius. Thus

the lesser camp was contained in the larger and served
as a kind of fortress and citadel. He also drew a line of
fortification about 400 paces long from the left corner
of the camp down to the river, so that his soldiers could
fetch water without exposing themselves. But Pompey
too changed his plan, for reasons we need not recount,
and abandoned the site. And so for many days the camp
remained empty with its fortifications undamaged.

67. It was to this spot, Caesar's scouts reported, that
the standards of a legion had been brought, and they asserted that the fact had been observed from some of the
higher redoubts also. The distance from the new camp
which Pompey built was 500 paces. In his desire to repair
the day's losses Caesar hoped he could overwhelm this
legion. He left two cohorts at labor, to maintain the appearance of carrying on the work of fortification, and
himself led the remaining cohorts, thirty-three in number
(these included the Ninth Legion, which was below
strength and had lost many centurions), by a different
route and as secretly as possible, in a double line towards
Pompey's legion and the lesser camp. His calculations
proved correct. He arrived at his objective before Pompey was aware of it, and though the camp was strongly
fortified, a quick attack on the left wing, where Caesar
himself was in command, dislodged the Pompeians from
the rampart. At the gates, which were barricaded with
studded beams, there was a short fight when our men
tried to crash in and the Pompeians put up a defense;
their champion was Titus Pulio, whose energy, as we
have pointed out, was responsible for the betrayal of
Gaius Antonius' army. Nevertheless our men won through
by their gallantry; they smashed through the barricade
and rushed first into the larger camp and then into the

fortress included within it. Here the defeated legion had
retreated, and some were still resisting; these our men
killed.

68. But fortune which is powerful generally is especially so in war; it produces revolutionary reversals,
as then happened, from insignificant beginnings. We
have pointed out that a fortification extended from the
camp down to the river; this the soldiers of Caesar's right
wing in their ignorance of the layout followed when
they were looking for the gate, for they thought it was
a side of the camp. When they found that the fortification connected with the river, they threw it down, none
opposing them, and crossed over, and the whole cavalry
followed these cohorts.

69. Meanwhile time had elapsed and Pompey had
been informed. He withdrew five legions from their work
and led them to the relief of his men; at the same time
his cavalry was drawing near ours and an advancing
battle line was sighted by our men who had occupied
the camp. The situation was suddenly transformed. The
Pompeian legion was heartened by the prospect of
speedy reinforcement; they resisted at the decuman gate
and even took the offensive against our men. Caesar's
cavalry was mounting over the earthworks on a narrow
track; they were afraid their retreat would be cut off
and were the first to fly. Upon the panic of the cavalry
the right wing (which was separated from the left) was
apprehensive of being caught inside the fortification and
retreated where it had thrown the fortification down; to
avoid the crush at the narrow opening many of these
men jumped from the ten-foot rampart into the trench,
and when these were trampled the others tried to make
their way through to safety over their bodies. On the left
wing, when our soldiers at the rampart saw Pompey ap-

proaching and their own comrades in flight, they were afraid of being caught in a narrow space with the enemy outside and inside, and they decided to retreat the way they had come. All was confusion, panic, flight, to such a degree that when Caesar laid hold of the standards of the men in flight and ordered them to halt, some coursed on at a gallop and others even let go the standards for fear. Not a one halted.

70. What saved the whole army from being destroyed in this great disaster was, I presume, Pompey's fear of an ambush; a little while before he had seen his men flying from the camp, and what had happened was completely unexpected. For a while he did not venture to approach the fortification, and the narrowness of the passage and the fact that it was occupied by Caesar's soldiers retarded pursuit by his cavalry. For either side an important result proceeded from a slight circumstance: the fortification leading from the camp to the river interrupted Caesar's victory, which was virtually achieved when the camp was stormed, and by delaying the dash of the pursuers that same fortification afforded our men safety.

71. In the day's two battles Caesar lost 960 soldiers, some well-known Roman equestrians—Tuticanus, a Gaul and the son of a senator; Gaius Fleginas of Piacenza, Aulus Granius of Puteoli; Marcus Sacrativir of Capua —and thirty-two military tribunes and centurions. Many of these were trampled in the trenches and fortifications and river banks in the panic and flight of their comrades and perished without a wound; thirty-two standards were lost. In this battle Pompey was hailed Imperator. He kept the title and was addressed by it thereafter, but did not regularly use it in dispatches and did not adorn his fasces with laurel. Upon Labienus' request Pompey

turned the prisoners over to him; to enhance his own credit, apparently, the turncoat paraded them, addressed them as messmates, asked them in most insulting language whether it was usual for veterans to run away, and then executed them in public view.

72. These events so increased the Pompeians' confidence and spirit that they took no thought for strategy but believed their victory was complete. They did not consider our numerical inferiority, the unfavorable position and lack of room when they had seized the camp, the simultaneous panic inside and outside the entrenchment, the splitting of our army into two parts—which was the occasion of their victory. They did not consider, further, that there was no sharp clash, no regular battle, and that our men had inflicted greater damage upon themselves by their crowding in a small space than they had received by enemy action. And finally, they did not reflect on the common chances of war where such trifling causes as groundless suspicion or sudden panic or superstitious scruples frequently produce great disasters, or when a general's mismanagement or a tribune's mistake is a stumbling block to an army. But by word of mouth and dispatches they proclaimed that day's victory throughout the world as if they had won it by prowess and as if the situation could undergo no change.

73. Dislodged from his earlier strategy, Caesar decided that a total change of plan was called for. He withdrew his garrisons simultaneously, abandoned the siege, concentrated the army in one spot, and harangued the soldiers. He urged them not to brood over what had happened nor to be dismayed at the situation: they had many successful battles to set against this one slight reverse. They had fortune to thank for having taken Italy without loss, for having subdued the two Spains with

their warlike peoples and experienced and expert generals, for having brought the neighboring grain-producing provinces under their control; and finally they must remember the good luck which enabled them to cross the Adriatic safely in the midst of enemy fleets which filled not only the harbors but also the coastline. If the throw was not always lucky, fortune must be bolstered by energy. For the reverse which had been sustained, he was the least chargeable of all. He had provided a favorable field for the fight, had won possession of the enemy camp, had driven them from their position, had beaten them in fight. Whether it was their nervousness or some mistake or even fortune that had blocked a victory already won and scored up, they must all make every effort to mend their reverse by their courage. If they would do this it would follow that their loss would be turned to gain, as had happened at Gergovia, and that those who had been afraid to fight would themselves volunteer to fight.

74. After this harangue Caesar publicly disgraced and demoted a number of standard-bearers. The army as a whole was so filled with remorse for their defeat and determination to repair their disgrace that no one looked to tribune or centurion for orders but each imposed even heavier labors upon himself by way of expiation. All were so keen on fighting that some of the higher officers calculated that it was advisable to remain on the spot and commit the issue to battle. But Caesar did not have the requisite confidence in troops which had been in panic and thought an interval should be allowed for recovering morale. In the absence of entrenchments, moreover, he was apprehensive about his food supply.

75. With no delay, then, except for attention to the sick and wounded, at nightfall Caesar silently sent all

the baggage ahead to Apollonia, with orders not to
rest till the journey was finished; one legion was sent
along for protection. When this had been arranged he
retained two legions in camp and about 3 A.M. sent the
remainder, out of several gates, on the same route. Then
after a short interval, to observe military usage and at
the same time delay advertising his departure as much
as possible, he ordered "Strike Camp" to be sounded and
marched out at once; he followed the rear column and
was quickly out of sight of the camp. Nor did Pompey
allow any delay in pursuing when he discovered Caesar's plan, but in the hope of overtaking our men on the
march while they were hampered and frightened, he led
his army out of camp and sent his cavalry ahead to slow
the rear of our column down. But Caesar had a head
start and was carrying no baggage, and they were unable to overtake him. They did overtake and engage
the rear guard when they arrived at the river Genusus,
which had difficult banks. Caesar countered Pompey's
cavalry with his own horse interspersed with 400 light-
armed shock troops: these were so effective that they
routed the whole enemy force in a cavalry skirmish,
killed many, and returned safe to their own column.

76. Upon completing his march for that day and taking his army across the Genusus, Caesar settled in his old
camp facing Asparagium. He kept his soldiers within
the rampart and ordered the cavalry, which had been
sent out to forage, to return promptly by the rear gate.
Pompey likewise settled in his old camp at Asparagium
when he completed the day's march. Because the entrenchments were intact and the soldiers therefore not
bound to a task, some went to a considerable distance to
fetch wood and fodder, and others, tempted by the
nearness of the last camp, left their arms in their quar-

ters and went back to recover baggage and packs which they had left behind when the decision to march was so hurriedly taken. When pursuit was thus impeded, as Caesar foresaw it would be, he gave the signal for departure about noon and led his army forward, and on that day advanced eight miles, twice the distance covered the day before. Pompey could not do the same because his men were dispersed.

77. Caesar's procedure on the next day was the same. At nightfall he sent his baggage ahead, and himself marched out about 3 A.M., so that if any need to fight should arise he could meet a sudden emergency with an unencumbered army. On the succeeding days he followed the same plan, and so was able to negotiate deep rivers and difficult roads without incurring loss. After the delay of the first day Pompey exerted himself greatly on the succeeding days with forced marches in his desire to overtake the men ahead of him, but in vain; on the fourth day he gave up the chase and decided to adopt some different plan.

78. Caesar had to go to Apollonia to billet his wounded, pay his army, secure his allies, and post garrisons in the cities. But to this business he devoted as little time as a man in a hurry could; it was most urgent that he join Domitius with all speed, for Domitius might be taken unaware by Pompey. His grand strategy was formulated with the following contingencies in view: If Pompey should follow Caesar's movements he would be drawn away from the sea, separated from his depots at Durazzo, and compelled to fight on equal terms; if Pompey should cross over to Italy Caesar would join with Domitius and march to Italy's assistance through Illyricum; if Pompey should attempt to storm Apollonia and Oricum and shut Caesar off from the whole coast, Cae-

sar would besiege Scipio and so compel Pompey to come
to his relief. And so Caesar sent messengers to Domitius
with written instructions for what he wanted done, left
four cohorts to garrison Apollonia, one Lissus, and three
Oricum, billeted the weak and wounded, and began his
march through Epirus and Athamania. Pompey con-
jectured Caesar's intentions and determined to push on
to Scipio; if Caesar should march against Scipio he
would support Scipio, but if Caesar should prove unwilling to leave Oricum and the seacoast because he
was expecting legions and cavalry from Italy, then Pompey would attack Domitius in full force.

79. For these reasons each of the generals was bent
on speed, to help his own people and not lose an opportunity to crush his adversary. But Apollonia had
drawn Caesar away from the direct route, whereas Pompey had an easy road to Macedonia through Candavia.
Another and unforeseen difficulty arose from the fact
that Domitius had, for reasons of commissariat, removed
his camp from near Scipio's, where he had kept it for
several days and had marched towards Monastir, which
is in reach of Candavia. Fortune herself seemed to have
put him in Pompey's way. But of this Caesar as yet knew
nothing. Immediately after the battle at Durazzo Pompey had sent dispatches to all the provinces and states
which enlarged upon and exaggerated that event, and
the rumor had spread that Caesar had been beaten and
was in flight and that almost all his forces were lost.
These made the roads dangerous, and turned a number
of states from attachment to Caesar. Consequently messengers sent by various routes from Caesar to Domitius
and from Domitius to Caesar could find no means of
reaching their destination. But Allobrogian associates of
Raucillus and Egus (we have told how these men de-

serted to Pompey) fell in with Domitius' scouts on the
road, and, whether because of their old familiarity as
fellow soldiers in the Gallic wars or because they loved
to boast, they gave Domitius' men a full account of what
had happened and explained that Caesar was on his
way to Macedonia and Pompey already there. With this
information, supplied by the enemy, Domitius, who had
barely four hours' start, avoided his danger and joined
with Caesar on his way to Aeginium, a town facing Thessaly.

80. With his united army Caesar arrived at Gomphi,
the first town in Thessaly on the way from Epirus. A
few months before, this people had voluntarily sent emissaries to Caesar, offering him the use of their resources
and asking him for a military garrison. But the rumor of
the battle at Durazzo, of which we have spoken above,
multiplied manifold, had preceded Caesar. Androsthenes,
governor of Thessaly, preferred to be associated with
Pompey in victory than with Caesar in defeat. He gathered all the populace, slave and free, from the fields into
the city, shut the gates, and sent messengers to Scipio
and Pompey to ask them to bring help. He could rely
on the town's fortifications, he said, if he received
prompt assistance, but could not support a long siege.
Scipio had brought his legions to Larissa when he heard
of the withdrawal of the armies from Durazzo, and
Pompey had not yet reached Thessaly. Caesar entrenched a camp and ordered scaling ladders, sheds,
and hurdles to be readied for a sudden assault. When
preparations were complete he exhorted his soldiers and
explained how useful the acquisition of a rich and well-
stocked city would be for supplying all their requirements, how effectively other states could be overawed
by making an example of Gomphi, and how this must

be done quickly, before reinforcements could arrive.
The extraordinary zeal of the soldiers enabled him to attack a city with very high walls at about four o'clock of
the day of reaching it and to take it before sunset. He
gave it to the soldiers to plunder, moved camp from the
city immediately, and reached Metropolis before messengers or rumor could bring word of the fall of Gomphi.

81. Actuated by the same rumors the Metropolitans
followed the same plan of closing their gates and filling
their walls with armed men. But Caesar had the captives from Gomphi brought up to the wall, and when
the Metropolitans learned the fate of Gomphi they
opened their gates. Caesar took care to protect the Metropolitans, and when their lot was compared with the
catastrophe of Gomphi there was no city of Thessaly
(except Larissa, which Scipio was holding with large
armies) that did not yield to Caesar and do his bidding.
Caesar found a suitable place in the countryside, where
crops were nearly ripe, and decided to await the arrival
of Pompey and concentrate his operations there.

82. A few days later Pompey arrived in Thessaly. In
a harangue to the whole army he thanked his own men
and exhorted Scipio's willingly to share the victory and
its plunder and prizes. All the legions were sheltered in
a single camp; Pompey shared his honors with Scipio—
he ordered a trumpeter for him and a pavilion to serve
as his headquarters. When Pompey's forces were thus
augmented by the union of two large armies the earlier
confidence of the soldiers was restored and their expectation of victory strengthened, so much so indeed that the
passing hours seemed only to postpone their return to
Italy. Whenever Pompey acted with hesitation or deliberation they declared that the business could be dispatched in a single day but that Pompey was luxuriating

in his authority and in treating men of consular and praetorian rank as menials. Already there were open disputes about priesthoods and magistracies, and they apportioned the consulship for years to come. Some put in claims for the houses and property of the men in Caesar's camp. There was a great debate in their council as to whether Lucilius Hirrus should be allowed to stand for the praetorship *in absentia* at the next elections. He had been sent to Parthia by Pompey, and his friends begged Pompey to keep the promise made to Hirrus when he left, so that it should not appear that Hirrus had been cheated through Pompey's position. Others objected to giving one man an advantage when all had shared the toil and danger.

83. In their daily bickering over Caesar's priesthood Domitius, Scipio, and Lentulus Spinther publicly stooped to abusive language. Lentulus made a show of his age, Domitius boasted of his popularity and reputation in the city, and Scipio relied on his kinship with Pompey. Acutius Rufus accused Lucius Afranius to Pompey of betraying an army, a crime he declared Afranius had committed in Spain. Lucius Domitius proposed in the council that everyone of senatorial rank who had been with them during the campaign should be given three judicial ballots for voting on individuals who had remained at Rome or had been in Pompey's occupied towns without doing military service: one for acquittal from all punishment, one for capital punishment, and the third for a monetary fine. In a word, everyone was busy with his own ambitions or monetary rewards or personal revenge, but took no thought of how they could gain the victory or how they should use it.

84. Caesar's commissary was assured, his troops had regained strength, and sufficient time had elapsed after

the battles at Durazzo to lend confidence in their morale, and Caesar decided to ascertain Pompey's intentions and temper in respect to fighting. Accordingly he led his men from the camp and deployed them in battle formation, at first on their own ground, at some distance from Pompey's camp, but on succeeding days progressively farther from his own camp and nearer the hills held by Pompey. This procedure increased his men's confidence daily. In respect to the cavalry he retained the practice described above, that is, since his cavalry was only a fraction of Pompey's, he assigned selected young shock troops, lightly armed to promote their nimbleness, to fight interspersed among the cavalry; daily practice gave them expertness in this mode of fighting. The result was that at need a thousand of our cavalry would venture, even in an open field, to withstand the charge of 7,000 Pompeians without being unduly frightened by their numbers. During the days of preparation he fought a successful cavalry engagement in which, among others, one of the two Allobrogians whose desertion to Pompey has been described above was killed.

85. Pompey kept drawing his line up on the lowest spurs of the hills on which he had his camp, apparently in the expectation that Caesar might put himself in an unfavorable position. Judging that there was no way to draw Pompey into battle Caesar decided that his best strategy would be to shift his camp and keep on the move; shifting to various localities would make the grain supply easier, might afford an opportunity of fighting on the march, and would wear down Pompey's army, which was not used to the fatigue of daily marches. This decision had been reached, the signal for departure given, and the tents had been struck when it was observed that Pompey's line had just advanced beyond its

customary distance from the rampart, so that it seemed we could fight in a not unfavorable position. When his column was already at the gate Caesar said to his men: "We must postpone our march for the present and think of fighting: this is what we have wanted. Let us be stout-hearted in the fight; we shall not easily find another opportunity." He led his forces out, stripped for battle, at once.

86. Pompey too, as was afterwards discovered, had decided, with the unanimous encouragement of his people, to give battle. He had even declared in council, during the days preceding, that Caesar's army would be thrown back even before the lines met. When some showed surprise he said: "I know that what I promise is nearly incredible, but listen to the tactic I have planned, and you will go into battle with stouter spirit. I have persuaded our cavalry (and they assure me they will do the thing) to attack Caesar's right wing on its unprotected flank as soon as the lines draw near and then take his line from the rear; they will confound and rout the enemy army before we fire a shot. We shall finish the war without imperiling the legions and almost without suffering a wound. The thing is not difficult, for we are very strong in cavalry." He bade them keep stout hearts for the morrow; they would have the opportunity to fight that they had repeatedly begged, and must not disappoint his and the others' expectations.

87. Labienus followed him, expressing contempt for Caesar's forces and praising Pompey's strategy in extravagant terms. Said he: "Do not imagine, Pompey, that this is the army which conquered Gaul and Germany. I was present at every battle and do not make rash pronouncements on a subject I do not know. Only a slight fraction of that army has survived; a great part in·

evitably perished in the numerous battles in Gaul, many were carried off by the pestilential autumn of Italy, many were discharged, and many were left behind on the mainland. You must have heard that the cohorts at Brindisi were made up of men who stayed behind because they were diseased. The forces before you have been brought up to their strength from recent levies in Hither Gaul; most are from the colonies across the Po. Even so, the flower of this army, such as it was, perished in the two battles at Durazzo." After this speech he swore he would never return to camp except as a conqueror and urged the others to do likewise. Pompey applauded and took the oath, and everyone else promptly followed suit. After these proceedings the council broke up, with everyone happy and hopeful. In their imagination they already anticipated victory, for it seemed impossible that so experienced a general would make empty promises on so important an issue.

88. The formation of Pompey's line, as Caesar observed when he came near Pompey's camp, was as follows: On the left wing were the two legions, called First and Third, which Caesar had handed over, in accordance with a decree of the senate, at the beginning of the hostility. Pompey himself was on the left. The center was held by Scipio with the Syrian legions. On the right was posted the Cilician legion together with the Spanish cohorts brought over, as we have explained, by Afranius. These legions Pompey regarded as his strongest; the others he posted between the center and either wing. He had 110 full cohorts, amounting to 45,000 men, about 2,000 of them veterans who had joined Pompey because of distinctions he had awarded them in previous armies; these latter he distributed along the whole line. The seven remaining cohorts he

assigned to garrison the camp and nearby strongholds. His right wing was protected by a river with steep banks, and hence he used all his cavalry, archers, and slingers to cover his left wing.

89. Caesar retained his regular practice of posting the Tenth Legion on the right wing and the Ninth on the left. The latter had been greatly weakened by the battles at Durazzo, and so he joined the Eighth to it to make virtually one legion out of two, instructing each to support the other. Caesar's line consisted of eighty cohorts, comprising 22,000 men; seven cohorts were left to garrison the camp. He placed Antony in command of the left, Publius Sulla of the right, and Cnaeus Domitius of the center. Caesar himself took a position opposite Pompey. In view of the dispositions detailed above Caesar feared that his right wing might be flanked by a preponderance of cavalry and so quickly withdrew one cohort from each legion of the third line and with them formed a fourth line to oppose the cavalry. He explained what he wished done and reminded them that the day's victory depended on the gallantry of these cohorts. At the same time he issued orders to the third line and the whole army not to engage without his specific order; he would himself give a flag signal when he wished them to engage.

90. In the exhortation to battle delivered to the soldiers according to military usage Caesar spoke of his constant concern for their welfare and particularly mentioned his great efforts to secure peace, as all the soldiers could testify. He spoke of his negotiations through Vatinius, of his pleading with Scipio through Aulus Clodius, of his efforts to persuade Libo at Oricum to open discussions with Pompey. He had never wished to squander soldiers' blood or to deprive the state of either

army. After this speech the men showed their ardor and clamored for action, and Caesar gave the order with a trumpet blast.

91. In Caesar's army there was a veteran called Gaius Crastinus, a man of outstanding courage, who had served as senior centurion of the Tenth Legion the year before. When the signal sounded this man cried: "Follow me, old comrades, and do your general the service you have always done. This is our last battle, and when it is done he will recover his dignity and we our freedom." Then he looked back to Caesar and said: "Today, general, my deeds, alive or dead, will deserve your thanks." When he had said this he led the charge from the right wing, and about 120 volunteers of the same cohort followed him.

92. Between the two armies there was only enough space for each to charge. But Pompey had instructed his men to await Caesar's attack without stirring from their position and allow his formation to be broken up. He is said to have done this on the advice of Gaius Triarius, the object being to diminish the impact of the enemy charge and loosen his formation, so that his own men held in their ranks could then attack the enemy when he was scattered. Further, missiles would strike with less force if his men kept their position than if they ran forward to meet the weapons, and moreover by charging double the distance Caesar's men would become breathless and exhausted. In our view Pompey's act seems very unwise, because in all men there is an innate excitability and drive which is kindled by the heat of the fight, and it is the function of the general not to quench but to heighten the excitement. There is sound sense in the ancient practice of sounding trumpet blasts on all sides and raising a battle cry from all throats; these things,

they thought, serve both to terrify the enemy and to heighten the ardor of one's own men.

93. Upon the signal our men charged forward with javelins at the ready but when they observed that the Pompeians were not advancing to meet them they checked their course of their own accord, as training and battle experience had taught them to do, and halted near the center of the field, not to approach the enemy with energy flagging; and after a short pause they resumed their charge, hurled their javelins, and promptly, as Caesar had instructed them, drew their swords. The Pompeians were equal to the situation. They received the volley of javelins, kept ranks under the charge of the legionaries, discharged their javelins, and took recourse to their swords. At the same time the cavalry dashed forward in a body from Pompey's left wing, according to instructions and the crowd of archers poured forth. Our cavalry did not withstand the attack but gradually gave ground, whereupon Pompey's cavalry pressed on the harder, deployed into squadrons, and began to surround our line on its open flank. When Caesar observed this he gave the signal to the fourth line which he had made up of six cohorts. These dashed forward quickly in force and attacked Pompey's horse with such violence that not one kept his ground but all turned tail and not only quitted their position but galloped off to the highest mountains in full flight. Their departure left the archers and slingers unprotected and helpless, and they were all killed. The same drive carried our cohorts against the Pompeian left, which continued resistance; they flanked the Pompeian line and attacked it from the rear.

94. At the same time Caesar ordered his third line, which had up to this moment kept inactive in its

assigned position, to charge. When fresh and vigorous
troops took the place of our men that were tired, while
others were attacking from the rear, the Pompeians could
no longer hold their ground but all turned tail. Caesar
had not been wrong in thinking, as he himself declared
in his address to the soldiers, that the victory would arise
from the cohorts of the fourth line which confronted the
cavalry. It was they who first repulsed the cavalry, they
who slaughtered the archers and slingers, they who surrounded Pompey's line on his left and started the rout.
When Pompey saw that his cavalry was driven off and
the part of his army he most relied upon in panic, he lost
confidence in the rest, left the battle line, rode off to
camp, and said to the soldiers he had posted at the
praetorian gate, in a voice loud enough for the soldiers
to overhear: "Guard the camp and defend it with care
if anything untoward happens. I shall visit the other
gates and hearten the garrisons of the camp." When he
had said this he retired to his headquarters, mistrusting
the outcome but yet waiting to see what would happen.

95. When the routed Pompeians had been driven
within their rampart Caesar thought no respite should
be given their terror and urged his soldiers to accept fortune's favor by storming the camp. The men were fatigued with the intense heat (the action had lasted till
noon), yet their spirits were ready for any exertion and
they obeyed orders. The cohorts left to garrison the camp
fought dutifully, and the Thracians and barbarian auxiliaries defended the camp with great spirit. But the soldiers who had fled from the battle were demoralized
and exhausted; most had thrown their weapons and
standards away and were more concerned to continue
running than to defend the camp. Those manning the

ramparts could not long withstand the hail of weapons;
weary and wounded they deserted their post, and with
the centurions and tribunes at their head made for the
highest mountains adjacent to the camp.

96. In Pompey's camp one could see dainty arbors,
great quantities of silver plate, tents paved with fresh
turf, and some—Lucius', Lentulus', and others'—shaded
with ivy. There were other indications of excessive luxury and confidence of victory; men so concerned for extravagant self-indulgence could have had no fears of the
day's outcome. And yet they had brought the charge of
luxury against Caesar's ill-conditioned and long-suffer-
ing army which had always been short of necessities.
When our men were moving about inside the camp Pompey procured a horse, ripped off his general's insignia,
and flung out of the rear gate, galloping straight for
Larissa. Nor did he stop there; he picked up a few fugitives and with an escort of thirty men continued, without stopping for darkness, to the seacoast, where he
boarded a grain ship. He repeatedly complained, it was
said, that his calculations had so far miscarried—the arm
he counted on for victory was the one that initiated the
rout—that it seemed almost as if he had been betrayed.

97. Once in possession of the camp Caesar begged his
soldiers not to let preoccupation with plunder lose them
the chance of finishing the remainder of the task. He
made his point and began to circumvallate the mountain.
The Pompeians distrusted their mountain because it had
no water and began to move in a body along the ridge
towards Larissa. Observing this Caesar divided his forces,
ordering some of the legions to remain in Pompey's camp,
some to return to his own camp, and four legions to follow him. He moved to intercept the Pompeians by a

shorter route, and after advancing six miles formed for
battle. Thereupon the Pompeians halted in a mountain
which had a river at its foot. Caesar heartened his troops,
and though they were tired with a whole day's continuous exertion and night was coming on, he cut the river
off from the mountain by an entrenchment to prevent
the Pompeians from watering by night. When this
work was done the Pompeians sent envoys to capitulate.
Some men of senatorial rank who had joined them made
their escape in the night.

98. At dawn Caesar ordered all those who had halted
on the mountain to descend to the plain and throw their
arms down. This they did without exception, and flung
themselves on the ground, and with tears and outstretched hands begged Caesar for their lives. He comforted them, bade them rise, and spoke to them briefly
of his leniency to lessen their fear, and then granted them
all safety and commended them to his soldiers, so that
none should be hurt or lose any of his belongings. This
precaution taken, he ordered replacements from his camp
and sent the legions with him back for a rest, and on the
same day arrived at Larissa.

99. Caesar had lost not more than 200 privates, but
about thirty gallant centurions. Crastinus, of whom we
have spoken above, received a sword thrust in his face
and died fighting bravely. It was no idle boast he made
as he went into battle, for Caesar rated his courage outstanding in the battle and judged that he owed him most.
Of the Pompeian army some 15,000 seem to have been
killed, and more than 24,000 surrendered, for even the
cohorts left to garrison the fortresses surrendered to
Sulla; many others took refuge in neighboring states.
Standards to the number of 180 and nine eagles were
brought to Caesar.

100. At this period Decimus Laelius came to Brindisi with a fleet and, following the tactic of Libo (which has been described above), occupied an island facing the harbor of Brindisi. Vatinius, again, who was then in command at Brindisi, enticed Laelius' ships out by means of some rowboats decked over and carefully equipped, and captured one quinquereme which had gone too far and two lesser craft in the narrows of the harbor. He also posted cavalry along the shore to keep the fleet from fresh water. But Laelius had better sailing weather and fetched water for his men in freighters from Corfu and Durazzo. He was not swayed from his purpose nor could the disgrace of losing ships or shortages of necessaries drive him from the harbor and the island until news came of the battle in Thessaly.

101. At about this same time Gaius Cassius arrived at Sicily with a fleet of Syrian, Phoenician, and Cilician vessels. Caesar's fleet was divided into two parts, one half at Bivona under command of the praetor Publius Sulpicius, and the other at Messina under Marcus Pomponius. Cassius swept into Messina before Pomponius could learn of his approach and found everything in confusion: there were no pickets and no systematic organization. He took advantage of a fresh breeze to send against Pomponius' fleet a number of freighters filled with pine, pitch, tow, and other combustibles and so burned all thirty-five of the ships, including twenty that were decked. The panic that ensued was so great that though there was a legion to guard it Messina was barely saved, and many are of the opinion that it would have been lost if news of Caesar's victory had not been brought in the nick of time by relays of mounted messengers. Their very opportune arrival stiffened the defense of Messina, and Cassius sailed off against Sulpicius' fleet at Bivona.

Employing the same tactic, Cassius waited for a favorable wind to send incendiary vessels against the fleet
which was moored to the shore: either end of the line
caught fire, and five vessels were burned out. As the fire
was spreading under the force of a stiff wind, disabled
soldiers of the veteran legions who had been left
to guard the fleet so resented the affront that they embarked of their own accord, cast off, and charged Cassius' fleet. They captured two quinqueremes (Cassius
was in one, but he was taken off in a boat and escaped)
and sank two triremes. Soon news of the battle in Thessaly convinced even the Pompeians; up to then they had
thought it an invention of Caesar's agents and friends.
Upon this intelligence Cassius and his fleet sailed away
from those parts.

102. Caesar judged that pursuit of Pompey, wherever
he might have taken refuge, must take precedence over
all else to prevent him from procuring fresh forces for
renewing the war. Each day he advanced as far as the
cavalry could go, and ordered one legion to follow by
easier stages. At Amphipolis an edict posted in Pompey's
name required all the young men of the province, Greeks
and Roman citizens alike, to assemble and be sworn in
for service. Whether Pompey had issued the order to
avert suspicion and conceal as long as possible his intentions to fly farther, or whether he would attempt to hold
Macedonia with new levies if no one prevented it, is impossible to judge. He lay at anchor at Amphipolis for
one night, summoned his friends and borrowed money
for necessary expenses, and when he learned of Caesar's
approach sailed for Mytilene, where he arrived in a few
days. There he was detained by bad weather for two
days, during which he was joined by some oar-propelled
boats. He crossed to Cilicia and thence to Cyprus, where

he learned that the people of Antioch and the Roman
citizens doing business there had agreed to keep him out
of the city by force of arms. They had also notified those
who had taken refuge in neighboring states to keep
away from Antioch at the peril of their lives. Lucius
Lentulus, who had been consul the year before, Publius
Lentulus, also an ex-consul, and sundry others fared similarly at Rhodes. They had followed Pompey's flight and
reached that island, but had not been received into the
town or harbor; when messengers bade them leave those
waters they reluctantly sailed away. News of Caesar's
approach was reaching the various states.

103. In view of this situation Pompey abandoned his
design of making for Syria. He confiscated the funds of
the tax corporation and borrowed from individuals, took
on board a large quantity of copper for soldiers' pay,
and armed 2,000 men, selected by himself from the slave-
establishment of the tax corporation or impressed from
the business men according to the latters' individual
choices, and so arrived at Pelusium.

At Pelusium, as it happened, King Ptolemy, who was
only a boy, with a large army was waging war against
his sister Cleopatra, whom he had driven from the throne
a few months before with the help of relatives and
friends. Cleopatra's camp was at no great distance from
Ptolemy's. Through messengers Pompey asked Ptolemy
to receive him in Alexandria, in view of his close rela-
tionship with his father, and protect him, in his misfortune, with his resources. After they had delivered their
formal message Pompey's emissaries began to speak
more freely with the king's soldiers and to urge them to
do their duty to Pompey and not despise him for his misfortune. Among Ptolemy's men were a number of Pompey's veterans whom Gabinius had taken over in Syria

and brought to Alexandria, and upon conclusion of his campaign had left with the Ptolemy who was this boy's father.

104. Because of the king's youth his kingdom was in charge of his friends, who dealt with the situation. Whether, as they later claimed, they were actuated by fear that Pompey might tamper with the army's loyalty and seize Alexandria and Egypt, or whether they despised his broken fortune—misfortune generally changes friends to enemies—they gave an ostensibly friendly reply to Pompey's messengers and bade him come to the king, but secretly they sent the royal prefect Achillas, a notably bold character, and Lucius Septimius, a tribune of soldiers, to assassinate Pompey. They greeted him cordially, and he was further reassured by his acquaintance with Septimius, who had held a command under him in the Pirate War; accordingly he embarked on a launch with a few of his men, and was there murdered by Achillas and Septimius. Lucius Lentulus was also arrested on the king's orders and done to death in prison.

105. When Caesar arrived in Asia he found that Titus Ampius had made an attempt on the treasury of the temple of Diana at Ephesus and for that purpose had summoned the senators in the province to serve as witnesses to the amount, but that Caesar's arrival had interrupted the proceedings, whereupon Ampius had fled. On two occasions, then, Caesar had saved the treasury at Ephesus. Similarly it was established by counting the days back that on the day of Caesar's success a statue of Victory in the temple of Minerva at Elis, which was placed in front of and facing Minerva's statue, had been turned round to face the lintel and entrance-doors of the temple. In Syrian Antioch on the same day an army's bat-

tle cry and the braying of trumpets was twice heard so
loudly that the armed citizens hurried to man the walls.
The same thing happened at Acre. In the secret recesses
of the temple at Pergamum, called *adyta* in Greek,
which none but priests are allowed to enter, drumrolls
resounded. In Tralles, likewise, in the temple of Victory
where they have dedicated a statue of Caesar, there
was exhibited a palm which had sprung up at that time
between the joints of the flagging of the pavement.

106. When he had spent a few days in Asia Caesar
heard that Pompey had been seen in Cyprus and con-
jectured that his destination was Egypt because of his
connections with that kingdom and other advantages it
offered. Accordingly Caesar proceeded to Egypt with
one legion which he had ordered to follow him from
Thessaly, another which he summoned from his legate
Quintus Fufius in Achaea, 800 horse, ten warships from
Rhodes, and a few from Asia. The legions contained
3,200 men; the remainder were disabled by battle
wounds, exhaustion, and the length of the journey and
unable to accompany the expedition. But Caesar did
not hesitate to proceed with weak support because he
was confident that the fame of his exploits would make
any place equally safe for him. At Alexandria he learned
of Pompey's death. Immediately on disembarking he
heard shouting from the soldiers the king had left to garrison the city and saw a crowd surging towards him.
This was because the fasces were being carried before
him, and this the crowd claimed was an infringement on
the king's majesty. This disturbance was put down, but
the mob rioted repeatedly day after day, and a number
of soldiers were killed in all quarters of the city.

107. In view of this situation Caesar ordered other
legions, made up of Pompeian troops, to be brought him

from Asia. He was himself immobilized by the Etesian winds, which made it impossible to sail out from Alexandria. In the meanwhile he decided that the quarrel between Ptolemy and Cleopatra affected the Roman people and himself as consul; it was all the more his duty to intervene because it was in his earlier consulship that an alliance with the elder Ptolemy had been concluded by enactment of law and senatorial decree. Accordingly Caesar declared it his will that King Ptolemy and his sister Cleopatra should disband the armies they controlled and settle their differences by legal proceedings under his jurisdiction rather than between themselves by force of arms.

108. Because of the king's youth his tutor, a eunuch named Pothinus, acted as regent. Pothinus was the first to express indignant complaint that the king should be summoned to plead his case. Presently he found supporters among the king's friends and secretly transferred the army from Pelusium to Alexandria. In general command of the forces he appointed the Achillas whom we have mentioned above, and through messengers and dispatches instructed him on what he wanted done. Promises in Pothinus' and the king's name were a further incentive to that self-important character.

Ptolemy's father had provided in his will that the elder of his two sons and the elder of his two daughters should jointly inherit, and in the same will he adjured the Roman people by all the gods and the covenants he had concluded at Rome to carry these provisions out. One copy of the will was brought to Rome by the king's ambassadors to be deposited in the treasury (this could not be done because of political distractions, and it was deposited with Pompey); the other identical copy, sealed and left in Alexandria, was now produced.

109. While Caesar was supervising the litigation and making every effort, as friend and referee for both parties, to settle their differences, word was suddenly brought that the royal army with all its cavalry was marching on Alexandria. Caesar's forces were far too small to hazard a battle outside the town, and his only course was to keep to his position inside the town and ascertain Achillas' intentions. He ordered his soldiers to remain under arms, however, and urged the king to send as emissaries to Achillas those of his connections whom he judged to merit the highest prestige, in order to communicate his desires to Achillas. Dioscorides and Serapion, both sometime ambassadors at Rome and most highly regarded by the elder Ptolemy, were sent. As soon as they came into Achillas' presence, before he could hear them or learn why they had come, he ordered them seized and executed. One was wounded and was taken up by his friends and carried away for dead; the other was killed. Thereupon Caesar arranged to keep the king in his own power, in the belief that the royal title carried great weight with his people, and in order to give the war the character of an unauthorized insurrection of a handful of brigands rather than of an official royal act.

110. The forces at Achillas' disposal were by no means contemptible in numbers or kind or military experience. He had under arms 20,000 of Gabinius' soldiers who had adopted the Alexandrian way of life with its license, had unlearned the name and discipline of the Roman, had married, and many had begotten children. In addition there were freebooters and brigands collected from Syria, the province of Cilicia, and neighboring regions, and these were joined by numerous condemned criminals and exiles. All our runaway slaves could be sure of a

refuge in Alexandria and of safety and maintenance provided they registered as soldiers. If any was seized by
his owner the soldiers would combine to rescue him, for
being involved in similar guilt they resisted violence to
one of their number as a peril to themselves. By a sort of
tradition of the Alexandrian army these men habitually
demanded the death of royal favorites, plundered the
property of the rich, besieged the palace to obtain increase of pay, drove certain individuals from the throne
and invited others to occupy it. There were also 2,000
cavalry. All these men were veterans of numerous wars
at Alexandria. They had restored the elder Ptolemy
to his throne, had killed the two sons of Bibulus, had
campaigned against the Egyptians. Such was their military experience.

111. With confidence in these forces and contempt for
the meager forces of Caesar, Achillas seized Alexandria
except for the part of the town Caesar was holding with
his troops. At his first onset he tried to force Caesar's
house, but Caesar resisted the assault with cohorts deployed in the streets. At the same time there was fighting at the harbor, which was the most hotly contested of
all. There was simultaneous fighting by scattered bands
in several streets, and the enemy in great numbers were
attempting to seize the warships. There were fifty of
these; they had been sent to support Pompey, and after
the battle in Thessaly had returned home. They were all
quinqueremes and quadriremes, completely equipped
and ready for sailing, and in addition there were the
twenty-two vessels regularly stationed at Alexandria to
protect the harbor, all decked. If they could take the
fleet Caesar would be without a navy and they would
control the entire seas and cut Caesar off from supplies
and reinforcements. The struggle was as intense as it was

bound to be when one side saw that speedy victory and
the other preservation depended on the issue. But Caesar succeeded; he burned all the ships and others in the
docks, because he could not protect so extensive an area
with his small force, and immediately ferried his men
over to Pharos.

112. On this island there is a wonderfully constructed
and very high tower, called Pharos after the island. It is
this island, lying in front of Alexandria, which forms the
harbor; earlier kings had joined it to the town by a causeway 800 paces long, in effect a bridge, supported by
piles. There are Egyptian houses on the island, and a
village as large as a town; the natives plundered any vessels that carelessness or bad weather had thrown off their
course, like pirates. So narrow is the passage that no vessel can enter the harbor if the occupiers of Pharos choose
to block it. This is what Caesar was afraid of, and so
while the enemy was preoccupied with fighting, he
landed his soldiers on Pharos, seized the island, and
posted a garrison on it. This ensured safe access by sea
for provisions and reinforcements; Caesar had sent for
reinforcements to all the neighboring provinces. Elsewhere in the city the fighting was indecisive; because of
the cramped streets neither side could be dislodged.
After a few casualties on either side Caesar marked
off the most strategic sector and barricaded it during
the night. That quarter contained a small wing of the
palace which had been assigned to Caesar as his residence upon his arrival, and adjoining it was a theater,
with approaches to the harbor and other docks, which
served as a citadel. On the days following Caesar
strengthened these structures to serve as a wall so that
he should not have to fight except on his own initiative.

Meanwhile King Ptolemy's younger daughter left the

palace to join Achillas, in the hope that she might succeed to the empty throne, and began to share the direction of operations. But they soon began to quarrel about priority; this multiplied their bounties to the soldiers, as each tried to win them over by extravagant largesse. In the course of these intrigues Pothinus (the king's tutor and agent in Caesar's sector) sent messengers to Achillas urging him not to slacken or lose heart; the messengers were informed against and intercepted, and Caesar executed them.

Such were the beginnings of the Alexandrine War.

THE ALEXANDRINE,
AFRICAN, AND
SPANISH WARS

*Regularly included in the Caesarian corpus but known
to be of uncertain authorship even in antiquity are three
books which carry the story of Caesar's campaigns from
the close of the Civil War to his return to Rome in September, 45 B.C. The* Alexandrine War *is probably the
work of Hirtius, who wrote the supplementary eighth
book of the* Gallic War, *though Hirtius did not himself
take part in the campaign. The* African *and* Spanish
Wars *are probably the work of two unnamed officers
who fought in those campaigns.*

The Alexandrine War, *in 78 chapters, carries the story
from the conclusion of the Civil War to Caesar's return
to Italy in September 47. First there is a vivid account
(Ch. 1-33), in continuation of Caesar's own, of the operations in Alexandria. Next the situation in other parts of
the empire during 48-47 is described: Calvinus' campaign against Pharnaces (Ch. 34-41), the war in Illyricum (Ch. 42-47), and Quintus Cassius' difficulties in
Spain (Ch. 48-64). Finally we have Caesar's own campaign against Pharnaces and his victory at Zela in Pontus
in August 47 (Ch. 65-78), won within five days of landing and within four hours of sighting the enemy. It was
this victory that Caesar reported in the famous dispatch,*

Veni, vidi, vici, "*I came, I saw, I conquered.*" *The* Alexandrine War *is the most readable of the three.*

The African War, *in 98 chapters, carries the story from Caesar's preparations for the campaign at Lily-baeum in Sicily in December 47, to his return to Rome in July 46. The account is pedestrian but meticulous. The climax of the campaign was the victory at Thapsus, after which Pompey's father-in-law Scipio and the Stoic Cato, who had commanded the survivors of Pompey's army, took their own lives.*

The Spanish War, *in 42 chapters, carries the story from Caesar's arrival in Spain in December 46 to his final return to Rome in September 45. The book is the most illiterate which has come down from antiquity. The battle of Munda (March 17, 45) was the most difficult and bloodiest of the war. Pompey's two sons had built the remaining anti-Caesarian elements into a formidable army, so that Caesar had to plead with his soldiers "not to hand him over to a pair of boys." Munda was Caesar's last victory.*

FRAGMENTS

The fragments of Caesar's lost writings occupy 65 pages in Alfred Klotz' standard Teubner edition (1927), but as in similar collections of quotations, there is a great preponderance of ancient comment on the works in question with only rare statements of what Caesar said and even rarer citations of his actual words. From Caesar's speeches and letters, about which most is said, there is nothing of special significance for the ordinary reader. Nor is there anything worth reproducing from the Collected Apophthegms or the work on astronomy. From the On Analogy, which dealt with correct usage of vocabulary and grammar, we have one notable piece of advice: "Avoid the far-fetched and rare word as you would a reef" (tamquam scopulum sic fugias inauditum atque insolens verbum). Caesar's juvenilia, as we read in Suetonius' summary (p. xvi, above), was suppressed by Augustus, but we do have quoted, in Suetonius' Life of Terence, Caesar's criticism of Terence in six perceptive hexameters:

Thou too, thou halved Menander, shall be reckoned with the best, thou lover of speech undefiled. Would that thy graceful writings were imbued with force as well, so that thy standing as a comic poet might be acclaimed on a par with the Greeks and thou wouldst not lie humble and neglected in that art. This is your one shortcoming, Terence, and it grieves and pains me.

GAZETTEER

In the listing below italic type indicates modern equivalents or derivatives, frequently merely conjectural; *tribal* names are sometimes represented by modern *cities* or *districts*. *Tribe* is abbreviated "tr," *town* "tn," *district* "dist," and *river* "r."

Acarnania dist, N Greece

Achaea dist, N Peloponnese; Roman name for Greece as administrative unit

Aduatica tn, *Tongres*

Aduatici tr, Belgium

Aedui tr, Depts. of Côte d'Or, Nièvre, Saône et Loire, Rhône

Aeginium tn, *Kalambaka* (Pindus range)

Aetolia dist, N Greece, E of Acarnania

Africa, Roman province centering on Carthage

Agedincum tn, *Sens*

Aisne r, Axona

Alba tn, *Albe*

Albici tr, Basses Alpes

Alesia tn, *Alise-Sainte-Reine* (Côte d'Or)

Aliacmon r, *Vistritza*

Allier r, Elaver

Allobroges tr, Savoy

Amantia tn, *Nivitza* (Epirus)

Amanus mountain, between Cilicia and Syria

Ambiani tr, *Amiens*

Ambracia dist and tn, *Arta*

Amphilochia dist, near Gulf of Arta

Amphipolis tn, *Neokhorio* (Macedonia)

Anartes tr, Transylvania

Anas r, *Guadiana* (between S Portugal and Spain)

Ancalites tr, Britain

Ancona tn, *Ancone*

Andes tr, *Angers*

Anquillaria tn, near Cape Bon (Africa)

Antioch tn, *Antakia* (Syria)

Apollonia tn, *Polina* (Illyria)

Apsus r, *Ergent* (Illyria)

Apulia dist, *Puglia*

Aquileia tn, *Aquileia*

Aquitania dist, between Garonne and Pyrenees

Aragon dist, Celtiberia

Arar r, Saône

Arduenna forest, *Ardennes*

Arecomici Volcae tr, *Nîmes*

Arelate tn, *Arles*

Arezzo, Arretium

Ariminum tn, *Rimini*

Arles, Arelate

Arretium tn, *Arezzo*

Arverni tr, *Auvergne*

Ascoli, Asculum

Asculum tn, *Ascoli*

Asparagium tn, *Iskarpar* (Illyricum)

Asturia, Cantabri

Athamania dist, Epirus

Atrebates tr, *Artois*

Aulerci tr, *Eure* (Normandy)

Ausci tr, *Auch*

Ausetani tr, S slope of Pyrenees on coast

Auximum tn, *Osimo*

Avaricum tn, *Bourges*

Axona r, *Aisne*

Bacenis forest, *Thuringia*

Bagrada r, *Medjerdah* (Africa)

Baleares islands, *Majorca, Minorca*

Batavi tr, Holland

Belgae tr, Belgium

Bellovaci tr, *Beauvais*

Besançon tn, Vesontio

Bessi tr, Thrace

Bibracte tn, *Autun en Bourgogne*

Bibrax tn, *Beurieux*

Bibroci tr, *Bray* (Britain)

Bigerriones tr, *Bigorre*

Bithynia dist, NW Asia Minor

Bituriges tr, *Bourges*

Bivona, Vibo

Boeotia dist, N of Attica

Boii tr, *Bourbonnais*

Boulogne, Itium

Bourges, Avaricum

Brannovices tr, *Brionnais*

Bratuspantium tn, *Breteuil*

Brindisi, Brundisium

Brundisium tn, *Brindisi*

Bruttium dist, S Italy

Buthrotum tn, *Butrinto*

Byllis tn, Illyricum

Cabillonum tn, *Chalon-sur-Saône*

Cadiz, Gades

Cadurci tr, *Cahors*

Caeroesi tr, Belgium

Cagliari, Caralis

Calagurritani tr, *Loarre* (Spain)

Caletes tr, *Pays de Caux*

Calydon tn, Aetolia

Camerinum tn, *Camerino*

Candava dist, Illyricum

Cantabri tr, N coast of Spain

Cantium dist, *Kent*

Canusium tn, *Canosa*

Capua tn, *Sta. Maria di Capua*

Caralis tn, *Cagliari* (Sardinia)

Caralitani tr, Sardinia

Carcaso tn, *Carcassonne*

Carmonenses tr, Andalusia

Carnutes tr, *Chartres*

Casilinum tn, *Capua*

Cassi tr, *Herts* (Britain)

Castile dist, Celtiberia

Castulonensis forest, *Sierra de Segura* (Castile)

Caturiges tr, Hautes-Alpes

Celtiberia dist, Guadalajara and Cuenca

Cenabum tn, *Orléans*

Cenimagni tr, Britain

Cevenna mountains, *Cevennes*

Cherusci tr, on Weser and Lippe

Cilicia dist, S Asia Minor

Cimbri tr, N Germany

Cinga r, *Cinca* (Spain)

Cingulum tn, *Cingulo*

Clupea tn, *Kalibia* (Africa)

Cocosates tr, Aquitaine

Condrusi tr, *Condroz*

Corcyra island, *Corfu*

Corduba tn, *Cordova*

Corfinium tn, *Pentima*

Cosa tns, in S Italy and in Etruria

Cremona tn, near Mantua

Curicum island, *Veglia* (Fiume)

Curiosolites tr, *Corseult*

Daci tr, on Danube

Danuvius r, *Danube*

Decetia tn, *Décize*

Diablintes tr, La Sarthe

Dubis tn, *Doubs*

Durocortorum tn, *Reims*

Dyrrachium tn, *Durazzo* (Albania)

Ebro r, Hiberus

Eburones tr, *Liège*

Eburovices tr, *Évreux*

Elaver r, *Allier*

Elusates tr, *Eauze*

Ephesus tn, capital of Roman Asia Minor

Epirus dist, N Greece-Albania

Fanum tn, *Fano*

Firmum tn, *Fermo*

Frentani tr, Abruzzo

Gabali tr, *Gévaudan*

Gades tn, *Cadiz*

Garumna r, *Garonne*

Geidumni tr, subjects of Nervii

Genava tn, *Geneva*

Genusus r, *Shkumbe*

Gergovia tn, *Gergovie,* near Clermont-Ferrand

Gomphi tn, *Palaeo-Episkopi* (Macedonia)

Gorgobina tn, *Charlieu*

Grudii tr, *Groede*

Guadiana r, Anas

Gubbio tn, Iguvium

Hadrumetum tn, *Susa* (Tunis)

Harudes tr, Jutland

Helvetii tr, Switzerland

Helvii tr, *Ardèche*

Heraclia tn, *Monastir*

Hercynian forest, Schwarzwald to Harz

Hibernia dist, Ireland

Hispalis tn, *Seville*

Huesca tn, Oscenses

Igilium tn, *Giglio*

Iguvium tn, *Gubbio*

Ilerda tn, *Lerida*

Illurgavonenses tr, near mouth of Ebro

Illyricum dist, Dalmatia and Albania

Issa tn and island, *Lissa, Vis* (Adriatic)

Italica tn, *Santiponce* (Spain)

Itius tn, *Boulogne*

Jacetani tr, N Spain

Jura mountain range, from Rhine to Rhone

Kalibia tn, Clupea (Africa)

Larinates, of Larinum (*Larino*)

Larisa tn, *Larissa* (Thessaly)

Latobrigi tr, adjoining Helvetii

Lemannus lake, of Geneva

Lemonum tn, *Poitiers*

Lemovices tr, *Limoges*

Lepanto tn, Naupactus

Lepontii tr, N Italy

Leptis tn, *Lebdah* (Africa)

Lerida tn, Ilerda

Leuci tr, Liège

Levaci tr, Belgium

Lexovii tr, *Lisieux*

Liger r, *Loire*

Lilybaeum tn, *Capo Boeo* (Sicily)

Lingones tr, *Langres*

Lissus tn, *Lesh* (Dalmatia)

Loarre tn, Calagurritani (Spain)

Loire r, Liger

Lucania dist, S Italy

Luceria tn, *Lucera* (Apulia)

Lusitania dist, Portugal

Lutetia tn, *Paris*

Macedonia dist, between Thessaly and Thrace

Mandubii tr, Côte d'Or

Marcomani tr, connected with Suevi

Marne r, Matrona

Marrucini tr, Abruzzo

Marseilles tn, Massilia

Marsi tr, central Italy

Massilia tn, *Marseilles*

Matisco tn, *Macôn*

Matrona r, *Marne*

Mauretania dist, N Africa

Mediomatrici tr, *Metz*

Meldi tr, *Meaux*

Menapii tr, between Meuse and Scheldt

Mequinenza tn, Octogesa (Spain)

Messana tn, *Messina*

Metiosedum tn, *Melun*

Metropolis tn, *Palaeo-Kastro* (Thessaly)

Meuse r, Mosa

Mona island, *Man*

Monastir tn, Heraclia

Morini tr, near English Channel

Mosa r, *Meuse*

Munda tn, *Monda* (Spain)

Mytilene tn, on Lesbos

Namnetes tr, *Nantes*

Nantuates tr, Provence

Naples, Neapolis

Narbo tn, *Narbonne*

Naupactus tn, *Lepanto*

Neapolis tn, *Naples*

Nemetes tr, *Spires*

Nervii tr, Hainault

Nitiobriges tr, *Agen*

Noreia tn, *Neumarkt* (Carinthia)

Noricum dist, between Danube and Alps

Noviodunum, tns, *Nevers, Villate, Pommiers*

Numidia dist, N Africa

Nymphaeum tn, *Capo di Redeni* (Illyria)

Ocelum tn, *Drubiaglio*

Octodurus tn, *Martigny*

Octogesa tn, *Mequinenza* (Spain)

Orchomenus tn, Boeotia

Oricum tn, *Palaeo-Kastro* (Illyria)

Oscenses tr, *Huesca* (Spain)

Osimo tn, Auximum

Padus r, *Po*

Paemani tr, *Pays de Famenne*

Palaeste tn, Epirus

Parisii tr, *Paris*

Parthini tr, N of Dyrrachium

Peligni tr, central Italy

Pelusium tn, at Nile mouth

Pergamum tn, *Bergama* (Asia Minor)

Petra headland, *Sasso Bianco* (Illyria)

Petrocorii tr, *Périgueux*

Pharos island, Alexandrian lighthouse

Piacenza, Placentia

Picenum dist, between Apennines and Adriatic

Pictones tr, Poitiers

Pirustae tr, Illyria

Pisaurum tn, *Pesaro*

Placentia tn, *Piacenza*

Pleumoxii tr, Belgium

Pontus dist, Asia Minor on Euxine

Puteoli tn, Pozzuoli

Rauraci tr, near Basle

Ravenna tn, *Ravenna*

Redones tr, *Rennes*

Remi tr, *Reims*

Rhenus r, *Rhine*

Rhodanus r, *Rhône*

Rimini tn, Ariminum

Ruteni tr, *Rodez*

Sabis r, *Sambre*

Sallyes tr, N of Marseilles

Salonae tn, *Salona* (Dalmatia)

Samarobriva tn, *Amiens*

Sambre r, Sabis

Santoni tr, *Saintes*

Sasonae tn, *Saseno* (Illyria)

Scaldus r, *Scheldt*

Seduni tr, *Sion*

Sedusii tr, Germany

Segni tr, *Signi*

Segontiaci tr, Hampshire

Segusiavi tr, *Feurs*

Seine r, Sequana

Senones tr, *Sens*

Sequana r, *Seine*

Seville tn, Hispalis (Spain)

Shkumbe r, Genusus

Sibuzates tr, *Sobusse*

Sicoris r, *Segre* (tributary of Ebro)

Sotiates tr, *Sos*

Suebi tr, NE Germany

Suessiones tr, *Soissons*

Sugambri tr, between Sieg and Ruhr

Sulmo tn, *Sulmona*

Susa tn, Hadrumetum (Africa)

Tamesis r, *Thames*

Tarbelli tr, Aquitaine

Tarracina tn, *Terracina*

Tarraco dist, *Tarragona* (Spain)

Tarusates tr, Aquitaine

Tauroentum fort, *Taurois* (near Marseilles)

Tectosages Volcae tr, Provence

Tencteri tr, Rhineland

Tergestini tr, *Trieste*

Teutoni tr, Jutland

Thurii tn, S Italy

Tigurini dist, *Zurich*

Tolosa tn, *Toulouse*

Tralles tn, Asia Minor

Treveri tr, Trèves

Triboci tr, Alsace

Trinobantes tr, Essex and Suffolk

Tulingi tr, Stühlingen

Turonis tr, Tours

Ubii tr, Rhineland

Usipetes tr, Rhineland

Utica tn, at mouth of Bagrada (Africa)

Vacalus r, Waal

Vangiones tr, Worms

Varus r, Var

Veliocassi tr, Vexin

Vellaunodunum tn, Montargis

Vellavii tr, Velay

Veneti tr, Venice

Veragri tr, Pennine Alps

Vesontio tn, Besançon

Vettones tr, Salamanca

Vibo tn, Bivona

Viromandui tr, Vermandois

Vis tn, Issa

Vistritza r, Aliacmon

Vocates tr, Aquitaine

Volcae Arecomici tr, Nîmes

Volcae Tectosages tr, Provence

Vosegus mountains, Vosges

Waal r, Vacalus